CISCO SYSTEMS

S0-DZC-230

Cisco Networking Academy Program
CCNA 3.0 Training Edition

Cisco Press

201 West 103rd Street

Indianapolis, Indiana 46290 USA

www.ciscopress.com

Cisco Networking Academy Program
CCNA 3.0 Training Edition

Published by:
Cisco Press
201 West 103rd Street
Indianapolis, IN 46290 USA

ISBN: 1-58713-126-9

Warning and Disclaimer

This book is a training edition and is designed to help Networking Academy instructors optimize their CCNA 3.0 training experience while providing advance insight into the CCNA 3.0 texts and companion products from Cisco Press. Every effort has been made to make this training edition as complete and as accurate as possible, but no warranty or fitness is implied.

The information is provided on an "as is" basis and is based on pre-publication material and subject to change. The authors, Cisco Press, and Cisco Systems, Inc., shall have neither liability nor responsibility to any person or entity with respect to any loss or damages arising from the information contained in this book or from the use of the discs or programs that may accompany it.

The opinions expressed in this book belong to the author and are not necessarily those of Cisco Systems, Inc.

Trademark Acknowledgments

All terms mentioned in this book that are known to be trademarks or service marks have been appropriately capitalized. Cisco Press or Cisco Systems, Inc., cannot attest to the accuracy of this information. Use of a term in this book should not be regarded as affecting the validity of any trademark or service mark.

This book is part of the Cisco Networking Academy® Program series from Cisco Press. The products in this series support and complement the Cisco Networking Academy Program curriculum. If you are using this book outside the Networking Academy program, then you are not preparing with a Cisco trained and authorized Networking Academy provider.

CISCO SYSTEMS

For information on the Cisco Networking Academy Program or to locate a Networking Academy, please visit www.cisco.com/edu.

Feedback Information

At Cisco Press, our goal is to create in-depth technical books of the highest quality and value. Each book is crafted with care and precision, undergoing rigorous development that involves the unique expertise of members from the professional technical community.

Readers' feedback is a natural continuation of this process. If you have any comments regarding how we could improve the quality of this book, or otherwise alter it to better suit your needs, you can contact us through e-mail at networkingacademy@ciscopress.com. Please make sure to include the book title and ISBN in your message.

We greatly appreciate your assistance.

Publisher	John Wait	
Editor-in-Chief	John Kane	
Executive Editor	Carl Lindholm	
Cisco Representative	Anthony Wolfenden	
Cisco Press Program Manager	Sonia Torres Chavez	
Manager, Marketing Communications, Cisco Systems	Scott Miller	
Cisco Marketing Program Manager	Edie Quiroz	
Production Manager	Patrick Kanouse	
Assistant Editor	Sarah Kimberly	
Development Editors	Chris Cleveland	Andrew Cupp
Project Editors	Sheri Cain	San Dee Phillips
Copy Editors	Karen Gill	Kevin Kent
Team Coordinator	Tammi Ross	
Cover Designer	Louisa Adair	
Production Team	Mark Shirar	

CISCO SYSTEMS

Corporate Headquarters
Cisco Systems, Inc.
170 West Tasman Drive
San Jose, CA 95134-1706
USA
www.cisco.com
Tel: 408 526-4000
     800 553-NETS (6387)
Fax: 408 526-4100

European Headquarters
Cisco Systems International BV
Haarlerbergpark
Haarlerbergweg 13-19
1101 CH Amsterdam
The Netherlands
www-europe.cisco.com
Tel: 31 0 20 357 1000
Fax: 31 0 20 357 1100

Americas Headquarters
Cisco Systems, Inc.
170 West Tasman Drive
San Jose, CA 95134-1706
USA
www.cisco.com
Tel: 408 526-7660
Fax: 408 527-0883

Asia Pacific Headquarters
Cisco Systems, Inc.
Capital Tower
168 Robinson Road
#22-01 to #29-01
Singapore 068912
www.cisco.com
Tel: +65 6317 7777
Fax: +65 6317 7799

Cisco Systems has more than 200 offices in the following countries and regions. Addresses, phone numbers, and fax numbers are listed on the
Cisco.com Web site at www.cisco.com/go/offices.

Argentina • Australia • Austria • Belgium • Brazil • Bulgaria • Canada • Chile • China PRC • Colombia • Costa Rica • Croatia • Czech Republic Denmark • Dubai, UAE • Finland • France • Germany • Greece • Hong Kong SAR • Hungary • India • Indonesia • Ireland • Israel • Italy Japan • Korea • Luxembourg • Malaysia • Mexico • The Netherlands • New Zealand • Norway • Peru • Philippines • Poland • Portugal Puerto Rico • Romania • Russia • Saudi Arabia • Scotland • Singapore • Slovakia • Slovenia • South Africa • Spain • Sweden Switzerland • Taiwan • Thailand • Turkey • Ukraine • United Kingdom • United States • Venezuela • Vietnam • Zimbabwe

Contents at a Glance

Contents

CISCO SYSTEMS

Cisco Networking Academy Program
CCNA 3.0 Training Edition

Cisco Press

201 West 103rd Street

Indianapolis, Indiana 46290 USA

www.ciscopress.com

Cisco Press Product Family Overview

Cisco Press works in conjunction with the Cisco Systems Worldwide Education Group to develop the only official books and resources for the Cisco Networking Academy Program. There are three types of core Networking Academy textbooks that Cisco Press publishes—Companion Guides, Lab Companions, and Engineering Journals and Workbooks. These materials enhance your students' learning experiences and lend support to you and the web-based curriculum developed for the Cisco Networking Academy Program.

Companion Guides

The Companion Guide textbook serves as the main volume for the course. These comprehensive texts contain key objectives, Skillbuilder activities, figures and tables, margin notes, chapter summaries, and "Check Your Understanding" review questions. CD-ROMs that contain additional enrichment tools such as practice exam questions within a customizable test engine, e-Lab Activities, PhotoZooms, and instructional videos are included with the hardbound textbook. Often Companion Guides also include additional chapters and exercises that reach beyond the online curriculum.

Lab Companions

Practice the concepts presented in the correlating Companion Guide. The Lab Companion serves as a tool for hands-on practice within the lab environment and can used for homework and tests. Most Lab Companions contain bonus labs or additional questions for further study.

Engineering Journal and Workbooks

Have your students begin the best-practice method of keeping an engineering journal for the workplace with this resource tool that includes training exercises to reinforce classroom learning. Each chapter includes review questions and focus questions to prepare students for the corresponding course exam.

Cisco Press Companion Guide Features

Interior Design

Interior design features of Cisco Press Companion Guides support your teaching efforts and present components that are distinctive, readily identified, and facilitate better comprehension of course content.

Margin Notes

Important and interesting concepts are highlighted using various types of margin notes:

- **Test tips** identify facts students need to know for certification exam success
- **Notes** mark ideas and concepts students will find interesting
- **Cautions** instruct students when to be careful or risk damage to equipment
- **Warnings** indicate dangers and hazards students must know for their personal safety

---

110   Chapter 2: How Computers Work

> **TEST TIP**
>
> Sometimes, it is necessary to adjust the system BIOS (CMOS) to enable the use of parity RAM or nonparity RAM, depending on the type of motherboard. The relevant information is found in the system's manual.

DRAM—Inexpensive and somewhat slow, and requires an uninterrupted power supply to maintain its data. When the power is turned off, the data is lost.

RAM can be installed on the motherboard, either as a permanent fixture or in the form of small chips, referred to as SIMMs (single inline memory modules) or DIMMs (dual inline memory modules). SIMMs and DIMMs are removable cards that can be replaced with larger or smaller increments of memory. Although having more memory installed in your computer is a good thing, most system boards have limitations on the amount and type of RAM that can be added or supported. Some systems might require that only SIMMs be used, while others might require that SIMMs be installed in matched sets of two or four modules at a time. Additionally, some systems use only RAM with parity (built-in error checking) while others use nonparity RAM (having no error-checking capability).

Identifying SIMMs and DIMMs

A *SIMM* plugs into the motherboard with a 72-pin or 30-pin connector. The pins connect to the system bus, creating an electronic path through which memory data can flow to and from other system components. Two 72-pin SIMMs can be installed in a computer that supports 64-bit data flow. With a SIMM board, the pins on opposite sides of the module board are connected to each other, forming a single row of contacts, as shown in Figure 2-10.

Figure 2-10   A 72-Pin SIMM

> **NOTE**
>
> SIMMs are available in 30-pin and 72-pin versions, while DIMMs take the form of larger, 168-pin circuit boards.

A *DIMM* plugs into the system's memory bank using a 168-pin connector. The pins establish a connection with the system bus, creating an electronic path through which data can flow between the memory chip and other system components. A single 168-pin DIMM supports 64-bit (nonparity) and 72-bit (parity) data flow. This configuration is now being used in the latest generation of 64-bit systems. Recall that parity refers to error-checking capability built into the RAM chip to ensure data integrity. An important feature is that the pins on a DIMM board are not connected side to side (as with SIMMs); the pins form two sets of contacts, as shown in Figure 2-11.

Book Features

In addition to distinctive design elements, Cisco Press builds the following book features into every Companion Guide:

Figures and Tables

Figures and tables are clearly rendered and labeled, and are plainly positioned near corresponding text, making it easy for students to refer to them while studying.

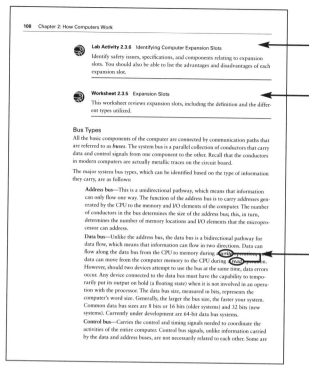

Skill Builders

Make a connection between theory and practice with the aid of skill builders. Clearly marked by icons, skill builders refer to **worksheets** and **lab activities** from the corresponding Lab Companion that reinforce hands-on training. References to the companion CD-ROM for **PhotoZooms** of actual equipment and **instructional videos** on complex topics are also included within chapters.

Key Terms

Key terms are clearly introduced within text, then listed at the end of each chapter for quick review, and compiled within a glossary of terms for easy reference.

Objectives

Each chapter starts with a succinct list of objectives that should be mastered by the end of the chapter.

Chapter Summaries

Appearing at the end of each chapter, chapter summaries provide topic synopses and serve as study aids.

"Check Your Understanding" Review Questions

Reinforce concepts and assess knowledge before moving on to subsequent chapters with these review questions presented at the end of each chapter.

Key Elements of CCNA 3.0 Texts from Cisco Press

Companion Guides include
- expanded coverage on complex CCNA topics
- exclusive content that extends the curriculum
- strong textbook pedagogy and learning aids
- clear references to practical activities within Lab Companions

Expanded CD-ROMs within Companion Guides incorporate
- more CCNA preparation questions
- new e-Lab Activities
- additional tools such as
  - PhotoZooms
  - instructional videos

Lab Companions contain
- bonus labs on complex CCNA topics
- a new reduced price

Engineering Journal and Workbooks have
- concept and focus questions
- vocabulary exercises

Overall, CCNA 3.0 textbooks are
- mapped fully to revised 3.0 curriculum
- written by the curriculum developers
- the only textbooks approved by Cisco Systems

Instructor Resource Center (IRC) Information

Visit the Cisco Press Networking Academy Instructor Resource Center at www.ciscopress.com/irc for product information, release news, and details on how to sample the classroom textbook companions.

Networking Academy Newsletter Registration Information

While visiting the Instructor Resource Center, sign up for the Cisco Press Networking Academy e-mail newsletter. This monthly newsletter is filled with upcoming release information and other important new for Networking Academy instructors. Click "newsletter" to learn more.

How to Request a Cisco Press Review Copy

U.S. Review Copy Requests

Option I—Request a review copy

You may request a review copy of the current and upcoming Networking Academy products by visiting **www.ciscopress. com/networkingacademy** and following these easy steps:

Step 1 Browse the Academy catalog and select the book you would like to review.

Step 2 Click on "Request a Review Copy" beneath the "More Information" bar.

Step 3 Select your customer type and follow the instructions given. Your Prentice Hall representative will be automatically notified to follow up and sample.

Option II—Contact your Prentice Hall Representative

Cisco Press is a division of Pearson Education and is represented in the U.S. by the Prentice Hall Education sales force. We have specialized our sales departments to provide the best service to you.

To locate your U.S. Prentice Hall representative

Instructors in high schools and vocational/technical schools may reach their sales and service representatives by calling **(866) 466-2539** (toll free).

Instructors in two-year colleges, community colleges, and four-year universities may contact their Prentice Hall sales and service representative by calling **(800) 526-0485** (toll free) or by visiting **www.prenhall.com/replocator** to locate their representative.

International review copy requests

Cisco Press is represented internationally through a global network of Pearson companies and partners. Visit **www.ciscopress.com/irc** and click on "Review Copies" for instructions on how to request a deskcopy.

How to Order Cisco Press Resources

U.S. Orders

To place a book order, call the Pearson Customer Service line at **(800) 922-0579** with your PO number and the ISBN(s) of the title(s) you would like to order. If you do not already have an account with Pearson, your sales representative will be located and an account will be established. You may also fax your order to **(800) 445-6991**.

International Orders

Please visit **www.ciscopress.com/international** for a complete listing of Pearson contacts for Cisco Networking Academy Program orders outside the United States.

Use the order form on the following page to help prepare your class adoption request for your school bookstore or school administrator.

Order Form

Use this form as you prepare the CCNA order for your bookstore.

School Name _____

Instructor _____

Department _____

Course Name/Section Name _____

Expected Enrollment _____

Title	ISBN	U.S. Net Price*	Quantity
CCNA 1 and 2—Third Editions from Cisco Press			
Discounted Value Packs—Order and Save			
CCNA 1 and 2 Complete Pack Companion Guide, Lab Companion, Engineering Journal and Workbook	0-13121-711-9	$80.10	_____
CCNA 1 and 2 Lab Pack Companion Guide, Lab Companion	0-13113-557-0	$65.25	_____
CCNA 1 and 2 Engineering Pack Companion Guide, Engineering Journal and Workbook	0-13113-553-8	$59.85	_____
Individual Titles			
CCNA 1 and 2 Companion Guide, Third Edition	1-58713-110-2	$50.00	_____
CCNA 1 and 2 Lab Companion, Third Edition	1-58713-111-0	$22.46	_____
CCNA 1 and 2 Engineering Journal and Workbook, Third Edition	1-58713-112-9	$16.46	_____
CCNA 3 and 4—Third Editions from Cisco Press			
Discounted Value Packs—Order and Save			
CCNA 3 and 4 Complete Pack Companion Guide, Lab Companion, Engineering Journal and Workbook	0-13121-712-7	$80.10	_____
CCNA 3 and 4 Lab Pack Companion Guide, Lab Companion	0-13113-556-2	$65.25	_____
CCNA 3 and 4 Engineering Pack Companion Guide, Engineering Journal and Workbook	0-13113-554-6	$59.85	_____
Individual Titles			
CCNA 3 and 4 Companion Guide, Third Edition	1-58713-113-7	$50.00	_____
CCNA 3 and 4 Lab Companion, Third Edition	1-58713-114-5	$22.46	_____
CCNA 3 and 4 Engineering Journal and Workbook, Third Edition	1-58713-115-3	$16.46	_____

* For pricing outside of the U.S., please contact your local Pearson representative or send an email to international@pearsoned.com.

Cisco Press also has titles and discount value packages available for the other Cisco Networking Academy Program courses. Ask your Prentice Hall representative for more details.

Bridging CCNA v2.0 and CCNA v3.0

CCNA1

Module 3—Networking Media

Lesson 3.2: Optical Media

See Chapter 3, "Networking Media," of the Cisco Press Companion Guide, Third Edition, for more information.

Optical fiber is the most frequently used medium for the longer, high-bandwidth, point-to-point transmissions required on LAN backbones and on WANs. Using optical media, light is used to transmit data over a thin glass fiber or plastic. Electrical signals cause a fiber-optic transmitter to generate the light signals sent down the fiber. The receiver produces electrical signals at the far end of the fiber. However, there is no electricity in the fiber-optic cable itself. In fact, the glass used in fiber-optic cable is a very good electrical insulator.

Optical fiber is used in networks because of the following:

- Fiber is not susceptible to lightning, electromagnetic interference (EMI), or radio frequency interference (RFI), and it does not generate EMI or RFI.
- Fiber has much greater bandwidth capabilities than other media.
- Fiber allows significantly greater transmission distances and excellent signal quality because very little signal attenuation occurs.
- Fiber is more secure than other media because it is difficult to tap into a fiber and easy to detect someone placing a tap on the fiber.
- Current fiber transmitter and receiver technologies can be replaced by newer, faster devices as they are developed so that greater transmission speeds can be achieved over existing fiber links with no need to replace the fiber.
- Fiber costs less than copper for long-distance applications.

- The raw material that fiber is made from is sand, a very plentiful substance.
- With fiber, there are no grounding concerns as there are when signaling using electricity.
- Fiber is light in weight and easily installed.
- Fiber has better resistance to environmental factors, such as water, than copper wire.
- Lengths of fiber can easily be spliced together for very long cable runs.

For these reasons, when very large numbers of bits need to be sent over distances greater than 100 meters, fiber-optic cable is often used.

This section explains the basics of fiber-optic cable. You learn about how fibers can guide light for long distances. You also learn about the types of cable used, how fiber is installed, the type of connectors and equipment used with fiber-optic cable, and how fiber is tested to ensure that it functions properly.

The light used in optical-fiber networks is one type of electromagnetic energy. When an electric charge moves back and forth, or accelerates, a type of energy called *electromagnetic energy* is produced. This energy in the form of waves can travel through a vacuum, the air, and through some materials such as glass. An important property of any energy wave is the wavelength, as shown in Figure 1.

Figure 1 Wavelengths

The part of an optical fiber through which light rays travel is called the *core* of the fiber and is shown in Figure 2. Light rays can only enter the core if their angle is inside the numeric aperture of the fiber. Likewise, after the rays have entered the core of the fiber, a light ray can follow only a limited number of optical paths through the fiber. These optical paths are called *modes*. If the diameter of the fiber core is large enough so that there are many paths that light can take through the fiber, the fiber is called *multimode* fiber. Single-mode fiber has a much smaller core that only allows light rays to travel along one mode inside the fiber, as shown in Figure 3.

Figure 2 Fiber-Optic Cable

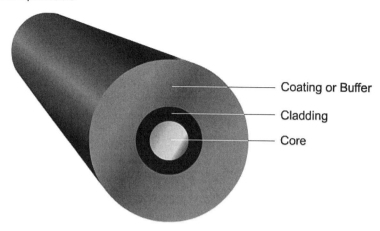

- Coating or Buffer
- Cladding
- Core

Figure 3 Multimode and Single-Mode Fiber

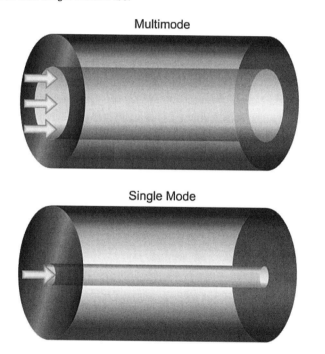

Multimode

Single Mode

Lesson 3.3: Wireless Media

See Chapter 3, "Networking Media," of the Cisco Press Companion Guide, Third Edition, for more information.

The introduction of wireless technology removes the restraints of cables and brings true portability to the computing world. The current state of wireless technology does not provide the high-speed transfers nor the security and uptime reliability of cabled networks. However, the flexibility has justified the tradeoff.

Administrators often consider wireless when installing a new network or when upgrading an existing network. A simple wireless network could be working just a few minutes after the workstations are turned on. Connectivity to the Internet is provided through a wired connection, router, cable, or digital subscriber line (DSL) modem and a wireless access point that acts as a hub for the wireless nodes. In a residential or small office environment, these devices may be combined into a single unit.

Wireless signals are electromagnetic waves that can travel through the vacuum of outer space or through a medium such as air. No physical copper-based or fiber-optic medium is necessary for wireless signals. This makes utilizing wireless signals a very versatile way to build a network. Wireless transmissions can cover large distances by using high-frequency signals. Each signal uses a difference frequency, measured in hertz (Hz) so that they remain unique from one another.

Wireless technologies have been around for many years. Satellite TV, AM/FM radio, cellular phones, remote-control devices, radar, alarm systems, weather radios, cordless phones, and retail scanners are integrated into everyday life. Today, wireless technologies are a fundamental part of business and personal life.

The radio spectrum is the part of the electromagnetic spectrum used to transmit voice, video, and data. It uses frequencies from 3 kilohertz (kHz) to 300 gigahertz (GHz). This section considers only the part of the radio spectrum that supports wireless data transmission.

Many different types of wireless data communications exist, as Figure 4 shows.

Figure 4 Wireless Data Networks

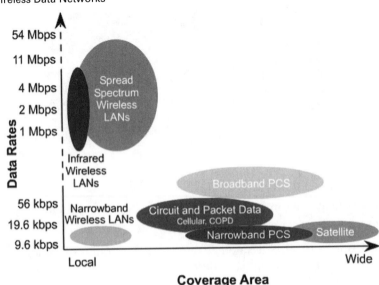

Each type of wireless data communication has its advantages and drawbacks, as follows:

- **Infrared (IR)**—Very high data rates and lower cost, but very short distance.
- **Narrowband**—Low data rates and medium cost. Requires a license and covers a limited distance.
- **Spread spectrum**—Medium cost and high data rates. Limited to campus coverage. Cisco Aironet products are spread spectrum.
- **Broadband personal communications service (PCS)**—Low data rates, medium cost, and citywide coverage. Sprint is an exception; Sprint PCS provides nationwide and international coverage.
- **Circuit and packet data (cellular and cellular digital packet data [CDPD])**—Low data rates, high packet fees, and national coverage.
- **Satellite**—Low data rates, high cost, and nationwide or worldwide coverage.

Module 4—Cable Testing

Lesson 4.2: Signals and Noise

See Chapter 4, "Cable Testing and Cabling LANs and WANs," of the Cisco Press Companion Guide, Third Edition, for more information.

This lesson describes the issues relating to the testing of media used for physical layer connectivity in LANs. For the LAN to function properly, the physical layer medium must meet the industry standard specifications.

Noise refers to any interference on the physical medium that makes it difficult for the receiver to detect the data signal. There are many sources of noise when copper cabling is used, but far fewer sources of noise when optical fiber is used as the transmission medium. Some level of noise on the medium is inevitable, but that acceptable level of noise must be kept as low as possible. Just as it is difficult to carry on a conversation when the background noise of the room is high compared to the volume of the participants' voices, data signals can be overwhelmed by the strength of noise to the point that the desired signal cannot be interpreted.

Proper cable installation techniques and proper attachment of connectors at both ends of a cable are vital. If standards are followed, the data signal experiences less attenuation, and noise levels remain a minimum.

After cable has been installed, it must be tested and meet the specifications of the TIA/EIA-568-B standards. Problems must be identified and corrected prior to further installation of network hardware. Installed cable should also be tested periodically after the installation to determine whether it still meets specifications. Cable and connectors experience wear and deterioration over a period of time and potential problems must be identified and corrected ensure reliable network operation. All cable testing and troubleshooting requires the use of quality cable testers.

Attenuation is the decrease in signal amplitude over the length of a link, as shown in Figure 5. Long cable lengths and high signal frequencies contribute to greater signal attenuation. For this reason, attenuation on a cable is measured by a cable tester using the highest frequencies that the cable is rated to support. Attenuation is measured from only one direction on all wire pairs of the cable because the attenuation of a wire pair is the same in either direction.

Figure 5 Attenuation

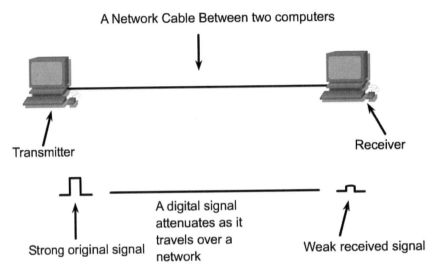

Impedance is a measurement of the resistance of the cable to an alternating current (AC) and is measured in ohms. The normal (characteristic) impedance of a Category 5 cable is 100 ohms. If a connector is improperly installed on Category 5, it will have a different impedance value than the cable. This is called an *impedance discontinuity* or an *impedance mismatch*.

Impedance discontinuities cause attenuation because a portion of a transmitted signal is reflected back to the transmitting device instead of continuing to the receiver, much like an echo. This effect is compounded if multiple discontinuities cause additional portions of the remaining signal to reflect back to the transmitter. When this returning reflection strikes the first discontinuity, some of the signal rebounds in the direction of the original signal, creating multiple echo effects. The echoes strike the receiver at different intervals making it difficult for the receiver to accurately detect data values on the signal. This effect is called *jitter* and results in data errors.

The combination of the effects of signal attenuation and impedance discontinuities on a communications link is called *insertion loss*. Proper network operation depends on constant characteristic impedance in all cables and connectors, with no impedance discontinuities in the entire cable system.

Crosstalk involves the transmission of signals from one wire pair to nearby pairs. When voltages change on one pair of wires, electromagnetic energy is generated. This energy radiates outward from the transmitting wire pair like a radio signal from a transmitter. Adjacent wire pairs in the cable act like antennas generating a weaker but similar electrical signal onto the nearby wire pairs. This causes interference with data that may be present on the adjacent wires. Signals from a completely separate nearby cable can also cause crosstalk. When a signal from outside the cable causes crosstalk, it is called *alien crosstalk*.

The three distinct types of crosstalk are as follows:

- Near-end crosstalk (NEXT), shown in Figure 6
- Far-end crosstalk (FEXT), shown in Figure 7
- Power sum near-end crosstalk (PSNEXT), shown in Figure 8

Figure 6 Near-End Crosstalk (NEXT)

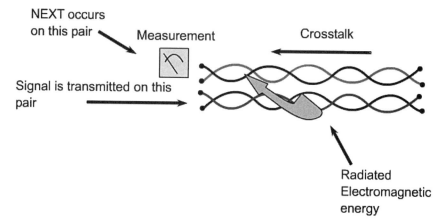

Figure 7 Far-End Crosstalk (FEXT)

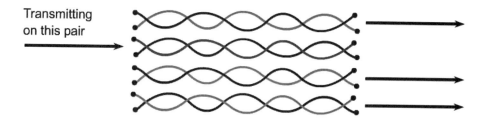

Figure 8 Power Sum Near-End Crosstalk (PSNEXT)

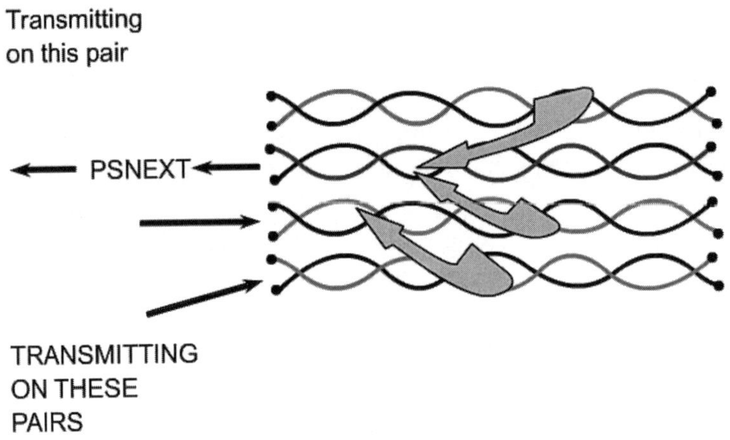

Transmitting
on this pair

←—— PSNEXT←

TRANSMITTING
ON THESE
PAIRS

Module 6—Ethernet Fundamentals

Lesson 6.1: Ethernet Fundamentals

See Chapter 5, "Ethernet Fundamentals," of the Cisco Press Companion Guide, Third Edition, for more information.

Ethernet, in its various forms, is the most widely used LAN technology. Ethernet was designed to fill the middle ground between long-distance, low-speed networks and specialized, computer-room networks carrying data at high speeds for very limited distance.

Ethernet is well suited to applications in which a local communication medium must carry sporadic, occasionally heavy traffic at high-pack data rates. It was designed to enable sharing resources on a local workgroup level. Design goals include simplicity, low cost, compatibility, fairness, low delay, and high speed.

In this module, you learn about history of Ethernet and IEEE Ethernet standards. In addition, this module introduces collision domains and broadcast domains. Finally, this module describes segmentation and the devices used to create network segments.

Ethernet is the dominant LAN technology in the world. Most of the traffic on the Internet originates and ends with an Ethernet connection. From its beginning in the 1970s, Ethernet has evolved to meet the increasing demand for high-speed LANs. When a new media, fiber-optic cable, was produced, Ethernet adapted to take advantage of fiber's great bandwidth and low error rate. Now, the same basic protocol that transported data at 3 megabits per second (Mbps) in 1973 is carrying data at 10 gigabits per second (Gbps).

The original technology that today's Ethernet is based on was wireless. This work later formed the basis for the famous Ethernet MAC method known as carrier sense multiple access/collision detect (CSMA/CD). CSMA/CD is discussed in more detail later in this module.

The original idea for Ethernet grew out of the problem of allowing two or more users to use the same medium without each user's signals interfering with the other's.

During the mid-1980s, Ethernet's 10-Mbps bandwidth was more than enough for the PCs of that era. By the early 1990s, PCs had become much faster and people were beginning to complain about the bottleneck caused by the small bandwidth of Ethernet LANs. In 1995, the IEEE announced a standard for a 100-Mbps Ethernet. This was followed by standards for Gigabit (1 billion bits per second) Ethernet in 1998 and 1999. IEEE approved the standards for 10 Gigabit Ethernet in June 2002. These more modern standards are still Ethernet (802.3).

Like the International Organization for Standardization (ISO), the IEEE is a standards-making organization. The manufacturers of networking equipment are not required to fully comply with all the specifications of any standard. The goals of IEEE are as follows:

- To supply the engineering information necessary to build devices that comply with an Ethernet standard
- To not stifle innovation by manufacturers

Lesson 6.1: Ethernet Operation

See Chapter 5, "Ethernet Fundamentals," of the Cisco Press Companion Guide, Third Edition, for more information.

This section discusses the operation of Ethernet, Ethernet framing, error handling, and the different types of the collisions on Ethernet networks. When multiple stations (nodes) must access physical media and other networking devices, various media access control strategies have been invented. This lesson briefly reviews the access control strategies, and then the discussion focuses on the Ethernet access control method: CSMA/CD.

Note that although CSMA/CD has immense historical importance and practical importance in original Ethernet, it is diminishing somewhat in implementation for two reasons:

- When four-pair unshielded twisted-pair (UTP) is used, separate wire pairs for transmission (Tx) and reception (Rx) exist, making copper UTP potentially collisionless and capable of full duplex depending on whether it is deployed in a shared (hub) or switched environment.
- Similar logic applies to optical-fiber links, where separate optical paths—a transmission fiber and an reception fiber—are used.

One new form of Ethernet—1000BASE-TX, Gigabit Ethernet over copper—uses all four wire pairs simultaneously in both directions, resulting in a permanent collision. In older forms of Ethernet, such a permanent collision would preclude the system from working. In 1000BASE-TX, however, sophisticated circuitry can accommodate this permanent collision resulting from an attempt to get as much data as possible over UTP.

Three well-known Layer 2 technologies are Token Ring, FDDI, and Ethernet. Of these, Ethernet is by far the most common; however, they all serve to illustrate a different approach to LAN requirements. All three specify Layer 2 elements (for example, logical link control [LLC], naming, framing, and MAC), as well as Layer 1 signaling components and media issues. Figure 9 shows the specific technologies for each, and the following list describes each element.

Figure 9 Common LAN Technologies

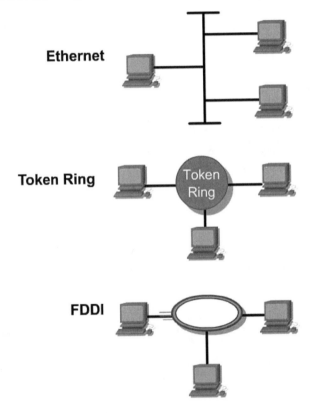

- **Ethernet**—Logical bus topology (information flow is on a linear bus) and physical star or extended star (wired as a star)
- **Token Ring**—Logical ring topology (in other words, information flow is controlled in a ring) and a physical star topology (wired as a star)
- **FDDI**—Logical ring topology (information flow is controlled in a ring) and physical dual-ring topology (wired as a dual-ring)

Ethernet is a shared-media broadcast technology. The access method CSMA/CD used in Ethernet performs three functions:

- Transmitting and receiving data packets
- Decoding data packets and checking them for valid addresses before passing them to the upper layers of the OSI model
- Detecting errors within data packets or on the network

In the CSMA/CD access method, networking devices with data to transmit over the networking media work in a listen-before-transmit mode (CS standing for carrier sense). With shared Ethernet, this means that when a device wants to send data, it must first check to see whether the networking media is busy—that is, whether there are any signals on the networking media. After the device determines the networking media is not busy, it begins to transmit its data. While transmitting its data in the form of signals, it also listens, to ensure no other stations are transmitting data to the networking media at the same time. If two stations send data at the same time, a collision occurs, as shown in the upper half of Figures 10 and 11. After it completes transmitting its data, the device returns to listening mode. With traditional shared Ethernet, only one device can transmit at a time. This is not true with switched Ethernet.

Figure 10 CSMA/CD Process

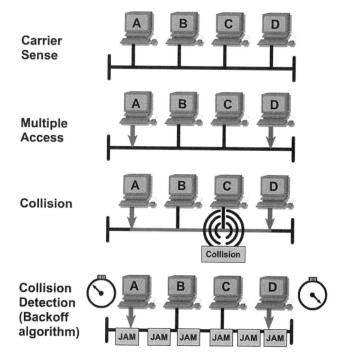

Figure 11 CSMA/CD Process

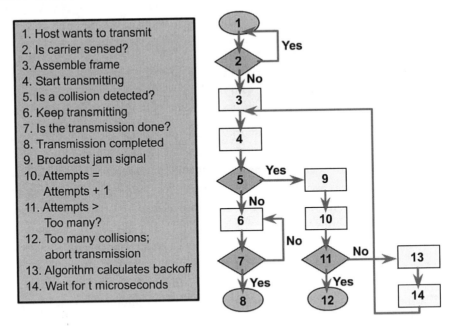

1. Host wants to transmit
2. Is carrier sensed?
3. Assemble frame
4. Start transmitting
5. Is a collision detected?
6. Keep transmitting
7. Is the transmission done?
8. Transmission completed
9. Broadcast jam signal
10. Attempts =
    Attempts + 1
11. Attempts >
    Too many?
12. Too many collisions;
    abort transmission
13. Algorithm calculates backoff
14. Wait for t microseconds

Module 7—Ethernet Technologies

Lesson 7.1: 10/100-Mbps Ethernet

See Chapter 6, "Ethernet Technologies and Ethernet Switching," of the Cisco Press Companion Guide, Third Edition, for more information.

Ethernet has been the most successful LAN technology largely because of its simplicity of implementation compared to other technologies. Ethernet has also been successful because it has been a flexible technology that has evolved to meet changing needs and media capabilities. This lesson introduces the specifics of the most important varieties of Ethernet.

Changes in Ethernet have resulted in major improvements over the 10-Mbps Ethernet of the early 1980s. The 10-Mbps Ethernet standard remained virtually unchanged until 1995 when IEEE announced a standard for a 100-Mbps Fast Ethernet. The power, versatility, and cost effectiveness of 10BASE-T coincided with an explosion in the number of LAN users, the number of Internet users (which also increased LAN traffic), and the complexity of applications. Demand for higher bandwidth grew, and Fast Ethernet was introduced. The copper-cable version of Fast Ethernet that became commercially successful was 100BASE-TX, and many clever features were developed for interoperability with 10BASE-T systems (the emergence of "10/100" interfaces, for example). To compete with the backbone/LAN technology of FDDI, fiber-based 100BASE-FX was introduced. Throughout all of these Ethernet technologies, the MAC addressing concept, the frame format, and CSMA/CD MAC method were maintained.

10BASE-T (originally 802.3i-1990) substituted the cheaper and easier-to-install UTP copper cable for coaxial cable. This cable plugged into a central connection device, a hub or a switch, that contained the shared bus. The type of cable used in 10BASE-T, the distances that the cable could extend from the hub, and the way in which the UTP was installed, interconnected, and tested—all these factors were standardized in a "structured cabling system," which increasingly specified a star or extended star topology. 10BASE-T was originally a half-duplex protocol, but full-duplex features were added later. The explosion in Ethernet's popularity in the 1990s—when Ethernet came to dominate LAN technology—was 10BASE-T running on Category (Cat) 5 UTP.

10BASE-T links generally consist of a connection between the station and a hub or switch. Hubs should be thought of as multiport repeaters and count toward the limit on repeaters between distant stations. Switches can be thought of as multiport bridges and are subject to 100-meter length limitations but no limit on switches between distant stations.

100-Mbps Ethernet, also known as Fast Ethernet (in comparison to the original 10-Mbps Ethernet), was a series of technologies. The two technologies that became commercially important are 100BASE-TX (copper-UTP based) and 100BASE-FX (multimode optical-fiber based). This section examines what these technologies have in common and then examines their individual differences.

100BASE-TX and 100BASE-FX have three things in common:

- The timing parameters
- The frame format
- Parts of the transmission process

Table 1 shows the parameters for 100-Mbps Ethernet operation.

Table 1 Parameters for 100-Mbps Ethernet Operation

Parameter	Value
Bit time	10 ns*
Slot time	512 bit times
Interframe spacing	96 bits
Collision attempt limit	16
Collision backoff limit	10
Collision jam size	32 bits
Maximum untagged frame size	1518 octets
Minimum frame size	512 bits (64 octets)

*ns = nanosecond

100BASE-TX and 100BASE-FX both share timing parameters. Note that 1 bit time in 100-Mbps Ethernet is 10 ns = .01 microseconds = 1 100-millionth of a second.

The 100-Mbps frame format is the same as the 10-Mbps frame. Unlike 10-Mbps Ethernet where the process was the same for all technologies until the signal was applied to the medium, the encoding process differs for each 100-Mbps technology and has multiple steps.

Fast Ethernet represents a 10-fold increase in speed. With this increase in speed comes extra requirements. The bits being sent are getting shorter in duration and occurring more frequently. They require more careful timing, and their transmission requires frequencies closer to medium bandwidth limitations and become more susceptible to noise. In response to these issues of synchronization, bandwidth, and signal-to-noise ratio (SNR), 100-Mbps Ethernet uses two separate encoding steps. The basic idea is to use codes—which can be engineered to have desirable properties—to represent the user data in a way that is efficient to transmit, including achievement of synchronization, efficient usage of bandwidth, and improved SNR characteristics. The first part of the encoding uses a technique called 4-bit/5-bit (4B/5B); the second part of the encoding is the actual line encoding specific to copper or fiber.

The two forms of 100-Mbps Ethernet of consideration in this course, 100BASE-TX and 100BASE-FX, take nibbles (4-bit groupings) from the upper parts of the MAC sublayer and encode them.

The need for faster networks led to the announcement of the 100BASE-T Fast Ethernet and autonegotiation standard in 1995 (originally 802.3u-1995). 100BASE-T increased Ethernet's bit rate to 100 Mbps. 100BASE-TX was the Category 5 UTP version of 100BASE-T that became commercially successful.

Why use 100BASE-FX (introduced as part of the 802.3u-1995 standard)? At the time copper-based Fast Ethernet was introduced, a fiber version was desired for backbone applications, connections between floors and buildings where copper is less desirable and high-noise environments. 100BASE-FX was also positioned as an alternative to the then-popular FDDI (100-Mbps token-passing, dual-ring LAN using fiber-optic cable). However, the vast majority of Fast Ethernet installations today are 100BASE-TX. One reason for the relative lack of adoption of 100BASE-FX was the rapidity of the introduction of Gigabit Ethernet copper and fiber standards, which are now the dominant technology for backbone installations, high-speed cross-connects, and general infrastructure needs.

Lesson 7.2: 1000-Mbps/10-Gbps Ethernet

See Chapter 6, "Ethernet Technologies and Ethernet Switching," of the Cisco Press Companion Guide, Third Edition, for more information.

Fast Ethernet (100 Mbps) represented a major improvement over Legacy Ethernet (10 Mbps). Yet the even more rapid progression from Fast to Gigabit Ethernet is testimony to the power of IEEE standards, engineering advances, and market forces. Gigabit Ethernet, 1000 Mbps, is a 100-fold increase in network speed over the wildly popular 10BASE-T. Although MAC addressing, CSMA/CD, and most importantly the frame format from earlier versions of Ethernet are preserved, many other aspects of the MAC sublayer, the physical layer, and the medium have been changed.

Copper interfaces capable of "10/100/1000" operation are now common. Gigabit switch and router ports and blades are becoming routine in wiring closets. More multimode and single-mode optical fiber is being installed. A major emphasis of Gigabit Ethernet is fiber-optic technology, but the need for a copper version led to a very clever scheme to get 1000 Mbps down the same Category 5 UTP used so successfully in 10-Mbps and 100-Mbps Ethernet. (The copper version is necessary take advantage of existing cable plants and to utilize the ruggedness of copper in user environments.) All the Gigabit technologies are intrinsically full duplex. The inexorable forward march of technology continues as standards and technologies for 40 Gbps, 100 Gbps, and 160 Gbps are currently being implemented. Most dramatic is the evolution of Ethernet from LAN applications only to an end-to-end LAN, metropolitan-area network (MAN), and WAN technology.

1000-Mbps Versions of Ethernet (Gigabit)

In 1998, the 1000BASE-X standard was adapted by the IEEE 802.3z committee. This standard raised the data transmission rate to 1 Gbps full duplex over optical fiber, a 100-fold increase in speed over 10BASE-T. The 1000BASE-T standard, specifying 1 Gbps full duplex over Category 5 or higher UTP was adopted in 1999.

Table 2 shows the parameters for 1000-Mbps Ethernet operation.

Table 2 Parameters for Gigabit Ethernet Operation

Parameter	Value
Bit time	1 ns
Slot time	4096 bit times
Interframe spacing	96 bits*
Collision attempt limit	16
Collision backoff limit	10
Collision jam size	32 bits
Maximum untagged frame size	1518 octets
Minimum frame size	512 bits (64 octets)
Burst limit	65,536 bits

*The value listed is the official interframe spacing.

1000BASE-T, 1000BASE-SX, and 1000BASE-LX all share the same timing parameters. Note that bit time at 1000 Mbps = 1 ns = .001 microseconds = 1 billionth of a second. Also note that some differences in timing relative to Legacy and Fast Ethernet are now appearing because of the special issues that arise with such short bit and slot times.

The 1000-Mbps (Gigabit) Ethernet frame has the same format as is used for 10- and 100-Mbps Ethernet. 1000-Mbps Ethernet has different paths for the process of converting frames to bits on the cable, depending on which implementation is used.

Gigabit Ethernet is a 10-fold increase in speed over Fast Ethernet. Just as with Fast Ethernet, with this increase in speed comes extra requirements—the bits being sent are getting shorter in duration (1 ns). The bits are occurring more frequently, they require more careful timing, their transmission requires frequencies closer to medium bandwidth limitations, and they become more susceptible to noise. In response to these issues of synchronization, bandwidth, and SNR, Gigabit Ethernet uses two separate encoding steps. The basic idea is to use codes—which can be engineered to have desirable properties—to represent the user data in a way that is efficient to transmit, including achievement of synchronization, efficient usage of bandwidth, and improved SNR characteristics.

1000BASE-T

Goals for 1000BASE-T (introduced as 802.3ab-1999 1000BASE-T Gigabit Ethernet over twisted-pair) included the following:

- Functioning over existing Category 5 copper-cable plants
- Ensuring this cable would work by passing a Category 5e test, which most cable can pass after a careful determination
- Interoperability with 10BASE-T and 100BASE-TX
- Applications such as building backbones, inter-switch links, wiring-closet applications, server farms, and high-end desktop workstations
- Providing 10x bandwidth of Fast Ethernet, which became very widely installed by end users helping to necessitate more speed upstream in the network

To achieve this speed running over Category 5e copper cable, 1000BASE-T needed to use all four pairs of wires. Category 5e cable can reliably carry up to 125 Mbps of traffic. Using sophisticated circuitry, full-duplex transmissions on the same wire pair allow 250 Mbps per pair, multiplied by four wire pairs gives a total of 1000 Mbps (1 Gbps). For some purposes, it is helpful to think of these four wire pairs as "lanes" over which the data travels simultaneously (to be carefully reassembled at the receiver).

Gigabit Ethernet over fiber is one of the better recommended backbone technologies. Its benefits are tremendous:

- 1000-Mbps data transfer can aggregate groupings of widely deployed Fast Ethernet devices.
- Noise immunity.

- Lack of any ground potential problems between floors or buildings.
- An explosion in 1000BASE-X device options.
- Excellent distance characteristics.

Gigabit Ethernet over fiber was originally introduced in the IEEE 802.3 supplement titled 802.3z-1998 1000BASE-X Gigabit Ethernet. The only application for which 1000BASE-SX and 1000BASE-LX has not caught on as rapidly is to the office desktop—1000BASE-TX is considered more "user proof" in terms of day-to-day wear and 10/100/1000-Mbps copper interfaces are common.

10-Gbps Versions of Ethernet

Most recently, in 2002, IEEE 802.3ae was adopted. This standard specifies 10-Gbps full-duplex transmission over fiber-optic cable. Taken as a whole, the similarities between 802.3ae and 802.3 (the original Ethernet) and all of the other varieties of Ethernet are remarkable. Metcalfe's original design has evolved, but it is still very apparent in the modern Ethernet. Recently 10 Gigabit Ethernet (10GbE) has emerged as the latest example of the extensibility of the Ethernet system. Usable for LANs, storage-area networks (SANs), MANs, and WANs, 10GbE offers exciting new networking possibilities. What is 10GbE and why should it be used?

Legacy Ethernet, Fast Ethernet, and Gigabit Ethernet now dominate the LAN market. The next step in the evolution of Ethernet is to move to 10GbE, operating at 10,000,000,000 bps. By maintaining the frame format and other Ethernet Layer 2 specifications, increasing bandwidth needs can be accommodated with the low-cost, easily implementable, and easily interoperable 10GbE. 10GbE will only run over optical-fiber media. End-to-end Ethernet networks become possible.

Because of massive growth in Internet and intranet-based traffic, and the rapidly increasing use of Gigabit Ethernet, even higher-bandwidth interconnections are needed. Internet service providers (ISPs) and network service providers (NSPs) can use 10GbE to create high-speed, low-cost, easily interoperable connections between co-located carrier switches and routers. Points of presence (POPs), intranet server farms comprised of Gigabit Ethernet servers, digital video studios, SANs, and backbones are already envisaged applications.

Perhaps most significantly, a major conceptual change comes with 10GbE. Ethernet is traditionally thought of as a LAN technology. But 10GbE physical layer standards allow both an extension in distance (to 40 kilometers [km] over single-mode fiber) and compatibility with Synchronous Optical Network (SONET)/Synchronous Digital Hierarchy (SDH) networks. Operation at a 40-km distance makes 10GbE a viable MAN technology. Compatibility with SONET/SDH networks operating up to OC-192 speeds (9.584640 Gbps) make 10GbE a viable WAN technology. 10GbE might also compete with Asynchronous Transfer Mode (ATM) for certain applications.

The following summarizes how 10GbE compares to other varieties of Ethernet:

- Frame format is the same, allowing interoperability between all varieties of Legacy, Fast, Gigabit, and 10GbE, with no reframing or protocol conversions.
- Bit time is now 0.1 ns; all other time variables scale accordingly.
- Because only full-duplex fiber connections are used, CSMA/CD is not necessary.
- The IEEE 802.3 sublayers within OSI Layers 1 and 2 are mostly preserved, with a few additions to accommodate 40-km fiber links and interoperability with SONET/SDH technologies.
- Flexible, efficient, reliable, relatively low-cost, end-to-end Ethernet networks become possible.
- TCP/IP can run over LANs, MANs, and WANs with one Layer 2 transport method.

CCNA2

Module 8—TCP/IP Messages

Lesson 8.1: Overview of TCP/IP Error Messages

See Chapter 17, "TCP/IP Error and Control Messages," of the Cisco Press Companion Guide, Third Edition, for more information.

IP is limited in that it is a best-effort delivery system and an unreliable method for delivery of network data (the reason it is known as a "best-effort" delivery mechanism). It has no built-in processes to ensure that data is delivered in the event that problems exist with network communication. If an intermediary device such as another router fails or if a destination device is disconnected from the network, delivery will not happen. Additionally, nothing in its basic design allows IP to notify the sender that a data transmission has failed. Internet Control Message Protocol (ICMP), shown in Figure 12, is the component of the TCP/IP protocol stack that addresses this basic limitation of IP. ICMP does not overcome the unreliability issues in IP. Upper-layer protocols must provide reliability if needed. This lesson describes the various types of ICMP error messages and some of the ways they are used.

ICMP is an error-reporting protocol for IP. When datagram delivery errors occur, ICMP is used to report these errors back to the sender of the datagram. If Workstation 1 in Figure 13 sends a datagram to Workstation 6, but the corresponding interface on Router C goes down, for example, Router C uses ICMP to send a message back to Workstation 1 indicating that the datagram could not be delivered. ICMP does not correct the encountered network problem. In the example from Figure 13, ICMP does not attempt to correct the problem with the interface on Router C that is preventing datagram delivery. The only capability of ICMP is to report the errors back to Workstation 1.

Figure 12 ICMP

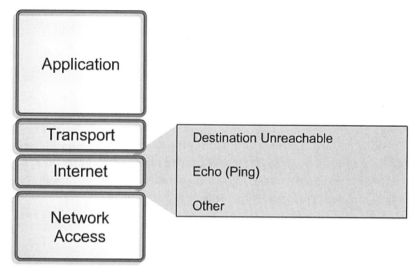

NOTE

Router C does not notify the intermediary devices of the delivery failure. That is, in this example, Router C does not send ICMP messages to Router A and Router B; Router C just sends the message to the originating device. Neither does Router C know the path the datagram has taken to arrive there. Datagrams contain only source and destination IP addresses. They do not contain information about all the intermediary devices. Therefore, the reporting device has only the sender's IP address with which to communicate. This is not to say that Routers A and B will never become aware of the down interface on Router C, but the dissemination of this information to neighbor routers is not the function of ICMP. ICMP reports on the status of the delivered packet to the sender. Its function is not to propagate information about network changes.

Figure 13 Error Reporting and Error Correction

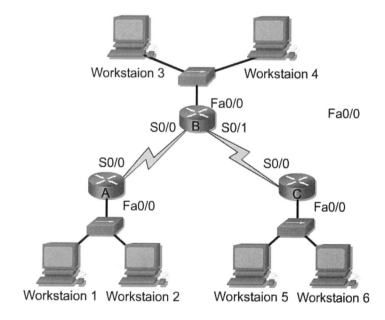

Note the following key points:

- IP is a best-effort delivery method that uses ICMP messages to alert the sender that the data did not reach its destination.
- ICMP echo request and echo reply messages allow the network administrator to test IP connectivity to aid in the troubleshooting process.
- ICMP messages are transmitted using the IP protocol, so their delivery is unreliable.
- ICMP packets have their own special header information starting with a type field and a code field.

Lesson 8.2: Overview of TCP/IP Control Messages

See Chapter 17, "TCP/IP Error and Control Messages," of the Cisco Press Companion Guide, Third Edition, for more information.

Because IP does not have a built-in mechanism for sending error and control messages, it uses ICMP to send and receive error and control messages to hosts on a network. This lesson focuses on control messages, which are messages that provide information or configuration parameters to hosts. Knowledge of ICMP control messages is an essential part of network troubleshooting and is a key to a full understanding of IP networks.

Students completing this lesson should be able to

- Identify potential causes of specific ICMP error messages.
- Describe ICMP control messages.
- Identify a variety of ICMP control messages used in networks today.
- Determine the causes for ICMP control messages.

The Internet Control Message Protocol (ICMP) is an integral part of the TCP/IP protocol suite. In fact, all IP implementations must include ICMP support. The reasons for this are simple. First, because IP does not guarantee delivery, it has no inherent method to inform hosts when errors occur. Second, IP has no built-in method to provide informational or control messages to hosts. For this reason, ICMP performs these functions for IP.

Unlike error messages, control messages are not the results of lost packets or error conditions that occur during packet transmission. Instead, they are used to inform hosts of conditions such as network congestion or the existence of a better gateway to a remote network. Like all ICMP messages, ICMP control messages are encapsulated within an IP datagram, as shown in Figure 14. ICMP uses IP datagrams to traverse multiple networks.

Figure 14 Control Messages

Frame Header Header	Datagram Header Header	ICMP Header Header	ICMP Data
Frame Header Header	Datagram Header Header	Datagram Data Area	
Frame Header Header	Frame Data Area		

Figure 15 ICMP Message Types

ICMP Message Types	
0	Echo Reply
3	Destination Unreachable
4	Source Quench
5	Redirect/ Change Request
8	Echo Request
9	Router Advertisement
10	Router Selection
11	Time Exceeded
12	Parameter Problem
13	Timestamp Request
14	Timestamp Reply
15	Information Request
16	Information Reply
17	Address Mask Request
18	Address Mask Reply

Module 9—Basic Router Troubleshooting

Lesson 9.1: Examining the Routing Table

See Chapter 18, "Basic Router Troubleshooting," of the Cisco Press Companion Guide, Third Edition, for more information.

One of a router's primary functions is to determine the best path to a given destination. A router learns paths, also called *routes*, from an administrator's configuration or from other routers via routing protocols. They store this routing information in "routing tables" using onboard random-access memory (RAM). A routing table contains a list of the best available routes and routers use this table to make packet-forwarding decisions.

The **show ip route** command displays the contents of the IP routing table. This table contains entries for all known networks and subnetworks (and a code that indicates how that information was learned). You can use the following additional commands with the **show ip route** command:

- **show ip route connected**
- **show ip route network**
- **show ip route rip**
- **show ip route igrp**
- **show ip route static**

A routing table maps network prefixes to an outbound interface. When RTA receives a packet destined for 192.168.4.46, it looks for the prefix 192.168.4.0/24 in its table. RTA then forwards the packet out an interface (Ethernet0) based on the routing table entry. If RTA receives a packet destined for 10.3.21.5, it sends that packet out Serial 0/0.

The example routing table, shown in Figure 16, shows four routes for directly connected networks. They are labeled with a C, and RTA drops any packet destined for a network that is not listed in the routing table. To forward to other destinations, the routing table for RTA must include more routes. These new routes may be added in one of two ways:

- **Static routing**—An administrator manually defines routes to one or more destination networks.
- **Dynamic routing**—Routers follow rules defined by a routing protocol to exchange routing information and independently select the best path.

Administratively defined routes are said to be static because they do not change until a network administrator manually programs the changes. Routes learned from other routers are dynamic because they can change automatically as neighboring routers update each other with new information. Each method has fundamental advantages and disadvantages (see Figures 17 and 18).

Figure 16 The **show ip route** Command

```
RTA#show ip route
Codes: C - connected, S - static, I - IGRP, R - RIP, M -
mobile, B - BGP
        D - EIGRP, EX - EIGRP external, O - OSPF, IA - OSPF
inter area
        N1 - OSPF NSSA external type 1, N2 - OSPF NSSA
external type 2
        E1 - OSPF external type 1, E2 - OSPF external type
2, E - EGP
        i - IS-IS, L1 - IS-IS level-1, L2 - IS-IS level-2,
ia - IS-IS inter area
        * - candidate default, U - per-user static route, o
- ODR
        P - periodic download static route
Gateway of last resort is not set
C    192.168.4.0/24 is directly connected, Ethernet0
     10.0.0.0/16 is subnetted, 3 subnets
C    10.3.0.0 is directly connected, Serial0
C    10.4.0.0 is directly connected, Serial1
C    10.5.0.0 is directly connected, Ethernet1
```

Figure 17 Static Routing Advantages and Disadvantages

Static Routing Advantages	Static Routing Disadvantages
Low processor overhead. Routers don't spend valuable CPU cycles calculating the best path. This requires less processing power and less memory (and therefore, a less expensive router).	*High maintenance configuration.* Administrators must configure all static routes manually. Complex networks may require constant reconfiguration.
No bandwidth utilization. Routers don't take up bandwidth updating each other about static routes.	*No adaptability.* Statically configured routes can't adapt to changes in link status.
Secure operation. Routers that don't send updates won't inadvertently advertise network information to an untrusted source. Routers that don't accept routing updates are less vulnerable to attack.	
Predictability. Static routes enable an administrator to precisely control a router's path selection. Dynamic routing sometimes yields unexpected results, even in small networks.	

Figure 18 Dynamic Routing Advantages and Disadvantages

Dynamic Routing Advantages	Dynamic Routing Disadvantages
High degree of adaptability. Routers can alert each other about links that are down or about newly discovered path. Routers automatically "learn" a network's topology and select optimum paths.	*Increased processor overhead and memory utilization.* Dynamic routing processes can require a significant amount of CPU time and system memory.
Low maintenance configuration. After the basic parameters for a routing protocol are set correctly, administrative intervention is not required.	*High bandwidth utilization.* Routers use bandwidth to send and recieve routing updates, which can detrimentally affect perfomance on slow WAN links.
Routers can alert each other about links that are down or about newly discovered path(s).	

Lesson 9.2: Network Testing

See Chapter 18, "Basic Router Troubleshooting," of the Cisco Press Companion Guide, Third Edition, for more information.

Basic testing of a network should proceed in sequence from one OSI reference model layer to the next, as shown in Figure 19. It is best to begin with Layer 1 and work to Layer 7, if necessary. Beginning with Layer 1, look for simple problems such as whether power cords are plugged into the wall. The most common problems that occur on IP networks result from errors in the addressing scheme. It is important to test the address configuration before continuing with further configuration steps.

Figure 19 Testing Process Overview

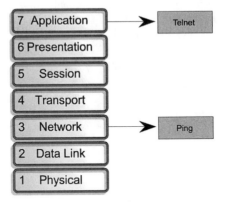

Each test presented in this section focuses on network operations at a specific layer of the OSI model. **telnet** and **ping** are just two of the commands that enable you to test of a network.

Troubleshooting is a process that enables a user to find problems on a network. Troubleshooting should follow an orderly process based on the networking standards set in place by an administration. Documentation is a very important part of the troubleshooting process, as shown in Figure 20.

Figure 20 Troubleshooting Steps

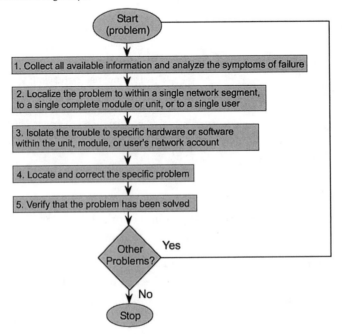

This troubleshooting model follows these steps:

Step 1   Collect all available information and analyze the symptoms of failure.

Step 2   Localize the problem to within a single network segment, to a single complete module or unit, or to a single user.

Step 3   Isolate the trouble to specific hardware or software within the unit, module, or user's network account.

Step 4   Locate and correct the specific problem.

Step 5   Verify that the problem has been solved.

Figure 21 shows one approach to troubleshooting. These two concepts are not the only ways to troubleshoot. To keep a network running smoothly and efficiently, however, an orderly troubleshooting process is of utmost importance.

Figure 21 OSI Layer Troubleshooting

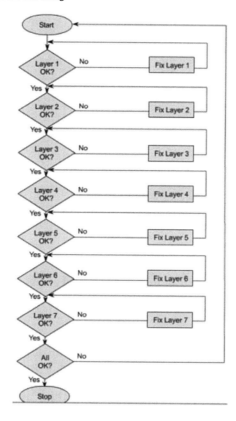

With a structured approach, members of the network know what each member has done in the attempt to solve a problem. A variety of ideas used without any organization results in a chaotic nature to the problem solving. In such cases, very few problems are usually solved.

Testing should begin with Layer 1 of the OSI model and work to Layer 7, if necessary.

Figure 22 shows Layer 1 errors, which may include the following:

- Broken cables
- Disconnected cables
- Cables connected to the wrong ports
- Intermittent cable connection
- Wrong cables used for the task at hand (must use rollovers, crossover cables, and straight-through cables correctly)
- Transceiver problems
- DCE cable problems
- DTE cable problems
- Devices turned off

Figure 22 Troubleshooting Layer 1

Figure 23 shows Layer 2 errors, which may include the following:

- Improperly configured serial interfaces
- Improperly configured Ethernet interfaces
- Improper encapsulation set (High-Level Data Link Control [HDLC] is the default for serial interfaces.)
- Improper clock rate settings on serial interfaces
- Network interface card (NIC) problems

Figure 23 Troubleshooting Layer 2

Figure 24 shows Layer 3 errors, which may include the following:

- Routing protocol not enabled
- Wrong routing protocol enabled
- Incorrect IP addresses
- Incorrect subnet masks
- Incorrect DNS-to-IP bindings

Figure 24 Troubleshooting Layer 3

If errors appear on the network, the process of testing through the OSI layers should begin. **ping** is a command at Layer 3 that may be used to test connectivity. At Layer 7, the **telnet** command enables you to verify the application layer software between source and destination stations. Both of these commands are discussed in detail in a later section.

Lesson 9.3: Troubleshooting Router Issues Overview

See Chapter 18, "Basic Router Troubleshooting," of the Cisco Press Companion Guide, Third Edition, for more information.

The Cisco IOS contains a rich set of commands for troubleshooting. Among the more widely used are the **show** commands. You can view every aspect of the router with one or more of the **show** commands. The **show** command used to check the status and statistics of the interfaces is the **show interfaces** command. You can use variations of this command to check the status of the different types of interfaces. To view the status of the Fast Ethernet interfaces, use **show interfaces FastEthernet**. You can also use the command to view the status of one particular interface. To view the status of Serial 0/0, for instance, use **show interface serial0/0**.

The **show interfaces** command enables you to view the status of two important portions of the interfaces: the physical (hardware) portion and logical (software) portion. These can be related to the Layer 1 and the Layer 2 functions.

The hardware includes cables, connectors, and interfaces showing the condition of the physical connection between the devices. The software status shows the state of messages that are passed between adjacent devices (messages such as keepalives, control information, and user information). This messaging relates to the condition of a data link layer protocol passed between two connected, neighboring router interfaces.

These important elements of the **show interfaces serial** command output are displayed as the line and data-link protocol status, as shown in Figure 25.

Figure 25 Interpreting **show interfaces serial** Output

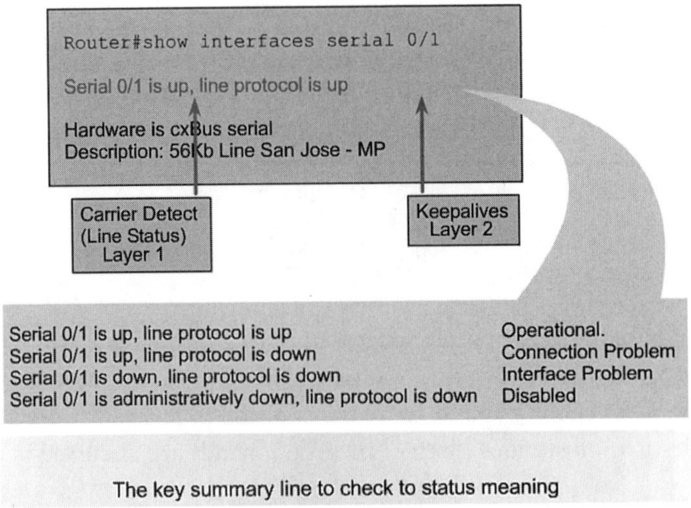

```
Router#show interfaces serial 0/1

Serial 0/1 is up, line protocol is up

Hardware is cxBus serial
Description: 56Kb Line San Jose - MP
```

Carrier Detect
(Line Status)
Layer 1

Keepalives
Layer 2

Serial 0/1 is up, line protocol is up	Operational.
Serial 0/1 is up, line protocol is down	Connection Problem
Serial 0/1 is down, line protocol is down	Interface Problem
Serial 0/1 is administratively down, line protocol is down	Disabled

The key summary line to check to status meaning

The **show interfaces** command is perhaps the single most important tool to discover Layer 1 and Layer 2 problems with the router. The first parameter (**line**) refers to the physical layer. The second parameter (**protocol**) indicates whether the IOS processes that control the line protocol consider the interface usable. This usability is determined by whether keepalives are successfully received. If the interface misses three consecutive keepalives, the line protocol is marked as down, as shown in Figure 26.

Figure 26 Is the Link Operational?

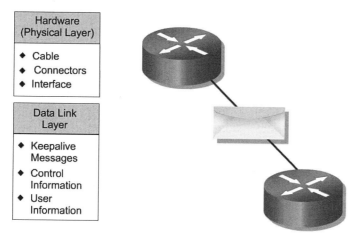

Cisco Discovery Protocol (CDP) advertises device information to its direct neighbors, including MAC and IP addresses and outgoing interfaces.

The output from the **show cdp neighbors** command displays information about directly connected neighbors. This information is useful for debugging connectivity issues. If you suspect a cabling problem, enable the interfaces with the **no shutdown** command and then execute the **show cdp neighbor detail** command before any other configuration. The command displays specific device detail, such as the active interfaces, the port ID, and the device. The version of Cisco IOS that is running on the remote devices also displays.

The **traceroute** command enables you to discover the routes that packets take when traveling to their destination. You can also use **traceroute** to test the network layer (Layer 3) on a hop-by-hop basis and to provide performance benchmarks.

The output of the **traceroute** command generates a list of hops that were successfully reached. If the data successfully reaches the intended destination, the output indicates every router that the datagram passes through. You can capture this output and use it for future troubleshooting of the internetwork.

traceroute output also indicates the specific hop at which the failure occurs. For each router in the path, a line of output is generated on the terminal indicating the IP address of the interface that the data entered. If an asterisk (*) appears, the packet failed. By obtaining the last good hop from the **traceroute** output and comparing it to a diagram of the internetwork, you can isolate the problem area.

traceroute also provides information indicating the relative performance of links. The round-trip time (RTT) is the time required to send an echo packet and get a response. This information enables you to approximate the length of the delay on the link. These figures are not precise enough to be used for an accurate performance evaluation. However, you can capture this output and use it for future performance troubleshooting of the internetwork.

The **show ip protocols** and **show ip route** commands display information about routing protocols and the routing table. You can use the output from these commands to verify the routing protocol configuration.

The **show ip route** command is perhaps the single most important command for troubleshooting routing issues. This command displays the contents of the IP routing table. Its output shows the entries for all known networks and subnetworks and how that information was learned.

Very often routers are remotely configured or troubleshot, and it is not possible to physically inspect the router connections. The **show controllers serial** command enables you to determine the type of cable connected without inspecting the cables.

By examining the **show controllers serial** command output, you can determine the type of cable that the controller detects. This information proves useful for finding a serial interface with no cable, the wrong type of cable, or a defective cable.

The **show controllers serial** command queries the integrated circuit (chip) that controls the serial interfaces and displays information about the physical interface. This output varies from controller chip to controller chip. Even within a router type, different controller chips may be used.

Module 11—Access Lists

Lesson 11.1: Access Control List Fundamentals

See Chapter 19, "Intermediate TCP," of the Cisco Press Companion Guide, Third Edition, for more information.

Network administrators must figure out how to deny unwanted access to the network while allowing internal users appropriate access to necessary services. Although security tools, such as passwords, callback equipment, and physical security devices are helpful, they often lack the flexibility of basic traffic filtering and the specific controls most administrators prefer. For example, a network administrator might want to allow users access to the Internet but might not want external users to use telnet to access the LAN.

Routers provide basic traffic-filtering capabilities, such as blocking Internet traffic, with access control lists (ACLs). An ACL is a sequential list of **permit** or **deny** statements that apply to addresses or upper-layer protocols. This lesson explains how to use standard and extended ACLs as a means to control network traffic and how ACLs are used as part of a security solution.

In addition, this lesson includes tips, considerations, recommendations, and general guidelines on how to use ACLs, including the commands and configurations needed to create ACLs. This lesson also provides examples of standard and extended ACLs and discusses how to apply ACLs to router interfaces.

ACLs are lists of conditions that are applied to traffic traveling across a router's interface, as shown in Figure 27. These lists tell the router what types of packets to accept or deny. Acceptance and denial can be based on specified conditions. ACLs enable management of traffic and secure access to and from a network.

Figure 27 ACL

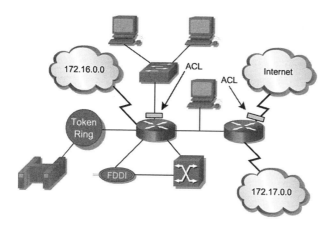

ACLs can be created for all routed network protocols, such as Internet Protocol (IP) and Internetwork Packet Exchange (IPX). ACLs can be configured at the router to control access to a network or subnet.

ACLs filter network traffic by controlling whether routed packets are forwarded or blocked at the router's interfaces, as shown in Figure 28. The router examines each packet to determine whether to forward or drop it, based on the conditions specified in the ACL. Some ACL decision points are source and destination addresses, protocols, and upper-layer port numbers.

Figure 28 ACLs Checking Packet Headers

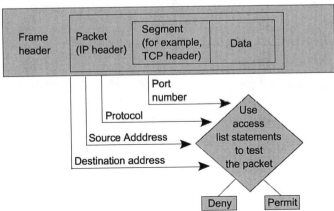

ACLs must be defined on a per-protocol, per-direction, per-port basis, as shown in Figure 29. To control traffic flow on an interface, an ACL must be defined for each protocol enabled on the interface. ACLs control traffic in only one direction on an interface; so for every protocol, two access lists need to be created (inbound and outbound). Finally, every interface can have multiple protocols and directions defined. If the router has two interfaces configured for IP, AppleTalk, and IPX, at least 12 separate ACLs are needed: one ACL for each protocol, times two, for direction in and out, times two for the number of ports.

Figure 29 Access List Groupings in a Router

IP
IPX
AppletTalk

IP
IPX
AppletTalk

One list, per point, per direction, per protocol

With two interfaces and three protocols running, this router could have a total of 12 separate ACLs.

The following are some of the primary reasons to create ACLs:

- Limit network traffic and increase network performance. By restricting video traffic, for instance, ACLs could greatly reduce the network load and consequently increase network performance.

- Provide traffic flow control. ACLs can restrict the delivery of routing updates. If updates are not required, because of network conditions, bandwidth is preserved.

- Provide a basic level of security for network access. ACLs can allow one host to access a part of the network and prevent another host from accessing the same area. Host A is allowed to access the Human Resources network, for example, and Host B is prevented from accessing it.

- Decide which types of traffic are forwarded or blocked at the router interfaces. Permit e-mail traffic to be routed but at the same time block all telnet traffic.

- Allow an administrator to control which areas a client can access on a network.

- Screen certain hosts either to allow or deny access to part of a network.

- Grant or deny user permission to access only certain types of files, such as FTP or HTTP.

If ACLs are not configured on the router, all packets passing through the router are allowed onto all parts of the network.

Lesson 11.2: Access Control Lists

See Chapter 19, "Intermediate TCP," of the Cisco Press Companion Guide, Third Edition, for more information.

Access control lists (ACLs) can be as simple as a single line intended to permit packets from a specific host, or they can be extremely complex sets of rules and conditions that can precisely define traffic and shape the performance of router processes. Many of the advanced uses of ACLs are beyond the scope of this course, but this lesson does cover standard and extended ACLs, the proper placement of ACLs, and some special applications of ACLs.

Standard ACLs check the source address of IP packets that are routed, as shown in Figure 30. The comparison results in either permit or deny access for an entire protocol suite, based on the network, subnet, and host addresses. For example, packets coming in Fa0/0 are checked for source address and protocol. If they are permitted, the packets are routed through the router to an output interface. If they are not permitted, they are dropped at the incoming interface.

Figure 30 Standard ACL

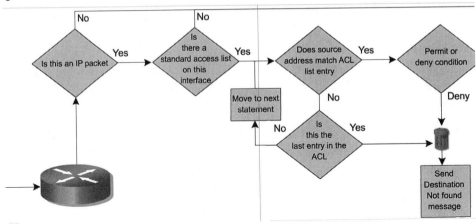

The standard version of the **access-list** global configuration enables you to define a standard ACL with a number in the range of 1 to 99, as shown in Figure 31. In the first ACL statement, notice that there is no wildcard mask. In this case where no list is shown, the default mask is used: 0.0.0.0.

Figure 31 Standard ACL Statements

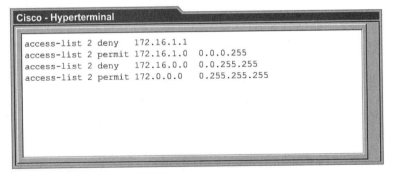

- Access list number range of 1-99
- Filter only on source IP address
- Wildcard masks
- Applied to port closest to destination

Extended ACLs are used more often than standard ACLs because they provide a greater range of control, as shown in Figure 32. Extended ACLs check the source and destination packet addresses and can check for protocols and port numbers (giving you greater flexibility to describe what the ACL will check). Packets can be permitted or denied access based on where the packet originated and its destination as well as protocol type and port addresses. An extended ACL can allow e-mail traffic from Fa0/0 to specific S0/0 destinations, while denying file transfers and web browsing. When packets are discarded, some protocols send an echo packet to the sender, stating that the destination was unreachable.

Figure 32 Extended ACL

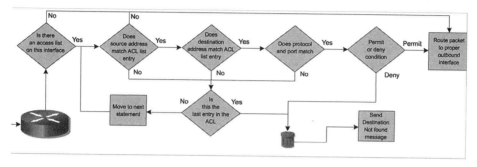

IP named ACLs were introduced in Cisco IOS Software Release 11.2, allowing standard and extended ACLs to be given names rather than numbers. A named access list provides the following advantages:

- Intuitively identify an ACL using an alphanumeric name.
- Eliminate the limit of 99 simple and 100 extended ACLs.
- Modify ACLs without deleting and then reconfiguring them. (Note that a named access list will allow the deletion of statements but will only allow for statements to be inserted at the end of a list.)

CCNA3

Module 1—Introduction to Classless Routing

Lesson 1.1: Variable-Length Subnet Masks (VLSM)

See Chapter 2, "Introduction to Classless Routing," of the Cisco Press Companion Guide, Third Edition, for more information.

A network administrator must anticipate and manage the physical growth of a network, perhaps by buying or leasing another floor of the building to house new networking equipment such as racks, patch panels, switches, and routers. The network designer must choose an addressing scheme that allows for growth. Variable-length subnet masking (VLSM) is a technique that allows for the creation of efficient, scalable addressing schemes.

Variable-length subnet masks (VLSMs) were developed to allow multiple levels of subnetworked IP addresses within a single network. You can use this strategy only when it is supported by the routing protocol in use, such as Open Shortest Path First (OSPF) and Enhanced Interior Gateway Routing Protocol (EIGRP). RIP version 1 is older than VLSM and cannot support it. RIP version 2, however, can support VLSM.

As IP subnets have grown, administrators have looked for ways to use their address space more efficiently. One technique is called variable-length subnet masks (VLSMs). VLSM allows an organization to use more than one subnet mask within the same network address space. VLSM enables an administrator to "subnet a subnet," and it can be used to maximize addressing efficiency, as shown in Figures 33 and 34.

Figure 33 What Is a Variable-Length Subnet Mask?

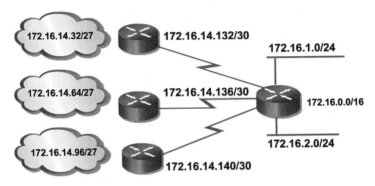

172.16.14.32/27
172.16.14.132/30
172.16.1.0/24
172.16.14.64/27
172.16.14.136/30
172.16.0.0/16
172.16.2.0/24
172.16.14.96/27
172.16.14.140/30

- Subnet 172.16.14/024 is divided into smaller subnets:
— Subnet with one mask (/27)
— Then further subnet one of the unused /27 subnets into mutiple /30 subnets

Figure 34 Calculating VLSMs

```
2
3
4
5
6
7
```

Subnetted Address: 172.16.32.0/20
In Binary 10101100.00010000.00100000.00000000

VLSM Address: 172.16.32.0/26
In Binary 101011100.00010000.00100000.00000000

	Network		Subnet	VLSM Subnet	Host	
1st subnet:	172	16	.0010	0000.00	000000 =	172.16.32.0/26
2nd subnet:	172	16	.0010	000.01	000000 =	172.16.32.64/26
3rd subnet:	172	16	.0010	0000.10	000000 =	172.16.32.128/26
4th subnet:	172	16	.0010	0000.11	000000 =	172.16.32.192/26
5th subnet:	172	16	.0010	001.00	000000 =	172.16.33.0/26

Within an autonomous system, most routing protocols insist that every network use the same subnet mask. Therefore, if 192.168.187.0, 192.168.188.0, and 192.168.200.0 are all in IGRP autonomous system number 2, these networks must all agree upon *one* subnet mask, such as 255.255.255.0.

VLSM is simply a feature that allows a single autonomous system to have networks with different subnet masks. If a routing protocol allows VLSM, use a 30-bit subnet mask on network connections, 255.255.255.252; a 24-bit mask for user networks, 255.255.255.0; or even a 22-bit mask, 255.255.252.0, for networks with up to 1000 users, as shown in Figure 35.

Figure 35 Subnet Masks

Subnet Masks		
255.255.255.252	11111111 11111111 11111111 11111100	30 bits
255.255.255.0	11111111 11111111 11111111 00000000	24 bits
255.255.255.0	11111111 11111111 11111100 00000000	22 bits

Lesson 1.2: RIP Version 2

See Chapter 2, "Introduction to Classless Routing," of the Cisco Press Companion Guide, Third Edition, for more information.

Networks must be scalable to meet the changing needs of users. When a network is scalable, it can grow in a logical, efficient, and cost-effective way. Which routing protocol is used in a network does much to determine the scalability of the network. Therefore, it is important that the routing protocol be chosen wisely. The Routing Information Protocol (RIP) is still considered suitable for very small networks but is not scalable to large networks because of many inherent limitations. To overcome these limitations yet maintain the simplicity of RIP version 1 (RIPv1), RIP version 2 (RIPv2) was developed.

Students completing this lesson should be able to

- Identify the key features of RIPv1 and RIPv2.
- Identify the important differences between RIPv1 and RIPv2.
- Configure RIPv2.
- Verify and troubleshoot RIPv2 operation.

The Internet is a collection of autonomous systems. Each autonomous system is generally administered by a single entity. Each autonomous system has its own routing technology, which may differ from other autonomous systems. The routing protocol used within an autonomous system is referred to as an Interior Gateway Protocol (IGP). A separate protocol, called an Exterior Gateway Protocol (EGP), is used to transfer routing information among autonomous systems. RIP was designed to work as an IGP in a moderate-sized autonomous system and is not intended for use in more complex environments.

RIPv1, shown in Figure 36, is considered an IGP that is classful. RIPv1 is a distance vector protocol that broadcasts its entire routing table to each neighbor router at pre-determined intervals, such as 30-second intervals. RIP uses hop count as a metric, with 15 as the maximum number of hops.

Figure 36 History of RIP

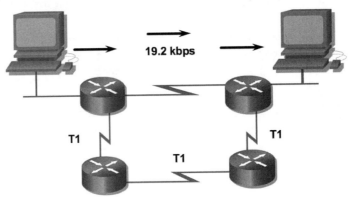

- Maximum is 6 paths (default = 4)
- Hop-count metric selects the path
- Routes update every 30 seconds

If the router receives information about a network, and the receiving interface belongs to the same network but is on a different subnet, the router applies the one subnet mask that is configured on the receiving interface.

For Class A addresses, the default classful mask is 255.0.0.0.

For Class B addresses, the default classful mask is 255.255.0.0.

For Class C addresses, the default classful mask is 255.255.255.0.

RIPv1 is a popular routing protocol because virtually all IP routers support it. The popularity of RIPv1 is based on the simplicity and the universal compatibility it demonstrates. RIPv1 is capable of load balancing over as many as six equal-cost paths; the default is four paths.

RIPv1 has the following limitations:

- It does not send subnet masks information in its updates.
- It sends updates as broadcasts on 255.255.255.255.
- It does not support authentication.
- It is not able to support VLSM or classless interdomain routing (CIDR).

RIPv2, an improved version of RIPv1, shares the following features with RIPv1:

- It is a distance vector protocol that uses a hop-count metric.
- It uses hold-down timers to prevent routing loops; the default is 180 seconds.

- It uses split horizon to prevent routing loops.
- It uses 16 hops as a metric for infinite distance.

RIPv2 provides prefix routing, which allows it to send out subnet mask information with the route update. Therefore, RIPv2 supports the use of classless routing in which different subnets within the same network can use different subnet masks and VLSM.

RIPv2 provides for authentication in its updates. A set of keys can be used on an interface as an authentication check. RIPv2 allows for a choice of the type of authentication to be used in RIPv2 packets. The choice can be either clear text or MD5 encryption. Clear text is the default. MD5 can be used to authenticate the source of a routing update. MD5 is typically used to encrypt enable secret passwords, and it has no known reversal.

RIPv2 multicasts routing updates using the Class D address 224.0.0.9, which provides for better efficiency.

Module 2—Single-Area OSPF

Lesson 2.2: Single-Area OSPF Concepts

See Chapter 3, "Single-Area OSPF," of the Cisco Press Companion Guide, Third Edition, for more information.

Link-state routing protocols differ from distance vector protocols. Link-state protocols flood link-state information and so allow every router to have a complete view of the network topology. Triggered updates allow efficient use of bandwidth and faster convergence because the news of the change in the state of a link is sent to all routers in the network as soon as the change happens.

One of the most important link-state protocols is Open Shortest Path First (OSPF). As should be apparent from its name, OSPF is based on open standards, which means it can be developed and improved by multiple vendors. Although it is a complex protocol that can be quite challenging to implement in a large network, the basics of OSPF are fairly straightforward and are the subject of this lesson.

Open Shortest Path First (OSPF) is a link-state routing protocol based on open standards. It is described in several standards of the Internet Engineering Task Force (IETF). The most recent description is RFC 2328. The "Open" in OSPF means that it is open to the public and is nonproprietary.

OSPF is becoming the preferred IGP when compared with RIPv1 and RIPv2 because it is scalable. RIP cannot scale beyond 15 hops, it converges slowly, and it can choose slow routes as it ignores critical factors such as bandwidth in route determination. OSPF deals with these limitations and has been proven to be a robust and scalable routing protocol suitable for the networks of today. OSPF can be used and configured as a single area, as shown in Figure 37, for small networks. It can also be used for large networks. OSPF routing scales to large networks if hierarchical network design principles are used, as shown in Figure 38.

Figure 37 Single-Area OSPF Network

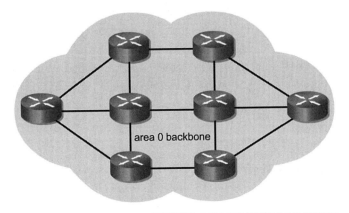

Large OSPF networks are hierarchical and divided into multiple areas.

Figure 38 Single-Area OSPF Network

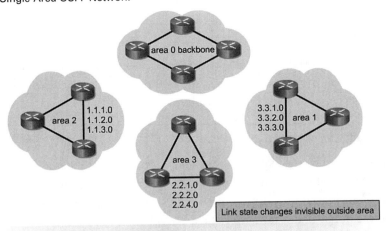

Large OSPF networks are hierarchical and divided into multiple areas.

Large OSPF networks use hierarchical design. Multiple areas connect to a distribution area, area 0, also called the *backbone*. This design approach allows for extensive control of routing updates. Defining areas reduces routing overhead, speeds up convergence, confines network instability to an area, and improves performance.

OSPF Terminology

As a link-state protocol, OSPF operates differently than distance vector routing protocols. Link-state routers identify neighboring routers and then communicate with the identified neighbors. OSPF comes with a new set of terms. Figure 39 lists these new terms.

Figure 39 OSPF Terminology

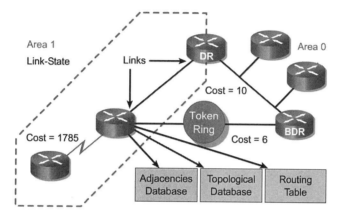

Information is gathered from OSPF neighbors about the status, or links, of each OSPF router, as shown in Figure 40. This information is flooded to all its neighbors. Flooding is a process that sends information out all ports, with the exception of the port on which the information was received. An OSPF router advertises its own link states, as shown in Figure 41, and passes on received link states.

Figure 40 OSPF Terminology

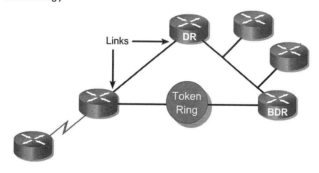

Link: An interface on a router.

Figure 41 OSPF Terminology

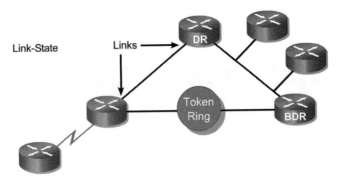

Link-State: The status of a link between two routers. Also a router's
interface and its relationship to its neighboring routers.

The routers process the information about link states and build a link-state database,
as shown in Figure 42. Every router in the OSPF area has the same link-state database,
as shown in Figure 43. Every router has the same information about the state of the
links and the neighbors of every other router.

Figure 42 OSPF Terminology

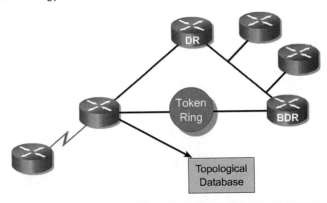

Link-state database (or topological database): A list of
information about all other routers in the internetwork. It shows the
internetwork topology.

Figure 43 OSPF Terminology

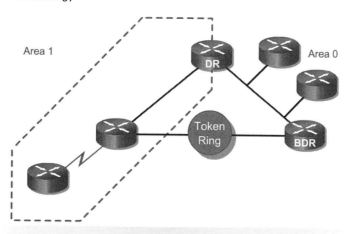

Area: A collection of networks and routers that has the same area identification. Each router within an area has the same link-state information. A router within an area is called an internal router.

Each router then runs the SPF algorithm on its own copy of the database. This calculation determines the best route to a destination. The SPF algorithm adds up the cost, which is a value that is usually based on bandwidth, as shown in Figure 44. The lowest-cost path is added to the routing table, which is also known as the *forwarding database*, as shown in Figure 45.

Figure 44 OSPF Terminology

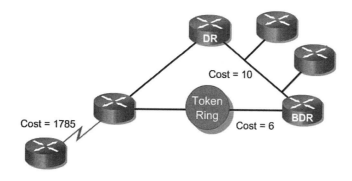

Cost: The value assigned to a link. Rather than hops, link-state protocols assign a cost to a link, which is based on the speed of the media.

Figure 45 OSPF Terminology

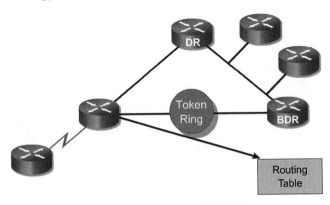

Routing table: The routing table (also known as forwarding database) generated when an algorithm is run on the link-state database. Each router's routing table is unique.

OSPF routers record information about their neighbors in the *adjacency database,* as shown in Figure 46.

Figure 46 OSPF Terminology

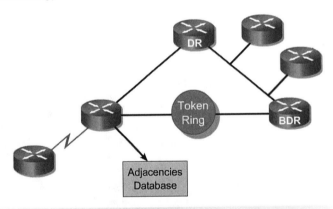

Adjacencies database: A listing of all the neighbors to which a router has established bidirectional communication.

To reduce the number of exchanges of routing information among several neighbors on the same network, OSPF routers elect a designated router (DR) and a backup designated router (BDR) that serve as focal points for routing information exchange, as shown in Figure 47.

Figure 47 OSPF Terminology

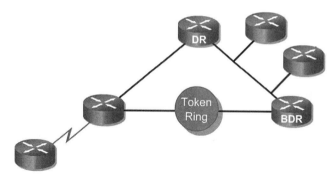

Designated router (DR) and backup designated router (BDR): A
router that is elected by all other routers on the same LAN to
represent all the routers. Each network has a DR and BDR.

Lesson 2.3: Single-Area OSPF Configuration

See Chapter 3, "Single-Area OSPF," of the Cisco Press Companion Guide,
Third Edition, for more information.

OSPF configuration on a Cisco router is in many ways much like the configuration of
other routing protocols. As with other routing protocols, the OSPF routing process
must be enabled and networks must be identified that will be announced by OSPF.
However, OSPF has a number of features and configuration procedures that are
unique to it. These features make OSPF a powerful choice for a routing protocol, but
they can also make OSPF configuration a very challenging proposition.

In large, complex networks, OSPF can be configured to span many areas and several
different area types. The ability to design and implement large OSPF networks begins
with the ability to configure OSPF in a single area. This lesson focuses on just that:
configuration of single-area OSPF.

OSPF routing uses the concept of areas. Each router contains a complete database of
link states in a specific area. If the OSPF network has only one area, that area is numbered 0 and known as *area 0*. In multi-area OSPF networks, all areas are required to
connect to area 0. Area 0 is also called the *backbone area*.

To use OSPF, you must configure it on the router and include network addresses and
area information, as shown in Figure 48. Network addresses are configured with a
wildcard mask and not a subnet mask. The wildcard mask represents the links or host
addresses that can be present in this segment. You can write area IDs as a whole number or in dotted-decimal notation.

Figure 48 Basic OSPF Configuration

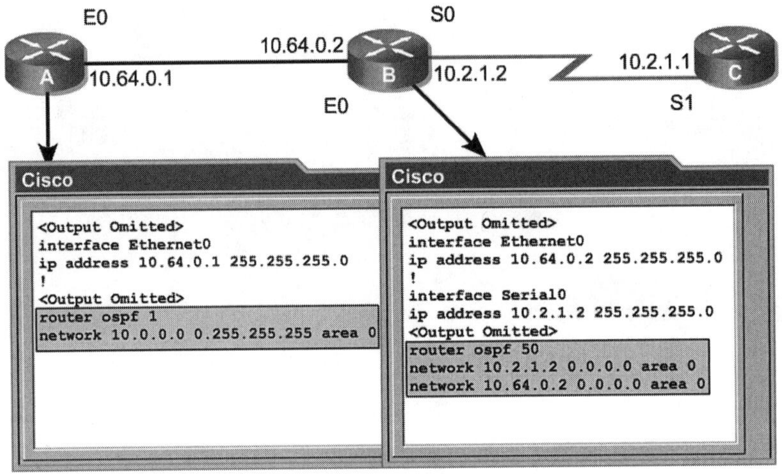

To enable OSPF routing, use the following global configuration command syntax:

```
Router(config)#router ospf process-id
```

The *process-id* refers to a number that is used to identify an OSPF routing process on the router. Multiple OSPF processes can be started on the same router. The number can be any value between 1 and 65,535. Most network administrators keep the same process ID throughout an autonomous system, but this is not a requirement. It is rarely necessary to run more than one OSPF process on a router. IP networks are advertised as follows in OSPF:

```
Router(config-router)#network address wildcard-mask area area-id
```

Each network must be identified with the area to which it belongs. The network address can be a whole network, a subnet, or the address of the interface. *wildcard mask* represents the set of host addresses that the segment supports. This differs from a subnet mask, which is used when configuring IP addresses on interfaces.

Module 3—EIGRP

Lesson 3.1: EIGRP Concepts

See Chapter 4, "Enhanced Interior Gateway Routing Protocol," of the Cisco Press Companion Guide, Third Edition, for more information.

Enhanced Interior Gateway Routing Protocol (EIGRP) is a Cisco proprietary routing protocol based on Interior Gateway Routing Protocol (IGRP).

Unlike IGRP, which is a classful routing protocol, EIGRP supports classless interdomain routing (CIDR), enabling network designers to maximize address space by using CIDR and variable-length subnet masking (VLSM). Compared to IGRP, EIGRP boasts faster convergence times, improved scalability, and superior handling of routing loops.

Furthermore, EIGRP can replace Novell Routing Information Protocol (RIP) and AppleTalk Routing Table Maintenance Protocol (RTMP), serving both IPX and Apple-Talk networks with powerful efficiency.

EIGRP is often described as a hybrid routing protocol offering the best of distance vector and link-state algorithms. Technically, EIGRP is an advanced distance vector routing protocol that relies on features commonly associated with link-state protocols. Some of the best features of OSPF, such as partial updates and neighbor discovery, are similarly put to use by EIGRP. However, EIGRP is easier to configure than OSPF.

Comparing EIGRP with IGRP

Cisco released EIGRP in 1994 as a scalable, improved version of its proprietary distance vector routing protocol, IGRP. The same distance vector technology found in IGRP is used in EIGRP, and the underlying distance information remains the same.

The convergence properties and the operating efficiency have improved significantly, resulting in an improved architecture while retaining the existing investment in IGRP.

Comparisons between EIGRP and IGRP fall into the following major categories:

- Compatibility mode
- Metric calculation
- Hop count
- Automatic protocol redistribution
- Route tagging

IGRP and EIGRP are compatible with each other. This compatibility provides seamless interoperability with IGRP routers. This interoperability is important because it enables users to take advantage of the benefits of both protocols. EIGRP offers multiprotocol support, but IGRP does not.

EIGRP and IGRP use different metric calculations. EIGRP scales the metric of IGRP by a factor of 256 (because EIGRP uses a metric that is 32 bits long, and IGRP uses a 24-bit metric). By multiplying or dividing by 256, EIGRP can easily exchange information with IGRP.

EIGRP also imposes a maximum hop limit of 224. This is more than adequate to support the largest, properly designed internetworks. IGRP has a higher hop-count limit: 255.

Enabling dissimilar routing protocols such as OSPF and RIP to share information requires advanced configuration. However, sharing, or redistribution, is automatic between IGRP and EIGRP as long as both processes use the same autonomous system number. In Figure 49, RTB automatically redistributes EIGRP-learned routes to the IGRP autonomous system and vice versa.

Figure 49 Using EIGRP with IGRP

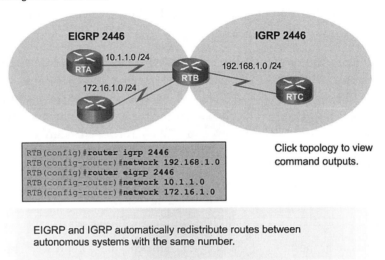

EIGRP and IGRP automatically redistribute routes between autonomous systems with the same number.

EIGRP will tag routes learned from IGRP or any outside source as external because they did not originate from EIGRP routers. IGRP cannot differentiate between internal and external routes.

Notice that in the **show ip route** command output for the routers in Figure 50, EIGRP routes are flagged with D, and external routes are denoted by EX. RTA identifies the difference between the network learned via EIGRP (172.16.0.0) and the network that was redistributed from IGRP (192.168.1.0). In the RTC table, the IGRP protocol makes no such distinction. RTC, which is running IGRP only, just sees IGRP routes, despite the fact that both 10.1.1.0 and 172.16.0.0 were redistributed from EIGRP.

Figure 50 show ip route Command Output

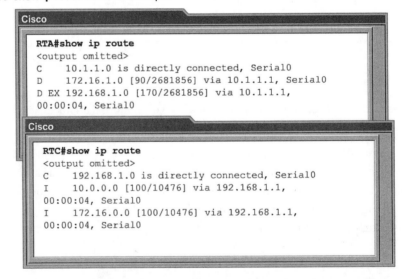

Lesson 3.2: EIGRP Configuration

See Chapter 4, "Enhanced Interior Gateway Routing Protocol," of the Cisco Press
Companion Guide, Third Edition, for more information.

Enhanced Interior Gateway Routing Protocol (EIGRP), the Cisco proprietary routing
protocol based on IGRP, has much of the functionality of OSPF but is much easier to
configure. In a networking environment that is primarily composed of Cisco routers,
EIGRP is an ideal choice for a dynamic routing protocol.

This lesson covers common EIGRP configuration tasks; particularly the ways in which
EIGRP establishes relationships with adjacent routers, calculates primary and backup
routes, and, when necessary, responds to failures in known routes to a particular destination, as shown in Figure 51.

Figure 51 Configuring EIGRP

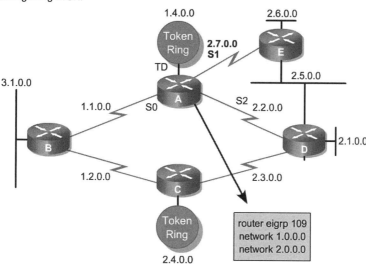

Despite the complexity of the Distributed Update Algorithm (DUAL), configuring
EIGRP can be relatively simple. EIGRP configuration commands vary depending on
the protocol that is to be routed. Some examples of these protocols are IP, IPX, and
AppleTalk. This section covers EIGRP configuration for the IP protocol.

Perform the following steps to configure EIGRP for IP:

Step 1   Use the following to enable EIGRP and define the autonomous system:

```
router(config)# router eigrp autonomous-system-number
```

The autonomous system number is the number that identifies the autonomous system. It is used to indicate all routers that belong within the
internetwork. This value must match all routers within the internetwork.

Step 2   Indicate which networks belong to the EIGRP autonomous system on the local router by using the following command:

```
router(config-router)# network network-number
```

The network number is the network number that determines which interfaces of the router are participating in EIGRP and which networks are advertised by the router.

The **network** command configures only connected networks. For example, network 3.1.0.0, which is on the far left of the main figure, is not directly connected to Router A. Consequently, that network is not part of the configuration of Router A.

Step 3   When you are configuring serial links using EIGRP, it is important to configure the bandwidth setting on the interface. If the bandwidth for these interfaces is not changed, EIGRP assumes the default bandwidth on the link rather than the true bandwidth. If the link is slower, the router may not be able to converge, routing updates might become lost, or suboptimal path selection may result. To set the interface bandwidth, use the following syntax:

```
router(config-if)# bandwidth kilobits
```

The value, *kilobits*, indicates the intended bandwidth in kilobits per second. For generic serial interfaces, such as PPP or HDLC, set the bandwidth to the line speed.

Step 4   Cisco also recommends adding the following command to all EIGRP configurations:

```
router(config-if)# eigrp log-neighbor-changes
```

This command enables the logging of neighbor adjacency changes to monitor the stability of the routing system and to help detect problems.

Lesson 3.3: Troubleshooting Routing Protocols

See Chapter 4, "Enhanced Interior Gateway Routing Protocol," of the Cisco Press Companion Guide, Third Edition, for more information.

A network is made up of many devices, protocols, and media that allow data communication to happen. When one piece of the network doesn't work properly, one or two users may be unable to communicate, or the entire network may fail. In either case, the network administrator must quickly identify and troubleshoot problems when they arise.

A network administrator should approach troubleshooting in a methodical manner using a general problem-solving model. It is often useful to check for physical layer problems first and then move up the layers in an organized manner. Although this lesson focuses on troubleshooting the operation of routing protocols, which work at Layer 3, it is important to eliminate any problems that may exist at lower layers.

All routing protocol troubleshooting should begin with a logical sequence, or process flow. This process flow is not a rigid outline for troubleshooting an internetwork. However, it is a foundation from which a network administrator can build a problem-solving process to suit a particular environment.

1. When analyzing a network failure, make a clear problem statement.
2. Gather the facts needed to help isolate possible causes.
3. Consider possible problems based on the facts that have been gathered.
4. Create an action plan based on the potential problems.
5. Implement the action plan, carefully troubleshooting each problem, one at a time, while testing to see whether the symptom disappears.
6. Analyze the results to determine whether the problem has been resolved. If it has, the process is complete.
7. If the problem has not been resolved, create an action plan based on the next most likely problem in the list. Return to Step 4, change one variable at a time, and repeat the process until you have solved the problem.
8. When the actual cause of the problem is identified, try to solve it.

Cisco routers provide numerous integrated commands to assist in monitoring and troubleshooting an internetwork:

- **show** commands help monitor installation behavior and normal network behavior, as well as isolate problem areas.
- **debug** commands assist in the isolation of protocol and configuration problems.
- TCP/IP network tools such as **ping**, **traceroute**, and **telnet**.

Cisco IOS **show** commands are among the most important tools for understanding the status of a router, detecting neighboring routers, monitoring the network in general, and isolating problems in the network.

Exec **debug** commands can provide a wealth of information about interface traffic, internal error messages, protocol-specific diagnostic packets, and other useful troubleshooting data. Use **debug** commands to isolate problems, not to monitor normal network operation. Only use **debug** commands to look for specific types of traffic or problems. Before using the **debug** command, narrow the problems to a likely subset of causes. Use the **show debugging** command to view which debugging features are enabled.

Module 6—Switch Configuration

Lesson 6.1: Starting the Switch

See Chapter 7, "Switch Configuration," of the Cisco Press Companion Guide, Third Edition, for more information.

A *switch* is a Layer 2 network device that acts as the concentration point for the connection of workstations, servers, routers, hubs, and other switches.

A *hub* is an earlier type of concentration device that, like a switch, provides multiple ports. Hubs are inferior to switches because all devices connected to a hub reside in the same bandwidth domain, and collisions will occur. In addition, hubs operate only in half-duplex mode. Half-duplex mode means the hubs can either send or receive data, but not both, at any given time. Switches can operate in full-duplex mode, which means they can send and receive data simultaneously.

Switches are multiport bridges. Switches are the standard technology for today's Ethernet LANs that utilize a star topology. A switch provides many dedicated, point-to-point virtual circuits between connected networking devices, so collisions are virtually impossible.

The ability to understand and configure switches is essential for network support because of the dominant role they play in modern networks.

A new switch has a preset configuration with factory defaults. This configuration is rarely what a network administrator needs. Switches can be configured and managed from a command-line interface (CLI). Increasingly, networking devices can also be configured and managed using a web-based interface and a browser.

Switches are dedicated, specialized computers, which contain a CPU, RAM, and an OS. Switches usually have several ports for connecting hosts and specialized ports for management. You can manage a switch by connecting it to the console port to view and make changes to the configuration.

Switches typically have no power switch to turn them on and off, but just connect or disconnect from a power source.

Lesson 6.2: Configuring the Switch

See Chapter 7, "Switch Configuration," of the Cisco Press Companion Guide, Third Edition, for more information.

A new switch has a preset configuration with factory defaults. This configuration is rarely what a network administrator needs. Switches can be configured and managed from a command-line interface (CLI). Increasingly, networking devices can also be configured and managed using a web-based interface and a browser.

To effectively manage a network with switches, a network administrator must be familiar with many tasks. Some tasks are associated with maintaining the switch and its Internetworking Operating System (IOS), whereas others involve managing the switch's interfaces and tables for optimal, reliable, and secure operation. Essential network administrator skills include basic switch configuration, upgrading the IOS, and performing password recovery.

A switch may already be configured and only passwords may need to be entered for the user EXEC, enable, or privileged EXEC modes. Switch configuration mode is entered from privileged EXEC mode.

In the CLI, the default privileged EXEC mode is Switch#. In user EXEC mode, the prompt is Switch>.

To ensure that a new configuration completely overwrites any existing configuration, follow these steps:

Step 1   Remove any existing VLAN information by deleting the VLAN database file vlan.dat from the Flash memory directory.

Step 2   Erase the backup configuration file startup-config.

Step 3   Reload the switch.

Security, documentation, and management are important for every internetworking device.

A switch should be given a hostname, and passwords should be set on the console and vty lines.

To allow the switch to be accessible by telnet and other TCP/IP applications, IP addresses and a default gateway should be set. VLAN 1 is, by default, the management VLAN. In a switch-based network, all internetworking devices should be in the management VLAN. This setup allows a single management workstation to access, configure, and manage all the internetworking devices.

The Fast Ethernet switch ports default to auto-speed and auto-duplex. This allows the interfaces to negotiate these settings. If a network administrator needs to ensure an interface has particular speed and duplex values, the administrator can set those values manually.

Intelligent networking devices can provide a web-based interface for configuration and management purposes. When a switch is configured with an IP address and gateway, it can be accessed in this way. A browser can be set to point at the IP address and port (default 80) for a web service. The HTTP service can be turned on or off and the port address for the service can be chosen.

Any additional software, such as an applet, can be downloaded to the browser from the switch and the network devices managed by a browser-based graphical user interface (GUI).

Module 7—Spanning Tree Protocol (STP)

Lesson 7.1: Redundant Topologies

See Chapter 8, "Spanning Tree Protocol," of the Cisco Press Companion Guide, Third Edition, for more information.

Redundancy in a network is extremely important because redundancy allows networks to be fault tolerant. Redundant topologies protect against network downtime due to a failure of a single link, port, or networking device. Network engineers are often required to make difficult decisions balancing the cost of redundancy with the need for network availability.

Redundant topologies based on switches and bridges are susceptible to broadcast storms, multiple frame transmissions, and MAC address database instability. Therefore, network redundancy requires careful planning and monitoring to function properly.

Switched networks provide the benefits of smaller collision domains, microsegmentation, and full-duplex operation. Put simply, switched networks provide better performance.

Redundancy in a network is required to protect against loss of connectivity due to the failure of an individual component. Providing this redundancy, however, often results in physical topologies with loops. Physical layer loops can cause serious problems in switched networks. Broadcast storms, multiple frame transmissions, and MAC database instability can make such networks unusable.

Many companies and organizations increasingly rely on computer networks for their operations. Access to file servers, databases, the Internet, intranets, and extranets is critical for successful businesses. If the network is down, productivity is lost and customers are dissatisfied.

Companies are increasingly looking for 24-hour, 7-days-a-week uptime for their computer networks. Achieving 100-percent uptime is perhaps impossible, but securing a 99.999-percent (or "five nines") uptime is a goal that organizations set. This is interpreted to mean 1 day of downtime, on average, for every 30 years, or 1 hour of downtime, on average, for every 4000 days, or 5.25 minutes of downtime per year.

Achieving such a goal requires extremely reliable networks. Reliability in networks is achieved by installing reliable equipment and by designing networks that are tolerant to failures and faults. The network is designed to reconverge rapidly so that the fault is bypassed.

Fault tolerance is achieved by redundancy. Redundancy means to be in excess or exceeding what is usual and natural. How does redundancy help achieve reliability?

Assume that the only way to get to work is by a car. If the car develops a fault that makes it unusable, going to work is impossible until the car is repaired and returned.

If the car fails and is unavailable on average 1 day in 10, there is 90-percent usage. Going to work is possible 9 days in every 10. Reliability is therefore 90 percent.

Buying another car will improve matters. There is no need for two cars just to get to work; however, the extra car does provide redundancy (backup) in case the primary vehicle fails. The ability to get to work is no longer dependent on a single car.

Both cars may become unusable simultaneously, 1 day in every 100. Purchasing a second redundant car improves reliability to 99 percent.

A goal of redundant topologies is to eliminate network outages caused by a single point of failure. All networks need redundancy for enhanced reliability.

Lesson 7.2: Spanning Tree Protocol (STP) Overview

See Chapter 8, "Spanning Tree Protocol," of the Cisco Press Companion Guide, Third Edition, for more information.

The Spanning Tree Protocol is used in switched networks to create a loop-free logical topology from a physical topology that has loops. Links, ports, and switches that are not part of the active loop-free topology do not participate in the forwarding of data frames. STP is a powerful tool that gives network administrators the security of a redundant topology without the risk of problems caused by switching loops.

Networking topologies are designed to ensure that networks continue to function in the presence of single points of failure. Users have less chance of interruption to their work because the network continues to function. Any interruptions that are caused by a failure should be as short as possible.

Reliability is increased by redundancy. A network based on switches or bridges introduces redundant links between the switches or bridges to overcome the failure of a single link. These connections introduce physical loops into the network, as shown in Figure 52. These bridging loops are created so that if one link fails another can take over the function of forwarding traffic.

Figure 52 Using Bridging Loops for Redundancy

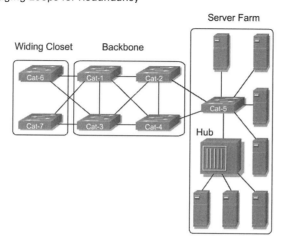

Switches operate at Layer 2 of the OSI model, and forwarding decisions are made at this layer. As a result of this process, switched networks must not have loops.

Switches flood traffic out all ports when it is for a destination that is not yet known. Broadcast and multicast traffic is forwarded out every port other than the port on which the traffic arrived. This traffic can be caught in a loop, as shown in Figure 53.

Figure 53 Broadcast Storm

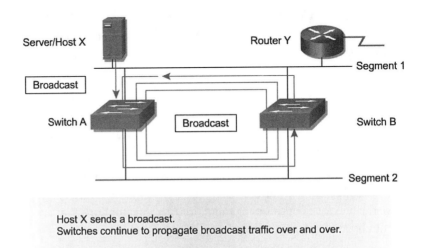

Host X sends a broadcast.
Switches continue to propagate broadcast traffic over and over.

The Layer 2 header does not contain a Time-To-Live (TTL). If a frame is sent into a Layer 2-looped topology of switches, it can loop forever. This wastes bandwidth and makes the network unusable.

At Layer 3, the TTL is decremented and the packet discarded when the TTL reaches zero. This creates a dilemma. A physical topology that contains switching or bridging loops is necessary for reliability, but a switched network cannot have loops.

The solution is to allow physical loops but create a loop-free logical topology, as shown in Figure 54. With this logical topology, traffic destined for the server farm attached to Category 5 from any user workstation attached to Category 4 travels through Category 1 and Category 2. This travel happens even though a direct physical connection exists between Category 5 and Category 4.

The loop-free logical topology created is called a *tree*. This topology is a star or extended star logical topology, the spanning tree of the network. It is a spanning tree because all devices in the network are reachable or spanned.

Figure 54 A Logical Loop-Free Topology Created by the Spanning-Tree Algorithm

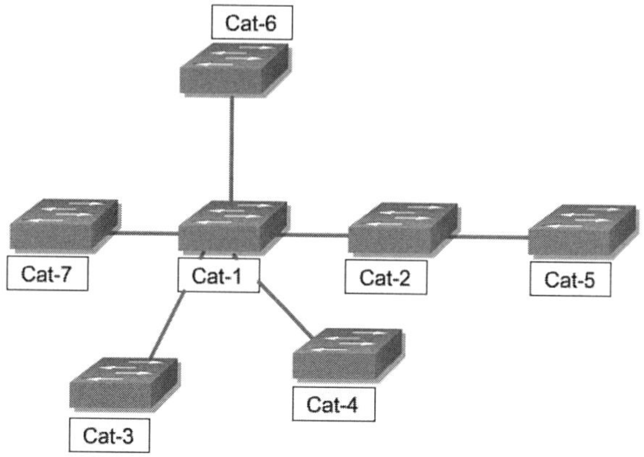

The algorithm used to create this loop-free logical topology is the spanning-tree algorithm. This algorithm can take a relatively long time to converge. A new algorithm called the *rapid spanning-tree algorithm* is being introduced to reduce the time for a network to compute a loop-free logical topology.

Module 8—VLANS

Lesson 8.1: VLAN Concepts

See Chapter 9, "Virtual LANs," of the Cisco Press Companion Guide, Third Edition, for more information.

An important feature of Ethernet switching is the virtual local-area network (VLAN). A *VLAN* may be defined as a group of ports or LANs that have different physical connections but which communicate as if they are connected on a single network segment. Devices on a VLAN are restricted to contacting other devices on their own VLAN unless a router is used to route traffic between VLANs. It is often difficult to get an exact definition for a VLAN because vendors take varied approaches to creating them.

VLANs increase overall network performance by grouping users and resources that communicate most frequently with each other. Businesses often use VLANs as a way to ensure that a particular set of users is logically grouped even if the users are geographically separated. People who work in the marketing section of the business are placed in the Marketing VLAN, for example, and people who work in the Engineering section are placed in the Engineering VLAN.

VLANs can enhance scalability, security, and network management. Routers in VLAN topologies provide broadcast filtering, security, and traffic-flow management.

VLANs are potentially powerful tools for network administrators. Properly designed and configured, VLANs can simplify the tasks of adds, moves, and changes. VLANs can also enhance network security and help with the control of Layer 3 broadcasts. However, improperly configured VLANs can make a network function badly or not at all. It is extremely important to carefully design a network that uses VLANs and to understand the different ways that VLANs are implemented on different switches.

A VLAN is a group of network services that is not restricted to a physical segment or switch, as shown in Figure 55.

Figure 55 VLANs and Physical Boundaries

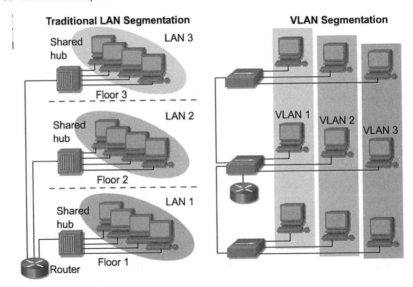

VLANs logically segment switched networks based on an organization's functions, project teams, or applications as opposed to a physical or geographical basis. For example, all the workstations and servers used by a particular workgroup team could be connected to the same VLAN, regardless of their physical connections to the network or location. Reconfiguration of the network can be done through software instead of by physically unplugging and moving devices or cables, as shown in Figures 56 and 57.

Figure 56 Introduction to VLANs

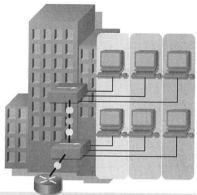

- A group of ports or users in same broadcast domain
- Can be based on port ID, MAC address, protocol, or application
- LAN switches and network management software provide a mechanism to create VLANs
- Frame tagged with VLAN ID

Figure 57 Multiple VLANs

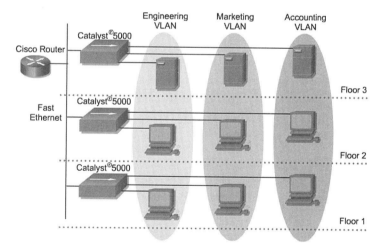

A client workstation on a VLAN is generally restricted to contacting only file servers on the same VLAN. A VLAN may be thought of as a broadcast domain that exists within a defined set of switches. VLANs consist of a number of end systems. These are either hosts or network equipment, such as bridges and routers, connected by a single bridging domain. The bridging domain is supported on various pieces of network equipment, such as LAN switches that operate bridging protocols, with a separate bridge group for each VLAN.

VLANs are created to provide the segmentation services traditionally provided by routers in LAN configurations. VLANs address scalability, security, and network management. Routers in VLAN topologies provide broadcast filtering, security, and traffic-flow management. Switches may not bridge any traffic between VLANs because this would violate the integrity of the VLAN broadcast domain. Traffic should only be routed between VLANs.

Lesson 8.2: VLAN Concepts

See Chapter 9, "Virtual LANs," of the Cisco Press Companion Guide, Third Edition, for more information.

Remember that each interface on a switch behaves like a port on a legacy bridge. Bridges filter traffic that does not need to go to segments other than the source. If a frame needs to cross the bridge, the bridge forwards the frame to the correct interface and to no others. If the bridge or switch does not know where the destination resides, it floods the frame to all ports in the broadcast domain VLAN, except the source port.

In a switched environment, a station usually sees only traffic destined specifically for it. The switch filters most of the other background traffic in the network. This allows the workstation to have full, dedicated bandwidth for sending or receiving interesting traffic. Unlike a shared-hub system where only one station can transmit at a time, the switched network allows many concurrent transmissions within a broadcast domain. The switched network does this without directly affecting other stations inside or outside of the broadcast domain, as shown in Figure 58. Station pairs A/B, C/D, and E/F can all communicate without affecting the other station pairs.

Figure 58 Concurrent Transmissions in a Catalyst

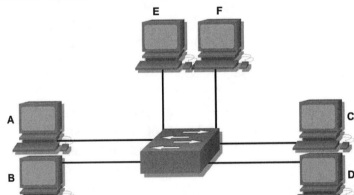

Each VLAN must have a unique Layer 3 network address assigned. This address enables switching of packets between VLANs with routers.

VLANs can exist either as end-to-end networks, which span the entire switch fabric, or they can exist inside of geographic boundaries.

An end-to-end VLAN network has the following characteristics:

- Users are grouped into VLANs independent of physical location, but according to group or job function.
- All users in a VLAN should have the same 80/20 traffic flow patterns.
- As a user moves around the campus, VLAN membership for that user should not change.

Each VLAN has a common set of security requirements for all members.

Starting in the wiring closet, 10-Mbps dedicated Ethernet ports are provisioned for each user. Each color represents a subnet. Because people have moved around over time, each switch eventually becomes a member of all VLANs. Fast Ethernet Inter-Switch Link (ISL) or IEEE 802.1Q is used to carry multiple VLAN information between the wiring closets and the distribution layer switches.

ISL is a Cisco proprietary protocol that maintains VLAN information as traffic flows between switches and routers. IEEE 802.1Q is an open-standard (IEEE) VLAN tagging mechanism that predominates in modern switching installations. Catalyst 2950 switches do not support ISL trunking.

Workgroup servers operate in a client/server model. For this reason, attempts have been made to keep users in the same VLAN as their server to maximize the performance of Layer 2 switching and keep traffic localized.

In the core, a router allows communication between subnets. The network is engineered, based on traffic-flow patterns, to have 80 percent of the traffic contained within a VLAN. The remaining 20 percent crosses the router to the enterprise servers and to the Internet and WAN, as shown in Figure 59.

Figure 59 End-to-End VLANs

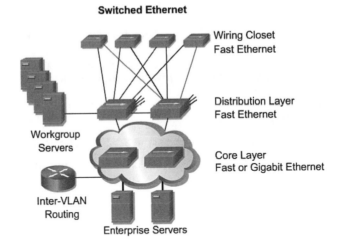

Switched Ethernet

Wiring Closet
Fast Ethernet

Distribution Layer
Fast Ethernet

Workgroup
Servers

Core Layer
Fast or Gigabit Ethernet

Inter-VLAN
Routing

Enterprise Servers

Lesson 8.3: Troubleshooting VLANs

See Chapter 9, "Virtual LANs," of the Cisco Press Companion Guide, Third Edition, for more information.

VLANs are now commonplace in campus networks. VLANs give network engineers flexibility in designing and implementing networks. VLANs also enable broadcast containment, security, and geographically disparate communities of interest. As with basic LAN switching, however, problems can occur when VLANs are implemented. This lesson covers some of the more common problems that can occur with VLANs and examines several tools and techniques for troubleshooting.

Students completing this lesson should be able to:

- Utilize a systematic approach to VLAN troubleshooting.
- Demonstrate the steps for general troubleshooting in switched networks.
- Describe how spanning-tree problems can lead to broadcast storms.
- Use **show** and **debug** commands to troubleshoot VLANs.

It is important to develop a systematic approach to troubleshooting switch-related problems. Figure 60 lists steps that can assist in isolating a problem on a switched network.

Step 1 Check the physical indications, such as LED status.

Step 2 Start with a single configuration on a switch and work outward.

Step 3 Check the Layer 1 link.

Step 4 Check the Layer 2 link.

Step 5 Troubleshoot VLANs that span several switches.

Figure 60 Problem Isolation in Catalyst Networks

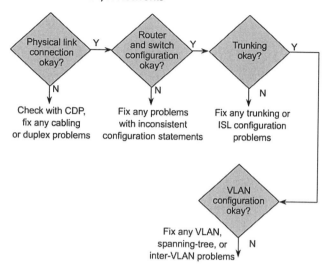

When troubleshooting, check to see whether the problem is a recurring one rather than an isolated fault. Some recurring problems result from growth in demand for services by workstation ports outpacing the configuration, trunking, or capacity to access server resources. For example, the use of web technologies and traditional applications, such as file transfer and e-mail, is causing network traffic growth that enterprise networks must handle.

Many campus LANs face unpredictable network traffic patterns that result from the combination of intranet traffic, fewer centralized campus server locations, and the increasing use of multicast applications. The old 80/20 rule, which stated that only 20 percent of network traffic went over the backbone, is obsolete. Internal web browsing now enables users to locate and access information anywhere on the corporate intranet. Traffic patterns are dictated by where the servers are located and not by the physical workgroup configurations with which they happen to be grouped.

If a network frequently experiences bottleneck symptoms, such as excessive overflows, dropped frames, and retransmissions, there may be too many ports riding on a single trunk or too many requests for global resources and access to intranet servers.

Bottleneck symptoms may also occur because a majority of the traffic is being forced to traverse the backbone. Another cause may be that any-to-any access is common, as users draw upon corporate web-based resources and multimedia applications. In this case, it may be necessary to consider increasing the network resources to meet the growing demand.

Module 9—Virtual Trunking Protocol (VTP)

Lesson 9.1: Trunking

See Chapter 10, "VLAN Trunking Protocol," of the Cisco Press Companion Guide, Third Edition, for more information.

Early VLANs were difficult to implement across large networks. Most VLANs were defined on a per-switch basis, which meant that defining VLANs over an entire network was a complicated task. Further complicating things, every switch manufacturer had a different idea of the best ways to make their switches VLAN capable. VLAN trunking solves many of the problems of early VLANs.

VLAN trunking allows many VLANs to be defined throughout an organization by adding special tags to frames to identify the VLAN to which they belong. This tagging allows many VLANs to be carried across a common backbone, or trunk. VLAN trunking is standards based, with the IEEE 802.1Q trunking protocol now widely implemented. Cisco's Inter-Switch Link (ISL) is a proprietary trunking protocol that can be implemented in all-Cisco networks.

VLAN trunking using specially tagged frames allows multiple VLANs to be carried throughout large switched networks over common backbones. Even with the use of trunks, however, manually configuring and maintaining VLANs on numerous switches can be difficult. VLAN Trunking Protocol (VTP) helps the network administrator by making many of the VLAN configuration tasks automatic.

As mentioned before, a trunk is a physical and logical connection between two switches across which network traffic travels. In few words, a trunk is a single transmission channel between two points that are usually switching centers.

In the context of a VLAN switching environment, a trunk is a point-to-point link that supports several VLANs. The purpose of a trunk is to save ports when creating a link between two devices implementing VLANs, typically two switches. Figure 61 illustrates two VLANs made available on two switches (Sa and Sb) using two physical links between the devices, each carrying the traffic for a separate VLAN. This is the simplest form of implementation, but it does not scale well.

Figure 61 VLANs

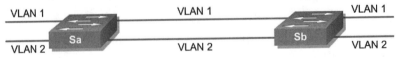

Adding a third VLAN would require two additional ports to be given up. This design is also inefficient in terms of load sharing, and the traffic on some VLANs may not justify a dedicated link. Trunking will bundle multiple virtual links over one physical link, as shown in Figure 62.

Figure 62 Trunking

Figure 63 uses the metaphor of a highway distributor to describe trunking. The roads with different starting and ending points share a main national highway for a few kilometers and then divide again to reach their particular destinations. This method is more cost effective than building an entire road from start to end for every, existing or new destination.

Figure 63 Highway Distributor

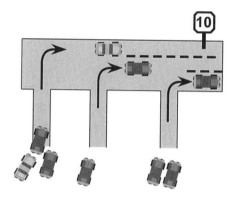

Lesson 9.2: Virtual Trunking Protocol (VTP)

See Chapter 10, "VLAN Trunking Protocol," of the Cisco Press Companion Guide, Third Edition, for more information.

VLAN trunking using specially tagged frames allows multiple VLANs to be carried throughout large switched networks over common backbones. Even with the use of trunks, however, manually configuring and maintaining VLANs on numerous switches can be difficult. VLAN Trunking Protocol (VTP) helps the network administrator by making many of the VLAN configuration tasks automatic.

This lesson explains the concept and operation of VTP as well as its implementation in a VLAN-switched LAN environment.

VLAN Trunking Protocol (VTP) was created to solve potential operational problems in a VLAN's network-switched environment.

Consider, for example, a domain with several interconnected switches that support several VLANs. To maintain connectivity within VLANs, each VLAN must be manually configured on each switch. As the organization grows and additional switches are added to the network, each new switch must be manually configured with VLAN information. A single incorrect VLAN assignment could cause two potential problems:

- Cross-connected VLANs due to VLAN configuration inconsistencies
- VLAN configuration reconciliations across mixed-media environments such as Ethernet and Fiber Distributed Data Interface (FDDI)

With VTP, VLAN configuration consistency is maintained across a common administration domain. Additionally, VTP reduces the complexity of managing and monitoring VLAN networks.

The role of VTP is to maintain VLAN configuration consistency across a common network administration domain. VTP is a messaging protocol that uses OSI Layer 2 trunk frames to manage the addition, deletion, and renaming of VLANs on a single domain. Further, VTP allows for centralized changes that are communicated to all other switches in the network.

VTP messages are encapsulated in either Cisco proprietary Inter-Switch Link (ISL) or IEEE 802.1Q protocol frames, and then passed across trunk links to other devices. In IEEE 802.1Q frames, a 4-byte field is added that tags the frame. Both formats carry the VLAN ID.

Whereas switch ports are normally assigned to only a single VLAN, trunk ports by default carry frames from all VLANs, as shown in Figure 64.

Figure 64 Highway Distributor

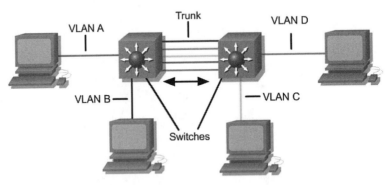

Lesson 9.3: Inter-VLAN Routing

See Chapter 10, "VLAN Trunking Protocol," of the Cisco Press Companion Guide, Third Edition, for more information.

VLAN technology provides network administrators with many advantages. Among other things, VLANs help control Layer 3 broadcasts, they improve network security, and they can help logically group network users. However, VLANs have an important limitation. They operate at Layer 2, which means that devices on one VLAN cannot communicate with users on another VLAN without the use of routers and network layer addresses.

When a host in one broadcast domain wants to communicate with another host, a router must be involved. The same situation exists with VLANs.

Port 1 on a switch is part of VLAN 1, and port 2 is part of VLAN 200, as shown in Figure 65. If all the switch ports were part of VLAN 1, the hosts connected to these ports could communicate. In this case, however, the ports are part of different VLANs, VLAN 1 and VLAN 200. A router must be involved if hosts from the different VLANs need to communicate, as shown in Figure 66.

Figure 65 Multiple VLANs

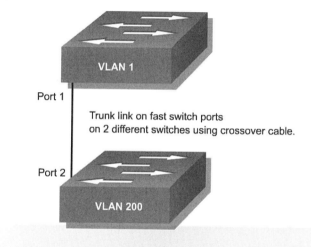

VLANs 1 and 200 cannot communicate without the assistance of a router.

The most important benefit of routing is its proven history of facilitating networks, particularly large networks. Although the Internet serves as the obvious example, this point is true for any type of network, such as a large campus backbone. Because routers prevent broadcast propagation and use more intelligent forwarding algorithms than bridges and switches, routers provide more efficient use of bandwidth. This simultaneously results in flexible and optimal path selection. For example, it is very easy to implement load balancing across multiple paths in most networks when routing. On the other hand, Layer 2 load balancing can be very difficult to design, implement, and maintain.

Figure 66 Multiple VLANs

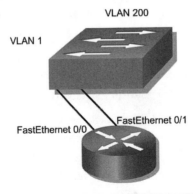

To route traffic between VLAN 1 and VLAN 200 in a non-ISL environment, a router must be connected to a port in VLAN1 and a port in VLAN 200.

If a VLAN spans across multiple devices, a trunk is used to interconnect the devices. A trunk carries traffic for multiple VLANs. A trunk can connect a switch to another switch, for instance, a switch to the inter-VLAN router, or a switch to a server with a special network interface card installed that supports trunking.

Remember that when a host on one VLAN wants to communicate with a host on another, a router must somehow be involved, as shown in Figure 67.

Figure 67 VLAN Components

Switches, Routers, Servers, Management

	Membership Establishment	• Switches—Membership determination
	Communication Across Fabric	• Trunking—Common VLAN exchange
	Inter-VLAN Communications	• Multiprotocol routing— Inter-VLAN exchange
	Server Communication	• Servers-Multi—VLAN communication
	Centralized Administration	• Management—Security, control, administration

CCNA4

Module 1—Scaling IP Addresses

Lesson 1.1: Scaling Networks with NAT and PAT

See Chapter 11, "Scaling IP Addresses," of the Cisco Press Companion Guide, Third Edition, for more information.

The rapid growth of the Internet has astonished most observers. One reason that the Internet has grown so quickly is the flexibility of the original design. This design has not remained static, and if it had, the supply of IP addresses would have been exhausted long ago. To cope with a potential shortage of addresses, several solutions have been proposed. Two of the solutions that have been widely implemented are classless interdomain routing (CIDR) and Network Address Translation (NAT).

NAT is a mechanism for conserving registered IP addresses in large networks and simplifying IP addressing management tasks. As a packet is routed across a NAT-capable device, which is usually a firewall or router, the source IP address on the packet from a private internal network address is translated to a legal, external IP address. This translation allows the packet to be transported over public external networks, such as the Internet. The reply traffic is then translated back to the private internal address for delivery within the internal network. A variation of NAT, called Port Address Translation (PAT), allows many addresses to be translated using a single, globally routable address.

RFC 1918 sets aside three blocks of IP addresses: 1 Class A address, 16 Class B addresses, and 256 Class C addresses, as shown in Figure 68. These addresses are for private, internal network usage only, providing more than 17 million private addresses.

Figure 68 Private IP Addresses

Class	RFC 1918 Internal Address Range	CIDR Prefix
A	10.0.0.0. - 10.255.255.255	10.0.0.0 / 8
B	172.16.0.0 - 172.31.255.255	172.16.0.0 /12
C	192.168.0.0 - 192.168.255.255	192.168.0.0 /16

Public Internet addresses must be registered by a company with an Internet authority (for example, American Registry for Internet Numbers [ARIN] or Réseaux IP Européens [RIPE]). These public Internet addresses can also be leased from an ISP. Private IP addresses are reserved and can be used by anyone. That means two networks, or two million networks, can each use the same private address. RFC 1918 addresses should never be seen on the public Internet. A router should never route RFC 1918 addresses because ISPs typically configure the border routers to prevent privately addressed traffic from being forwarded.

NAT provides great benefits to individual companies and the Internet. Before NAT, a host with a private address could not access the Internet. Using NAT, individual companies can address some or all of their hosts with private addresses and use NAT to provide access the Internet.

NAT is the process of altering the IP header of a packet. NAT changes the header so that the destination address, the source address, or both addresses are replaced in the header. A device that runs specialized NAT software or hardware performs this process. NAT is designed to conserve IP addresses and enable networks using private IP addresses to connect to the Internet. This is accomplished by translating those nonregistered addresses into globally registered IP addresses. NAT also increases network privacy by hiding internal IP addresses from external networks.

A NAT-enabled device typically operates at the border of a stub network. A stub network is a network that has a single connection to its neighbor network, as shown in Figure 69. When a host inside the stub network wants to transmit to a host on the outside, it forwards the packet to the border gateway router. The border gateway router for the host performs the NAT process, translating the internal private address to a public, external routable address, as shown in Figure 70. In NAT terminology, the internal network is the set of networks that are subject to translation. The external network refers to all other addresses.

Figure 69 Introducing NAT and PAT

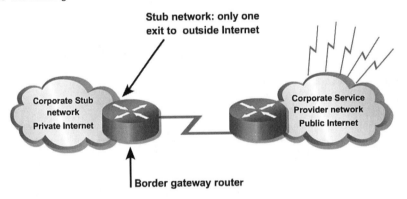

NAT can be configured to use only one address for the entire network. This function, static Port Address Translation (PAT) or "overload," effectively hides the internal network, providing additional security.

Figure 70 Introducing NAT and PAT

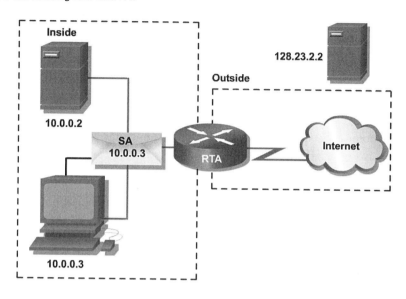

Lesson 1.2: DHCP

See Chapter 11, "Scaling IP Addresses," of the Cisco Press Companion Guide, Third Edition, for more information.

Routers, servers, and other key nodes usually require a static IP configuration, which is entered manually. However, desktop clients do not require a specific address but rather any one in a range of addresses. This range is typically within an IP subnet. A desktop client within a specific subnet can have any address within a range, and the other values are defaults, including subnet mask, gateway, and DNS server.

The Dynamic Host Configuration Protocol (DHCP) was designed to assign IP addresses and other important network configuration information dynamically. Because desktop clients typically make up the bulk of network nodes, DHCP is an extremely useful time-saving tool for network administrators.

DHCP works in a client/server mode. DHCP enables DHCP clients on an IP network to obtain their configurations from a DHCP server. Less work is involved in administrating an IP network when DHCP is used. The most significant configuration option the client receives from the server is its IP address. RFC 2131 describes DHCP.

The DHCP client is part of most modern operating systems, including Windows 2000, Windows NT, Solaris, Linux, and Mac OS. With DHCP, the client requests the configuration values from the network. There must be a DHCP server on the network. This server manages the allocation of the IP configuration values and answers configuration requests from clients. The DHCP server can be responsible for answering requests for many subnets. DHCP is not intended for use in configuring routers, switches, and servers. These hosts all need to have static IP addresses.

DHCP works by configuring a server to give out IP information to clients. Clients lease the information from the server for an administratively defined period. When the lease is up, the host must ask for another address, although the host is typically reassigned the same one.

Administrators typically prefer to use a Microsoft NT server or a UNIX computer to offer DHCP services because these solutions are scalable and relatively easy to manage. Even so, a Cisco IOS feature set, Easy IP, offers an optional, fully featured DHCP server. Easy IP leases configurations for 24 hours by default—a convenience for small offices and home offices, which can take advantage of DHCP and NAT without having a Windows NT or UNIX server.

Administrators set up DHCP servers to assign addresses from predefined pools. DHCP servers can also offer other information, such as DNS server addresses, WINS server addresses, and domain names. Most DHCP servers also allow the administrator to define specifically what client MAC addresses can be serviced and automatically assign them the same IP address each time.

DHCP uses User Datagram Protocol (UDP) as its transport protocol. The client sends messages to the server on port 67. The server sends messages to the client on port 68.

Module 2—WAN Technologies

Lesson 2.2: WAN Technologies

See Chapter 12, "WAN Technologies," of the Cisco Press Companion Guide, Third Edition, for more information.

As the enterprise grows beyond a single location, it is necessary to interconnect the LANs in the various branches to form a WAN. This lesson examines some of the options available for these interconnections, the hardware needed to implement them, and the terminology used to discuss them.

Many options are currently available for implementing WAN solutions. They differ in technology, speed, and cost. Familiarity with these technologies is an important part of network design and evaluation.

If all data traffic in an enterprise is within a single building, a LAN meets the needs of the organization. If data must flow between buildings on a single campus, the buildings can be interconnected with high-speed data links to form a campus LAN. If data must be transferred between geographically disparate locations, however, a WAN is needed to carry the data. Individual remote access to the LAN and connection of the LAN to the Internet are separate study topics and are not considered here.

Most students will not have the opportunity to design a new WAN but many will be involved in designing additions and upgrades to existing WANs and will be able to apply the techniques learned in this lesson.

A WAN is a data communications network that operates beyond the geographic scope of a LAN. One primary difference between a WAN and a LAN is that a company or organization must subscribe to an outside WAN service provider to use WAN carrier network services. A WAN uses data links provided by carrier services to access the Internet and connect the locations of an organization to each other, to locations of other organizations, to external services, and to remote users. WANs generally carry a variety of traffic types, such as voice, data, and video. Telephone and data services are the most commonly used WAN services.

WAN links are provided at various speeds measured in bits per second (bps), kilobits per second (kbps or 1000 bps), megabits per second (Mbps or 1000 kbps), or gigabits per second (Gbps or 1000 Mbps). The bps values are generally full duplex. This means that an E1 line can carry 2 Mbps, or a T1 can carry 1.5 Mbps, in each direction simultaneously.

Devices on the subscriber premises are called customer premises equipment (CPE), as shown in Figure 71. The CPE may be owned by the subscriber or leased from the service provider. A copper cable connects the CPE to the service provider's nearest exchange or central office (CO). The copper cabling is often called the local loop, or "last-mile." A dialed call is connected locally to other local loops, or nonlocally through a trunk to a primary center. It then goes to a sectional center and on to a regional or international carrier center as the call travels to its destination, as shown in Figure 72.

Figure 71 WAN Technology

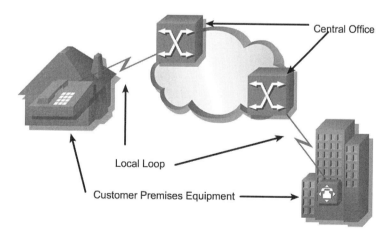

Central Office

Local Loop

Customer Premises Equipment

Figure 72 WAN Service Providers

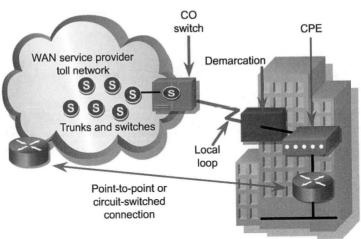

For the local loop to carry data, a device such as a modem is needed to prepare the data for transmission. Devices that put data on the local loop are called data circuit-terminating equipment or data communications equipment (DCE). The customer devices that pass the data to the DCE are called data terminal equipment (DTE), as shown in Figure 73. The DCE primarily provides an interface for the DTE into the communication link on the WAN cloud. The DTE/DCE interface uses various physical layer protocols such as High-Speed Serial Interface (HSSI) and V.35 that establish the codes the devices use to communicate with each other, as shown in Figure 74.

Figure 73 DCE and DTE

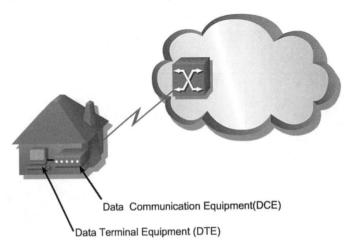

Figure 74 Physical Layer: WANs

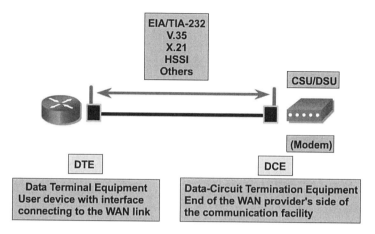

Module 4—ISDN and DDR

Lesson 4.1: ISDN Concepts

See Chapter 14, "ISDN and DDR," of the Cisco Press Companion Guide, Third Edition, for more information.

Integrated Services Digital Network (ISDN) is a network that provides end-to-end digital connectivity to support a wide range of services, including voice and data services.

ISDN allows multiple digital channels to be operated simultaneously through the same regular phone wiring used for analog lines, but ISDN transmits a digital signal rather than an analog one. Latency is much lower on an ISDN line than on an analog line.

Several WAN technologies are used to provide network access from remote locations. One of these technologies is ISDN. ISDN is specifically designed to solve the low-bandwidth problems that small offices or dial-in users have with traditional telephone dial-in services.

The traditional Public Switched Telephone Network (PSTN) was based on an analog connection between the customer's premises and the local exchange, also called the *local loop*, as shown in Figure 75. This analog signaling introduces limitations on the bandwidth that can be obtained on the local loop. Bandwidth restrictions do not permit analog data to travel faster than 3000 Hz. Removal of the bandwidth restriction has permitted the use of digital signaling on the local loop and hence better access speeds for the remote users, as shown in Figure 76.

Figure 75 Physical Layer: WANs

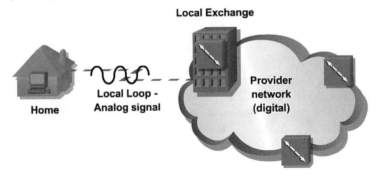

Figure 76 Physical Layer: WANs

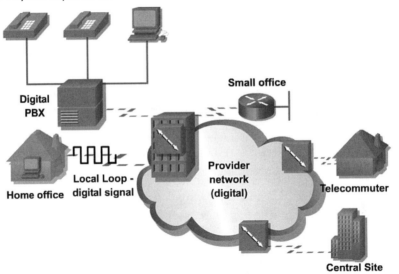

Telephone companies developed ISDN with the intention of creating a totally digital network. ISDN allows digital signals to be transmitted over existing telephone wiring. This became possible when the telephone company switches were upgraded to handle digital signals. ISDN is generally used for telecommuting and networking small and remote offices into the corporate LAN.

Telephone companies developed ISDN as part of an effort to standardize subscriber services. This standardization included the User-Network Interface (UNI), better known as the local loop. The ISDN standards define the hardware and call setup schemes for end-to-end digital connectivity. These standards help achieve the goal of worldwide connectivity by ensuring that ISDN networks easily communicate with one another. In an ISDN network, the digitizing function is done at the user site rather than the telephone company.

ISDN brings digital connectivity to local sites, and the benefits include the following:

- Carrying a variety of user traffic signals, including data, voice, and video.
- Offering much faster call setup than modem connections.
- Bearer channels (B channels) provide a faster data transfer rate than modems.
- B channels are suitable for negotiated Point-to-Point Protocol (PPP) links.

ISDN is a versatile service able to carry voice, video, and data traffic. It is possible to use multiple channels to carry different types of traffic over a single connection.

Unlike PSTN connections, ISDN uses out-of-band signaling, the delta (D channel), for call setup and signaling. To make a normal telephone call, the user dials the number one digit at a time. When all the numbers are received, the call can be placed to the remote user. ISDN allows all the numbers to be signaled to the switch simultaneously, thus reducing the time it takes to set up the call.

ISDN also provides more bandwidth than a traditional 56-kbps dialup connection. ISDN uses bearer channels, also called B channels, as clear data paths. Each B channel provides 64 kbps of bandwidth. With multiple B channels, ISDN offers more bandwidth for WAN connections than some leased services. An ISDN connection with two B channels provides a total usable bandwidth of 128 kbps.

Each ISDN B channel can make a separate serial connection to any other site in the ISDN network. Because PPP operates over both synchronous and asynchronous serial links, ISDN lines can be used in conjunction with PPP encapsulation.

Lesson 4.2: ISDN Configuration

See Chapter 14, "ISDN and DDR," of the Cisco Press Companion Guide, Third Edition, for more information.

The command **isdn switch-type** *switch-type* can be configured at the global or interface command mode to specify the provider ISDN switch.

Configuring the **isdn switch-type** command in the global configuration mode sets the ISDN switch type identically for all ISDN interfaces. Individual interfaces may be configured, after the global configuration command, to reflect an alternate switch type.

When the ISDN service is installed, the service provider issues information about the switch type and service profile identifiers (SPIDs). SPIDs are used to define the services available to individual ISDN subscribers. Depending on the switch type, these SPIDs may have to be added to the configuration. National ISDN-1 and DMS-100 ISDN switches require SPIDs to be configured, but the AT&T 5ESS switch does not. SPIDs must be specified when using the Adtran ISDN simulator.

The format of the SPIDs can vary depending on the ISDN switch type and specific provider requirements. Use the **isdn spid1** and **isdn spid2** interface configuration mode commands to specify the SPID required by the ISDN network when the router initiates a call to the local ISDN exchange.

Configuration of ISDN BRI is a mix of global and interface commands. To configure the ISDN switch type, use the **isdn switch-type** command in global configuration mode, as follows:

```
Router(config)#isdn switch-type switch-type
```

The argument *switch-type* indicates the service provider switch type. To disable the switch on the ISDN interface, specify **isdn switch-type none**. The following example configures the National ISDN-1 switch type in the global configuration mode:

```
Router(config)#isdn switch-type basic-ni
```

To define SPIDs, use the **isdn spid#** command in interface configuration mode. This command is used to define the SPID numbers that have been assigned for the B channels:

```
Router(config-if)#isdn spid1 spid-number [ldn]
Router(config-if)#isdn spid2 spid-number [ldn]
```

Lesson 4.3: DDR Configuration

See Chapter 14, "ISDN and DDR," of the Cisco Press Companion Guide, Third Edition, for more information.

Dial-on-demand routing (DDR) is a technique developed by Cisco that allows the use of existing telephone lines to form a WAN, instead of using separate, dedicated lines. Public Switched Telephone Networks (PSTNs) are involved in this process.

DDR is used when a constant connection is not needed, thus reducing costs. DDR defines the process of a router connecting via a dialup network when there is traffic to send, and then disconnecting when the transfer is complete.

This flowchart shows how a router decides whether to initiate a DDR connection.

DDR is triggered when traffic that matches a predefined set of criteria is queued to be sent out a DDR-enabled interface. The traffic that causes a DDR call to be placed is referred to as *interesting traffic*. After the router has transmitted the interesting traffic, the call is terminated.

The key to efficient DDR operation is in the definition of interesting traffic. Interesting traffic is defined with a dialer list. Dialer lists can allow all traffic from a specific protocol to bring up a DDR link, or they can query an access list to see which types of traffic should bring up the link. Dialer lists do not filter traffic on an interface. Even traffic that is not interesting is forwarded if the connection to the destination is active.

DDR is implemented in Cisco routers as follows:

1. The router receives traffic, performs a routing table lookup to determine whether there is a route to the destination, and identifies the outbound interface.
2. If the outbound interface is configured for DDR, the router does a lookup to determine whether the traffic is interesting.
3. The router identifies the dialing information necessary to make the call using a dialer map to access the next-hop router.
4. The router then checks to see whether the dialer map is in use. If the interface is currently connected to the desired remote destination, the traffic is sent. If the interface is not currently connected to the remote destination, the router sends call-setup information via the Basic Rate Interface (BRI) using the D channel.
5. After the link is enabled, the router transmits both interesting and uninteresting traffic. Uninteresting traffic can include data and routing updates.
6. The idle timer starts when no interesting traffic is seen during the idle timeout period and disconnects the call based on the idler timer configuration.

The idle timer setting specifies the length of time the router should remain connected if no interesting traffic has been sent. When a DDR connection is established, any traffic to that destination is permitted. However, only interesting traffic resets the idle timer.

Legacy DDR is a term used to define basic DDR configurations in which a single set of dialer parameters is applied to an interface. If multiple unique dialer configurations are needed on one interface, dialer profiles should be used.

To configure Legacy DDR, perform the following steps:

Step 1   Define static routes.

Step 2   Specify interesting traffic.

Step 3   Configure the dialer information.

Module 5—Frame Relay

Lesson 5.1: Frame Relay Concepts

See Chapter 15, "Frame Relay," of the Cisco Press Companion Guide, Third Edition, for more information.

Frame Relay was originally developed as an extension of ISDN to enable the circuit-switched technology to be transported on a packet-switched network. The technology has become a standalone and cost-effective means of creating a WAN.

Frame Relay switches create virtual circuits to connect remote LANs to a WAN. The Frame Relay exists between a LAN border device, usually a router, and the carrier switch. The technology used by the carrier to transport the data between the switches is irrelevant to Frame Relay.

The sophistication of the technology requires a thorough understanding of the terms used to describe how Frame Relay works. Without a firm understanding of Frame Relay, it is difficult to troubleshoot its performance.

Frame Relay is an International Telephony Union (ITU-T) and American National Standards Institute (ANSI) standard. Frame Relay is a packet-switched, connection-oriented, WAN service. It operates at the data link layer of the OSI reference model. Frame Relay does this by using a subset of the High-Level Data Link Control (HDLC) protocol called Link Access Protocol Frame (LAPF). Frames carry data between user devices, referred to as data terminal equipment (DTE), and the data communications equipment (DCE) at the edge of the WAN, as shown in Figure 77.

Figure 77 Frame Relay Operation

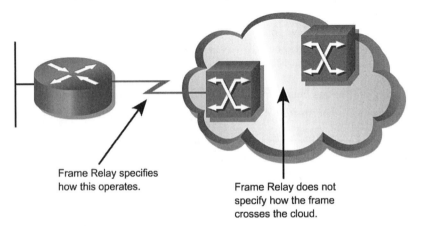

Frame Relay specifies
how this operates.

Frame Relay does not
specify how the frame
crosses the cloud.

Originally Frame Relay was designed to allow Integrated Services Digital Network (ISDN) equipment to have access to a packet-switched service on a B channel. However, Frame Relay is now a standalone technology.

A Frame Relay network may be privately owned but is more commonly provided as a service by a public carrier. It typically consists of many geographically scattered Frame Relay switches interconnected by trunk lines, as shown in Figures 78 and 79.

Figure 78 Frame Relay Switches Interconnected by Trunk Lines

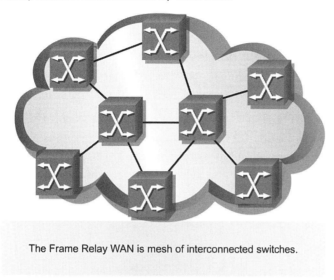

The Frame Relay WAN is mesh of interconnected switches.

Figure 79 Frame Relay Switches Interconnected by Trunk Lines

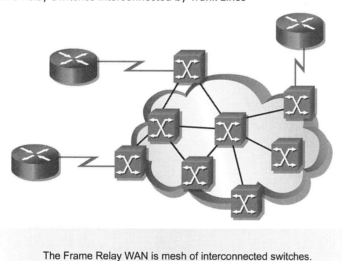

The Frame Relay WAN is mesh of interconnected switches.

Frame Relay is often used to interconnect LANs. When this is the case, a router on each LAN is the DTE. These routers have a serial connection, such as a T1/E1 leased line, to a Frame Relay switch at the carrier's nearest point of presence. The Frame Relay switch is a DCE device. Frames from one DTE are moved via DCEs, across the network, for delivery to the other DTE.

Computing equipment not on a LAN may also send data across a Frame Relay network. The computing equipment uses a Frame Relay access device (FRAD) as the DTE.

Lesson 5.2: Basic Frame Relay Configuration

See Chapter 15, "Frame Relay," of the Cisco Press Companion Guide, Third Edition, for more information.

This lesson explains how to configure a basic Frame Relay permanent virtual circuit (PVC), as shown in Figures 80 and 81. Frame Relay is configured on a serial interface, and the default encapsulation type is the Cisco proprietary version of HDLC. To change the encapsulation to Frame Relay, use the **encapsulation frame-relay** [*cisco* | *ietf*] command.

Figure 80 Frame Relay Overview

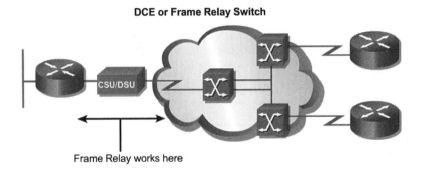

Figure 81 Configuring Basic Frame Relay

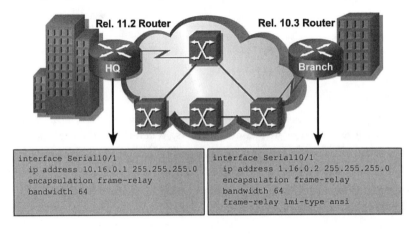

| cisco | Uses the Cisco proprietary Frame Relay encapsulation. Use this option if connecting to another Cisco router. Many non-Cisco devices also support this encapsulation type. This is the default. |
| ietf | Sets the encapsulation method to comply with the Internet Engineering Task Force (IETF) standard RFC 1490. Select this if connecting to a non-Cisco router. |

Cisco's proprietary Frame Relay encapsulation uses a 4-byte header, with 2 bytes to identify the data-link connection identifier (DLCI) and 2 bytes to identify the packet type. Use IETF Frame Relay encapsulation to connect to other vendors. RFCs 1294 and 1490 define the IETF standard.

Set an IP address on the interface using the **ip address** command. Set the bandwidth of the serial interface using the **bandwidth** command (using the kbps format). This command notifies the routing protocol that bandwidth is statically configured on the link. The bandwidth value is used by Interior Gateway Routing Protocol (IGRP), Enhanced Interior Gateway Routing Protocol (EIGRP), and Open Shortest Path First (OSPF) to determine the metric of the link. This command also affects bandwidth utilization statistics, which you can find by using the **show interfaces** command.

You can establish and configure the Local Management Interface (LMI) connection with the **frame-relay lmi-type** [*ansi* | *cisco* | *q933a*] command. This command is only needed if using Cisco IOS Release 11.1 or earlier; with IOS Release 11.2 or later, the LMI type is autosensed, so no configuration is needed. The default LMI type is Cisco. The LMI type is set on a per-interface basis and displays in the output of the **show interfaces** command.

These configuration steps are the same regardless of the network layer protocols operating across the network.

Module 6—Introduction to Network Administration

Lesson 6.1: Workstations and Servers

See Chapter 16, "Introduction to Network Administration," of the Cisco Press Companion Guide, Third Edition, for more information.

The first PCs were designed as standalone desktop systems. The operating system (OS) software enabled one user at a time to access files and system resources. The user had physical access to the PC. As PC-based computer networks gained popularity in the workplace, software companies developed specialized network operating systems (NOSs). Developers designed NOSs to provide file security, user privileges, and resource sharing among multiple users. The explosive growth of the Internet compelled developers to build the NOS of today around Internet-related technologies and services such as the World Wide Web.

Within a decade, networking has become of central importance to desktop computing. The distinction between modern desktop OSs, now loaded with networking features and services, and their NOS counterparts has blurred. Now, most popular OSs, such as Microsoft Windows 2000 and Linux, are found on high-powered network servers and on the desktops of end users.

Your knowledge of several different OSs will help you to select the "proper" OS, one that offers the wide range of services needed. Therefore, this lesson covers UNIX, Linux, Mac OS X, and several Windows OSs.

A workstation is a client computer that is used to run applications and is connected to a server from which it obtains data shared with other computers. A server is a computer that runs a network operating system (NOS). A workstation uses special software, such as a network shell program, to perform the following tasks:

- Intercept user data and application commands
- Decide whether the command is for the local operating system or for the NOS
- Direct the command to the local operating system or to the network interface card (NIC) for processing and transmission onto the network
- Deliver transmissions from the network to the application running on the workstation

Windows NT/2000/XP Professional operating systems can run on a personal computer. Any system that is running one of these operating systems is referred to as either a workstation or a server. A PC is a system running any of the other popular operating systems originally designed for the PC such as DOS, Windows 95, or Windows 98.

UNIX or Linux can serve as a desktop operating system but are most commonly found on high-end computers. These workstations are employed in engineering and scientific applications, which require dedicated high-performance computers. Some of the specific applications typically run on UNIX workstations include the following:

- Computer-aided design (CAD)
- Electronic circuit design
- Weather-data analysis
- Computer graphics animation
- Telecommunications equipment management

Most current desktop operating systems include networking capabilities and support multi-user access. For this reason, it is becoming more common to classify computers and operating systems based on the types of applications the computer runs. Such a classification reflects the role or function that the computer plays, such as workstation or server. Typical desktop or low-end workstation applications might include word processing, spreadsheets, and financial management. On high-end workstations, the applications might include graphical design or equipment management and others as listed previously.

The term *diskless workstation* refers to a special class of computer designed to run on a network. As the name implies, it has no disk drives but does have a monitor, keyboard, memory, booting instructions in ROM, and a NIC. The software that establishes a network connection is loaded from the bootable ROM chip located on the NIC.

Because a diskless workstation does not have disk drives, you cannot upload data from the workstation or download anything to it. A diskless workstation cannot pass on a virus to the network, nor can you use it to take data from the network (for instance, by copying information to a disk drive). As a result, diskless workstations offer greater security than ordinary workstations. For this reason, diskless workstations are used in networks where security is paramount.

Laptops can also serve as workstations on a LAN and can be connected through a docking station, external LAN adapter, or a PCMCIA card. A docking station is an add-on device that turns a laptop into a desktop.

In a network operating system (NOS) environment, many client systems access and share the resources of one or more servers. Desktop client systems are equipped with their own memory and peripheral devices, such as a keyboard, monitor, and a disk drive. The server systems must support multiple concurrent users and multiple tasks as clients make demands on the server for remote resources.

NOSs have additional network management tools and features that are designed to support access by large numbers of simultaneous users. On all but the smallest networks, NOSs are installed on powerful servers. Many users, known as clients, share these servers. Servers usually have high-capacity, high-speed disk drives, large amounts of RAM, high-speed NICs, and in some cases multiple CPUs. These servers are typically configured to use the Internet family of protocols, TCP/IP, and offer one or more TCP/IP services.

Servers running NOSs are also used to authenticate users and provide access to shared resources. These servers are designed to handle requests from many clients simultaneously. Before a client can access the server resources, the client must be identified and be authorized to use the resource. Identification and authorization is achieved by assigning each client an account name and password. The account name and password are then verified by an authentication service acting as a sentry to guard access to the network. By centralizing user accounts, security, and access control, server-based networks simplify the work of network administration.

Servers are typically larger systems with additional memory to support multiple tasks that are all active, or resident, in memory at the same time. Additional disk space is required on servers to hold shared files and to function as an extension to the internal memory on the system. Servers also typically require extra expansion slots on their system boards to connect shared devices, such as printers and multiple network interfaces.

Another feature of systems capable of acting as servers is the processing power. Ordinarily, computers have a single CPU, which executes the instructions that make up a given task or process. To work efficiently and deliver fast responses to client requests, an NOS server requires a powerful CPU to execute its tasks or programs. Single-processor systems with one CPU can meet the needs of most servers if the CPU has the necessary speed. To achieve higher execution speeds, some systems are equipped with more than one processor. Such systems are called multiprocessing systems. Multiprocessing systems are capable of executing multiple tasks in parallel by assigning each task to a different processor. The aggregate amount of work that the server can perform in a given time is greatly enhanced in multiprocessor systems.

Lesson 6.1: Network Management

See Chapter 16, "Introduction to Network Administration," of the Cisco Press Companion Guide, Third Edition, for more information.

Effective management of LANs and WANs is the key element to maintaining a productive environment in the networking world. As more services become available to more users, the performance of networks suffers. Network administrators, through constant monitoring, must recognize and be able to rectify problems before they become noticeable to the end users.

Various tools and protocols enable administrators to monitor the network on a local and remote basis. A comprehensive understanding of these tools is critical to effective network management.

As a network evolves and grows, it becomes a more critical and indispensable resource to the organization. However, the more resources the network offers its users and the more complex the network gets, the more things that can go wrong. Loss of network resources, or even to have the network perform poorly, is not acceptable to the users. The network administrator must actively manage the network, diagnose problems, prevent situations from occurring, and provide the best network performance possible for the users. At some point, networks become too large to manage without automated network management tools.

Network management tasks include the following:

- Monitor network availability
- Improve automation
- Monitor response time

- Maintain security
- Reroute traffic
- Restore capability
- Register users

The driving forces, or goals, of network management are as follows:

- **Control corporate assets**—Unless network resources are effectively controlled, they will not provide the payback that management requires.
- **Control complexity**—With massive growth in the number of network components, users, interfaces, protocols, and vendors, loss of control of the network and its resources threatens management.
- **Improve service**—Users expect the same or improved service as the network grows and the resources become more distributed.
- **Balance various needs**—Users must be provided with various applications at a given level of support, with specific requirements in the areas of performance, availability, and security.
- **Reduce downtime**—Network administrators, through effective redundant design, must ensure high availability of resources.
- **Control costs**—Network administrators must monitor and control resource utilization so that user needs can be satisfied at a reasonable cost.

Module 7—Emerging Technologies

Lesson 7.1: Basics of Optical Networks

See Chapter 17, "Optical Networking Fundamentals," of the Cisco Press Companion Guide, Third Edition, for more information.

Optical networks are an extremely efficient means of transporting data, video, and voice. Optical networks are not affected by electrical interference and may be used in a variety of topologies. This module covers the use of optical fiber in the backbone structure of LANs and MANs and discusses how optical fiber is used in WANs to cover long distances around the globe.

Optical fiber provides fast, reliable transport of information, high bandwidth availability, and network scalability. Optical networks use light pulses over fiber to achieve transfer speeds up to 10 Gbps.

This module introduces some of the advanced technologies used in fiber networking. These technologies are being developed to continue improving the performance and scalability of fiber installations.

Networks must be able to transmit data, voice, and video quickly, efficiently, and cost effectively. In comparison to any other resource, fiber optic is the most efficient medium for transmitting information. Fiber optic offers the highest bandwidth capacity for network traffic, and the technology is expanding exponentially.

The burgeoning Internet economy and surging amounts of data traffic call for scalable, multiservice platforms that can support next-generation, IP-based services and security. Today, service providers look for networks with the following characteristics:

- Capacity/scalability
- Reliability
- Accelerated profits
- Broad coverage
- End-to-end flexibility
- Adaptability
- Space efficiency
- Security

Fiber-optic technology is becoming the core of high-speed networks. Connecting both distant cities and many points within a metropolitan area, optical-fiber networks are made of thin glass strands that carry rapid light pulses, faster and more reliably than copper wires, at speeds up to 10 Gbps.

Information is transmitted at the speed of light in optical fiber. At approximately the diameter of a human hair, optical fiber is extremely strong and can carry a tremendous amount of information.

All communications systems have three things in common: a signal source, a medium for the signal to travel through, and a receiver. In fiber optics, the transmitter is a light source, the medium is a light guide or optical fiber, and the receiver is an optical sensor.

An optical transmitter is just a source of light, like a lightbulb. An electrical signal, such as a voice, data, or video transmission, is converted to light by using the electrical signal to turn the light on and off (for a digital signal) or to vary the intensity of the light (for an analog signal). In a digital signal, the presence of light is a one and the absence of light is a zero. In an analog signal, the intensity of the light matches the strength of the electrical signal level.

The receiver is a semiconductor that converts the light into a corresponding electrical signal. It is generically called an optical-to-electrical (O-E) converter. In a digital signal, the presence of light produces a higher electrical signal level. The absence of light produces a lower electrical signal level. In an analog system, the electrical level corresponds to the power level of the light received by the O-E converter.

Even with no light reaching an O-E converter, an electrical signal will still exist, caused by the dark current that exists in all detector circuits. (*Dark current* refers to the electrical noise that naturally occurs on every electrical circuit.)

Lesson 7.2: Optical Transmission and Multiplexing

See Chapter 17, "Optical Networking Fundamentals," of the Cisco Press Companion Guide, Third Edition, for more information.

In fiber optics, information is carried by modulating the light power, not the wavelength or frequency of the light. It is possible to mix two wavelengths of light on the same fiber without interference between them. This is called *wavelength-division multiplexing* (WDM). WDM allows more than one wavelength to be sent over a single fiber, thereby increasing the capacity, as shown in Figure 82.

Figure 82 Wavelength-Division Multiplexing

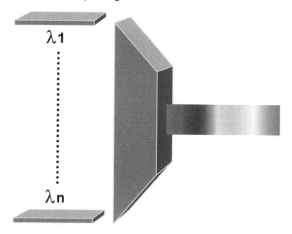

The light source used in the design of a system is an important consideration because it can be one of the most costly elements. The light source characteristics often constitute a strong limiting factor in the final performance of an optical link. Light emitting devices used in optical transmission must be compact, monochromatic, stable, and long lasting.

Figure 83 shows the two general types of light emitting devices used in optical transmission.

- Light emitting diodes (LEDs) and laser diodes
- Semiconductor lasers

Figure 83 LED

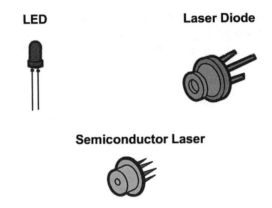

LEDs are relatively slow devices suitable for use at speeds of less than 1 Gbps, exhibit a relatively wide spectrum width, and transmit light in a relatively wide cone. LEDs and laser diodes are inexpensive devices, often used in multimode fiber communications.

Semiconductor lasers have performance characteristics better suited to longer-distance and higher-bandwidth applications.

Objectives

Upon completing this chapter, you will be able to

- Name a router
- Set passwords
- Examine **show** commands
- Configure a serial interface
- Configure an Ethernet interface
- Execute changes to a router
- Save changes to a router
- Configure an interface description
- Configure a message-of-the-day banner
- Configure host tables
- Describe backup documentation
- Recover passwords

Chapter 12

Router Configuration

This chapter covers the router modes and configuration methods to update a router's configuration file. It is important to have a firm understanding of Cisco IOS Software and know the procedures for starting a router. In addition, this chapter describes the tasks necessary for password recovery.

Please be sure to look at this chapter's associated e-labs, movies, and photozooms that you will find on the CD-ROM accompanying the full text of this title. These CD elements are designed to supplement the material and reinforce the concepts introduced in this chapter.

Command-Line Interface Command Modes

To gain access to a router, a login is required. After login, there is a choice of modes. The modes interpret the commands that are typed and carry out the operations. Two EXEC modes exist:

- User mode
- Privilege mode (or enable mode)

The sections that follow define the two command modes and their associated commands.

User Command List

A user is automatically in user EXEC mode upon first login to the router. *User mode* is a limited examination of the router. Table 12-1 provides the user mode commands and their descriptions.

Table 12-1 User Mode Commands

Command	Description
access-enable	Creates a temporary access list entry.
atmsig	Executes ATM signaling commands.
cd	Changes current device.
clear	Resets functions.
connect	Opens a terminal connection.

continues

NOTE

At this point, the list of commands displayed is context sensitive. You see a different list when you are in user mode versus enable mode and when in *global configuration mode* versus configure *interface* mode.

Table 12-1 User Mode Commands (Continued)

Command	Description
dir	Lists files on a given device.
disable	Turns off privileged commands.
disconnect	Disconnects an existing network.
enable	Turns on privileged commands.
exit	Exits EXEC.
help	Gets a description of the interactive help system.
lat	Opens a LAT connection.
lock	Locks the terminal.
login	Logs in as a particular user.
logout	Exits EXEC mode.
mrinfo	Requests neighbor and version information from a multicast router.
mstat	Shows statistics after multiple multicast traceroutes.
mtrace	Traces the reverse multicast path from destination to source.
name-connection	Names an existing network connection.
pad	Opens an X.29 PAD connection.
ping	Sends echo messages.
ppp	Starts IETF Point-to-Point Protocol (PPP).
pwd	Displays current device.
resume	Resumes an active network connection.
rlogin	Opens an rlogin connection.
show	Shows running system information.
slip	Starts Serial Line IP (SLIP).
systat	Displays information about terminal lines.
telnet	Opens a Telnet connection.
terminal	Sets terminal line parameters.

Table 12-1 User Mode Commands (Continued)

Command	Description
tn3270	Opens a TN3270 connection.
traceroute	Sets a traceroute to the destination.
tunnel	Opens a tunnel connection.
where	Lists active connections.
x3	Sets X.3 parameters on PAD.
xremote	Enters Xremote mode.

Privileged Mode Command List

Privileged EXEC mode provides a detailed examination of the router and allows configuration changes to be made to the router. A specific mode is entered depending on the configuration change required. From privileged EXEC mode, other modes can be entered; privileged EXEC mode must be entered before entering these other modes (see the next section, "Router Configuration Modes").

To access *privileged mode* from user EXEC mode, type **enable** (or the abbreviation **en**):

```
Router>enable
Password:

Router>en
Password:
```

You are prompted for a password. If you type a question mark (?) at the privileged mode prompt Router#, you see a longer list of commands than you do at the user mode prompt. Table 12-2 provides a complete list with descriptions of privileged mode commands.

Note that the list of commands varies depending on the type of router platform being configured.

Table 12-2 Privileged Mode Commands

Command	Description
access-enable	Creates a temporary access list entry.
access-template	Creates a temporary access list entry.
appn	Sends a command to the APPN subsystem.
atmsig	Executes ATM signaling commands.

continues

Table 12-2 Privileged Mode Commands (Continued)

Command	Description
bfe	Sets manual emergency modes.
calendar	Manages the hardware calendar.
cd	Changes the current device.
clear	Resets functions.
clock	Manages the system clock.
cmt	Starts or stops FDDI connection-management functions.
configure	Enters configuration mode.
connect	Opens a terminal connection.
copy	Copies configuration or image data.
debug	Uses debugging functions (see also **undebug**).
delete	Deletes a file.
dir	Lists files on a given device.
disable	Turns off privileged commands.
disconnect	Disconnects an existing network connection.
enable	Turn on privileged commands.
erase	Erases Flash or configuration memory.
exit	Exits EXEC mode.
format	Formats a device.
help	Gets a description of the interactive help system.
lat	Opens a LAT connection.
lock	Locks the terminal.
login	Logs in as a particular user.
logout	Exits EXEC mode.
mbranch	Traces the multicast route down the tree branch.
mrbranch	Traces the reverse multicast up the tree branch.

Table 12-2 Privileged Mode Commands (Continued)

Command	Description
mrinfo	Requests neighbor and version information from a multicast router.
mstat	Shows statistics after multiple multicast traceroutes.
mtrace	Traces reverse multicast path from destination source.
name-connection	Names an existing network connection.
ncia	Starts or stops an NCIA server.
pad	Opens an X.29 PAD connection.
ping	Sends echo messages.
ppp	Starts the IETF Point-to-Point Protocol (PPP).
pwd	Displays current device.
reload	Halts and performs a cold return.
resume	Resumes an active network connection.
rlogin	Opens an rlogin connection.
rsh	Executes a remote command.
sdlc	Sends SDLC test frames.
send	Sends a message over tty lines.
setup	Runs the **setup** command facility.
show	Shows running system information.
slip	Starts Serial Line IP (SLIP).
squeeze	Squeezes a device.
start-chat	Starts a chat script on a line.
Systat	Displays information about terminal lines.
tarp	Targets ID Resolution Process (TARP) commands.
telnet	Opens a Telnet connection.
terminal	Sets terminal-line parameters .
test	Tests subsystems, memory, and interfaces.

continues

Table 12-2 Privileged Mode Commands (Continued)

Command	Description
tn3270	Opens a TN3270 connection.
traceroute	Sets a traceroute to the destination.
tunnel	Opens a tunnel connection.
undebug	Disables debugging functions (see also **debug**).
undelete	Undeletes a file.
verify	Verifies the checksum of a Flash file.
where	Lists active connections.
which-route	Does an OSI route table lookup and displays results.
write	Writes running configuration to memory, network, or terminal.
x3	Sets X.3 parameters on PAD.
xremote	Enters Xremote mode.

Router Configuration Modes

Global configuration commands are used in a router to apply configuration statements that affect the system as a whole. Use the privileged EXEC command **configure** to enter global configuration mode. After this command is entered, a prompt asking for the source of the configuration commands appears, at which you can specify **terminal**, **nvram**, or **network**. The default selection is to type in commands from the terminal console. Pressing the Enter key begins this configuration method.

The first configuration mode is referred to as global configuration mode, or global config, for short. Table 12-3 describes some of the configuration modes that you access from global configuration mode.

Table 12-3 Router Configuration Modes

Configuration Mode	Prompt
Interface	Router(config-if)#
Subinterface	Router(config-subif)#
Controller	Router(config-controller)#
Map-list	Router(config-map-list)#
Map-class	Router(config-map-class)#

Table 12-3 Router Configuration Modes (Continued)

Configuration Mode	Prompt
Line	Router(config-line)#
Router	Router(config-router)#
IPX-router	Router(config-ipx-router)#
Route-map	Router(config-route-map)#

Typing **exit** at one of these specific configuration modes returns the router to global configuration mode. Pressing Ctrl-Z leaves the configuration modes completely and returns the router to privileged EXEC mode.

Example 12-1 demonstrates this sequence of transitioning between configuration modes.

Example 12-1 *Navigating Privileged EXEC, Global Config, and Specific Configuration Modes*

```
Router#configure terminal
Router(config)#(commands)
Router(config)#exit
Router#


Router#configure terminal
Router(config)#router protocol
Router(config-router)#(commands)
Router(config-router)#exit
Router(config)#interface type port
Router(config-if)#(commands)
Router(config-if)#exit
Router(config)#exit
Router#
```

Router Startup Modes

Whether it is accessed from the console or by a Telnet session through a vty port, a router can be placed in several modes. Each mode provides different functions:

- **ROM monitor** mode is generally a recovery mode. It allows certain configuration tasks, such as recovering a lost password or downloading software (IOS). The router boots into ROM monitor mode if the router does not find a valid system image or if the boot sequence is interrupted during startup. In many routers, Rommon> is the default prompt for ROM monitor mode.

- **Setup** mode is a prompted dialog that helps users create a first-time basic configuration. Setup mode consists of a series of questions with default answers in brackets. Setup mode does not have a defining default prompt. The router prompts the user to enter setup mode if a valid startup configuration file is not found. Setup can also be entered by typing **setup** from privileged mode. Note that setup mode also can be invoked manually if the user erased the NVRAM and rebooted the router.

- **RXBoot** mode is a special mode that the router can enter by changing the settings of the configuration register and rebooting the router. RXBoot mode provides the router with a subset of Cisco IOS Software and enters a streamlined setup mode. The streamlined setup mode differs from the standard setup mode because streamlined setup does not configure global router parameters. There are prompts only to configure interface parameters, which permit the router to boot. This allows the router to boot when it cannot find a valid Cisco IOS Software image in Flash memory. The default prompt is the host name followed by <boot>.

Table 12-4 describes briefly some of the commonly used configuration commands.

Table 12-4 Selection of Router Configuration Commands

Command	Description
configure terminal	Configures manually from the console terminal.
configure memory	Loads configuration information from NVRAM.
copy tftp running-config	Loads configuration information from a network TFTP server into RAM .
show running-config	Displays the current configuration in RAM.
copy running-config startup-config	Stores the current configuration from RAM into NVRAM.
copy running-config tftp	Stores the current configuration from RAM on a network TFTP server.
show startup-config	Displays the saved configuration, which is the contents of NVRAM.
erase startup-config	Erases the contents of NVRAM.

Use the commands shown in Figure 12-1 for routers running Cisco IOS Software Release 11.0 or later.

Figure 12-1 Configuration File Commands

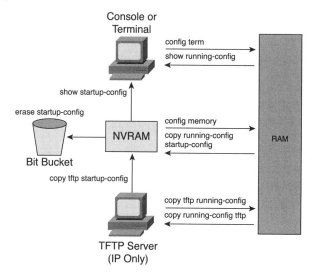

Configuring a Router Name

One of the first basic configuration tasks is to name the router, as shown in Example 12-2. Naming a router helps to better manage the network by uniquely identifying each router within the network. The router is named in global configuration mode. The name of the router is called the host name and is displayed as the system prompt. If a router is not named, the system default is Router.

Example 12-2 *Naming a Router*

```
Router(config)#hostname Cougars
Cougars#
```

e-Lab Activity   Basic Router Configuration

In this activity, you use the router's global configuration mode to make changes to the entire router.

Lab Activity CLI Modes and Router Identification

In this lab, you identify the basic router modes of user and privilege. You also use several commands that will enter specific modes to become familiar with the router prompt for each mode. In addition, you name the router.

Configuring and Protecting Router Passwords

A router can be secured to restrict access by using passwords. Passwords can be established for virtual terminal lines as well as the console line. Privileged EXEC mode also can have a password.

From global configuration mode, use the **enable password** command to restrict access to privileged mode. This password, however, will be visible from the router's configuration files. To enter an encrypted password in privileged mode, use the command **enable secret**. If an enable secret password is configured, it is used instead of the enable password. From the configuration files, a person can view only the encryption, not the actual password.

Enable secret passwords cannot be read; another user might be able to break into the configuration, but the only thing they can do is overwrite the password, because it is one-way encrypted and cannot be converted back to clear text.

Passwords can be further protected from display through the use of the **service password-encryption** command. This command is entered from global configuration mode.

The line console 0 configuration mode can be used to establish a login password on the console terminal. This is quite useful on a network on which multiple people have access to the router. This prevents anyone not authorized from accessing the router.

Telnet requires a password check. Different hardware platforms have different numbers of vty lines defined. The range 0 through 4 is used to specify five vty lines. These five incoming Telnet sessions can be simultaneous. The same password can be used for all lines, or one line can be set uniquely. This often is used in large networks with many network administrators. If a catastrophic problem occurs on a network and all common vty lines are used, the unique line can be reserved for recovery.

Use the command **line vty 0 4** to establish a login password on incoming Telnet sessions. Example 12-3 demonstrates the different ways to configure and protect passwords.

Example 12-3 *Configuring/Protecting Passwords*

```
! Console Password
Router(config)# line console 0
Router(config-line)# login
Router(config-line)# password cisco
! Virtual Terminal Password
Router(config)# line vty 0 4
Router(config-line)# login
Router(config-line)# password cisco
! Enable Password
Router(config)# enable password san-fran
!Perform Password Encryption
Router(config)# service password encryption set password here
Router(config)# no service password encryption
```

e-Lab Activity   Using Password Commands

In this activity, you use several password-related commands.

Lab Activity   Configuring Router Passwords

In this lab, you configure passwords for the console, virtual terminals, and a secret password.

Examining the show Commands

Many **show** commands exist, which help examine the contents of files in the router and are useful in troubleshooting. From each mode in the router, the **show ?** command can be used to see all the available options. Table 12-5 lists some of the **show** command options.

Table 12-5 show Commands

Command	Description
show interfaces	Displays all the statistics for all the interfaces on the router. If a user wants to view the statistics for a specific interface, he can enter the **show interfaces** command followed by the specific interface and port number. For example, `Router#show interfaces serial 1`

Table 12-5 **show** Commands (Continued)

Command	Description
show controllers serial	Displays information specific to the interface hardware.
show clock	Displays the time set in the router.
show hosts	Displays a cached list of host names and addresses.
show users	Displays all users who are connected to the router.
show history	Displays a history of commands that have been entered.
show flash	Displays information about Flash memory and what Cisco IOS Software files are stored there.
show version	Displays information about the Cisco IOS Software image that is running in RAM.
show arp	Displays the router's address resolution (ARP) table.
show protocol	Displays the global and interface-specific status of any configured Layer 3 protocols.
show startup-configuration	Displays the saved configuration located in NVRAM.
show running-configuration	Displays the configuration currently running in RAM.

Examples 12-4, 12-5, and 12-6 display sample output from the **show protocols, show version,** and **show interfaces** commands, respectively.

Example 12-4 show protocols *Command Output*

```
Router#show protocols
Global values:
Internet Protocol routing is enabled
DECnet routing is enabled
XNS routing is enabled
Vines routing is enabled
AppleTalk routing is enabled
Novell routing is enabled
--More--
```

Example 12-4 show protocols *Command Output (Continued)*

```
Ethernet0 is up, line protocol is up
Internet address is 183.8.126.2, subnet mask is 255.255.255.128
DECnet cost is 5
XNS address is 3010.aa00.0400.0284
CLNS enabled
Vines metric is 32
AppleTalk address is 3012.93, zone ld-e0
Novell address is 3010.aa00.0400.0284
--More--
```

Example 12-5 show version *Command Output*

```
Router#show version
Cisco Internetwork Operating System Software
IOS (tm) 4500 Software (C4500-J-M). Version 12.1.5
Copyright  1986-1996 by Cisco Systems, Inc.
Compiled Fri 28-Jun-96 16:32 by rbeach
Image text-base: 0x600088A0, data-base: 0x6076E000
ROM: System Bootstrap, Version 5.1(1) RELEASE SOFTWARE (fc1)
ROM: 4500-XBOOT Bootstrap Software, Version 10.1(1) RELEASE SOFTWARE (fc1)
router uptime is 1 week, 3 days, 32 minutes
System restarted by reload
System image file is c4500-j-mz, booted via tftp from 171.69.1.129
--More--
```

Example 12-6 show interfaces *Command Output*

```
Router#show interfaces
Serial0 is up, line protocol is up
Hardware is MK5025
Internet address is 183.8.64.129, subnet mask is 255.255.255.128
MTU 1500 bytes, BW 56 kbit, DLY 20000 usec, rely 255/255. load 9/255
Encapsulation HDLC, loopback not set, keepalive set (10 sec)
Last input 0:00:00, output 0:00:01, output hang never
Last clearing of show interfaces counters never
Output queue 0/40, 0 drops, input queue 0/75, 0 drops
Five minute input rate 1000 bits/sec, 0 packets/sec
331885 packets input, 62400237 bytes, no buffer
```

Example 12-6 show interfaces *Command Output (Continued)*

```
Received 230457 broadcasts, 0 runts, 0 giants
3 input errors, 3 CRC, 0 frame, 0 overrun, 0ignored, 0 abort
403591 packets output, 66717279 bytes, 0 underruns
0 output errors, 0 collisions, 8 interface resets, 0 restarts
45 carrier transitions
```

e-Lab Activity   **show interfaces**, **show version**, and **show protocols**

In this activity, you demonstrate how to use the **show interfaces, show version, and show protocols** commands.

e-Lab Activity   Router **show** Commands

This activity helps you become familiar with the router **show** commands available in user and privileged modes.

Lab Activity   Using the show Commands

This lab helps you become familiar with the router **show** commands. The show commands are the most important information-gathering commands available for the router.

Configuring a Serial Interface

A serial interface can be configured from the console or through a virtual terminal line. Serial interfaces require a clock signal to control the timing of the communications. In most environments, a data communications equipment (DCE) device such as a channel service unit/data service unit (CSU/DSU) provides the clock. By default, Cisco routers are data terminal equipment (DTE) devices, but they can be configured as DCE devices.

On serial links that are directly interconnected, one side must be considered as a DCE and provide a clocking signal. The clock is enabled and its speed is specified with the **clockrate** command. The available clock rates in bits per second are

1200	2400	9600	19,200	38,400	56,000
64,000	72,000	125,000	148,000	500,000	800,000
1,000,000	1,300,000	2,000,000	4,000,000		

To configure a serial interface, perform the following steps and refer to Example 12-7.

Step 1   Enter global configuration mode.

Step 2   Enter interface mode.

Step 3   Specify the bandwidth.

Step 4   Set the DCE clock rate (skip this step on a DTE).

Step 5   Turn on the interface.

Example 12-7 *Configuring a Serial Interface*

```
Router(config)# interface serial 1/0
Router(config-if)#bandwidth 56
Router(config-if)#clockrate 56000
Router(config-if)#no shutdown
```

By default, interfaces are turned off. To turn on an interface, you must enter the command **no shutdown**. The interface might need to be administratively turned off to perform hardware maintenance, change the interface configuration, perform troubleshooting, or perform other maintenance. The **shutdown** command turns off an interface.

The following command is used to administratively turn off the interface:

```
Router(config-if)#shutdown
```

The following command is used to turn on an interface that has been shut down:

```
Router(config-if)#no shutdown
```

The following command is used to quit the current interface configuration mode:

```
Router(config-if)#exit
```

e-Lab Activity   Assigning an IP Address to a Router Interface

In this activity, you demonstrate how to assign an IP address and a subnet mask to an interface.

e-Lab Activity   Defining Interface Physical Properties

In this activity, you demonstrate how to set various physical interface properties, such as clock rate and bandwidth.

Lab Activity Configuring a Serial Interface

In this lab, you configure a serial interface on two routers so that they can communicate with each other.

Configuring an Ethernet Interface

An Ethernet interface can be configured from the console or a virtual terminal line. Each Ethernet interface must have an IP address and subnet mask.

To configure an Ethernet interface, perform the steps that follow and refer to Example 12-8.

Step 1   Enter global configuration mode.

Step 2   Enter interface configuration mode.

Step 3   Specify the interface address and subnet mask.

Step 4   Turn on the interface.

Example 12-8 *Configuring an Ethernet Interface*

```
Router(config)#interface e0
Router(config-if)#183.8.126.2 255.255.255.128
Router(config-if)#no shutdown
```

By default, interfaces are turned off. To turn on an interface, enter the command **no shutdown**. The interface might need to be administratively turned off to perform hardware maintenance, change the interface configuration, perform troubleshooting, or perform other maintenance. The **shutdown** command turns off an interface.

Lab Activity Configuring an Ethernet Interface

In this lab, you configure an Ethernet or FastEthernet interface on the router for a LAN.

Executing Changes to the Router

If a change is needed to a configuration, enter the appropriate mode and make the change. For example, if an interface was not turned on, enter global configuration mode, enter interface mode, and issue the **no shutdown** command.

To verify changes, use the **show running-config** command. This command displays the current configuration. If the variables displayed are not what was intended, the environment can be corrected by doing the following:

- Issuing the **no** form of a configuration command
- Restarting the system and reloading the original configuration file from NVRAM
- Removing the startup configuration file with the **erase startup-configuration** command, restarting the router, and entering setup mode

To save the configuration variables to the startup configuration file in NVRAM, enter the following command at the privileged EXEC prompt:

```
Router#copy running-configuration startup-configuration
```

Table 12-6 shows commands used to manage the contents of NVRAM in Cisco IOS Software Release 11.*x* and later.

Table 12-6 Commands Used to Manage the Contents of NVRAM in Cisco IOS Software Release 11.x and Later

Command	Description
configure memory	Loads configuration information from NVRAM.
erase startup-config	Erases the contents of NVRAM.
copy running-config startup-config	Stores the current configuration in RAM (that is, the running configuration) into NVRAM (as the startup configuration).
show startup-config	Displays the saved configuration, which is the contents of NVRAM.

e-Lab Activity   Using NVRAM Configuration Commands

In this activity, you configure the router from NVRAM and work with other related commands.

e-Lab Activity   Using Configuration Modes

In this activity, you enter various configuration modes.

Lab Activity   Making Changes to a Configuration

In this lab, you prepare to make changes to the existing configuration in a router. You bring an interface down and then back up and view its status.

Finishing the Configuration

The following lists recommended tasks for finishing the configuration. (Some organizations do not have some of the recommended configuration tasks, such as a message of the day.)

- Establish configuration standards
- Provide and configuring interface descriptions
- Configure login banners
- Configure a message of the day (MOTD) banner
- Perform host name resolution
- Perform configuration backup and documentation

Importance of Configuration Standards

It is important to develop standards for configuring files within an organization. This facilitates control of the number of configuration files that must be maintained, how the files are stored, and where the files are stored.

A standard is a set of rules or procedures that are either widely used or officially specified. Without standards in an organization, a network could be in chaos if an interruption in service occurs.

To manage a network, there must be a centralized support standard. Configuration, security, performance, and other issues must be adequately addressed for the network to function smoothly. Creating standards for network consistency helps reduce network complexity, the amount of unplanned downtime, and exposure to events that might have an impact on network performance.

Providing Interface Descriptions

An interface description should be used to identify important information such as a distant router, a circuit number, or a specific network segment. A description of an interface can help a network user remember specific information about the interface, such as what network the interface services. The next section, "Configuring Interface Descriptions," provides a specific example.

The description is meant solely as a comment about the interface. Although the description appears in the configuration files that exist in router memory, a description does not affect the operation of the router. Descriptions are created by following a standard format that applies to each interface. The description can include the purpose and location of the interface, other devices or locations connected to the interface, and circuit identifiers. Descriptions enable support personnel to better understand the scope of problems related to an interface and allow for faster resolution of problems.

Configuring Interface Descriptions

Enter global configuration mode to configure an interface description. Perform the following steps and refer to Example 12-9:

Step 1   Enter global configuration mode by entering the command **configure terminal.**

Step 2   Enter specific interface mode (for example, interface Ethernet 0) by entering the command **interface ethernet 0.**

Step 3   Enter the command **description,** followed by the information that is to be displayed (for example, XYZ Network, Building 10).

Step 4   Exit interface mode back to privileged EXEC mode by pressing Ctrl-Z.

Step 5   Save the configuration changes to NVRAM by using the command **copy running-config startup-config.**

Example 12-9 *Configuring an Interface Description*

```
Router(config)#interface ethernet 0
Router(config-if)#description SkyDome LAN Communication Building
Router(config-if)#exit
! Results of issuing the show running-config command
interface Ethernet0
 description SkyDome LAN Communication Building
 ip address 198.133.215.1 255.255.255.0
```

Lab Activity   Configuring Interface Descriptions

In this lab, you choose a description for an interface and use interface configuration mode to enter that description.

Login Banners

A login banner is a message that is displayed at login. The login banner is useful for conveying messages that affect all network users, such as notices of impending system shutdowns.

Anyone can see login banners. Therefore, careful attention should be used in the wording of a banner message. "Welcome" is an invitation for anyone to enter a router and is probably not an appropriate message.

A login banner should be a warning not to attempt login unless authorized. A message such as, "This is a secure system, authorized access only!" instructs unwanted visitors that any further intrusion or attempt is unwanted and illegal. Example 12-10 shows an example of a login banner.

Example 12-10   *Login Banner*

```
Tokyo con0 is now available
Press RETURN to get started.



This is a secure system.  Authorized Access ONLY!!!
User Access Verification
Password:
Tokyo>enable
Password:
Tokyo#
```

Configuring a Message of the Day

A message-of-the-day (MOTD) or login banner can be displayed on all connected terminals.

Enter global configuration mode to configure a message-of-the-day banner. Use the **banner motd** command, followed by a space and a delimiting character such as the pound sign (#). Add a message of the day followed by a space and the delimiting character again.

Perform the following steps to create and display a message of the day and refer to Example 12-11:

Step 1   Enter global configuration mode by using the **configure terminal** command.

Step 2   Enter the command **banner motd # The message of the day goes here #**.

Step 3   Save changes by issuing the **copy running-configuration startup-configuration** command, or **copy run start** for a shortcut.

Example 12-11   *Message-of-the-Day Display*

```
Tokyo(config)#banner motd #
You have entered a secure system, authorized access ONLY!#
```

e-Lab Activity   Using the Message of the Day Command

In this activity, you demonstrate how to create a message of the day.

Lab Activity   Configuring Message of the Day

In this lab, you use global configuration mode to enter a message of the day into the router. This procedure enables all users to view the message upon entering the router.

Host Name Resolution

Host name resolution is the process that a computer system uses to associate a host name with a network address.

Protocols such as Telnet use host names to identify network devices. To use host names to communicate with other IP devices, network devices, such as routers, must be capable of associating the host names with IP addresses. A list of host names and their associated IP addresses is called a *host table*. Table 12-7 shows a sample host table.

Table 12-7 Host Table

Router Name	Router Type	E0	E1	S0
Tokyo	2601	205.7.5.1	192.5.5.1	201.100.11.1
Paris	2621	205.7.5.2		204.204.7.2

A host table might include all devices in a network organization. Each unique IP address can have a host name associated with it. Cisco IOS Software maintains a cache of host name-to-address mappings for use by EXEC commands. This cache speeds up the process of converting names to addresses.

Host names, unlike Domain Name System (DNS) names, are significant only on the router on which they are configured. Example 12-12 shows the configuration of a host table on a router.

Example 12-12 *Host Table Configuration*

```
Router(config)#ip host Auckland 172.16.32.1
Router(config)#ip host Beirut 192.168.53.1
Router(config)#ip host Capetown 192.168.89.1
Router(config)#ip host Denver 10.202.8.1
```

This host table enables the network administrator to type either the host name or the IP address to Telnet to a remote host. An example to use as the host name would be Auckland or 172.16.32.1 for the IP address. To display a list of hosts and their associated IP addresses that are defined for a particular router, use the command **show hosts**.

e-Lab Activity Creating an IP Host Table Entry

In this activity, you create an IP host table entry.

e-Lab Activity Displaying Host Names

In this activity, you display a list of host names and IP addresses defined for a router.

Lab Activity Configuring Host Tables

In this lab, you use global configuration mode to create IP host tables to allow a router to translate router names with all the attached interfaces on that router.

Configuration Backup and Documentation

The configuration of network devices determines the way the network behaves or acts. Management of device configuration includes the following tasks:

- Listing and comparing configuration files on running devices
- Storing configuration files on network servers
- Performing software installations and upgrades

Configuration files should be stored as backup files in case a problem arises. Configuration files can be stored on a network server, on a TFTP server, or on a disk stored in a safe place. Documentation should be included with this offline information.

The configuration on the router also can be saved to a disk by capturing text in the router and saving it to the disk or hard drive. If the file needs to be copied back to the router, it can be pasted into the router. These methods of saving and restoring the router configuration are covered in greater detail in Chapter 14, "Managing Cisco IOS Software."

Figure 12-2 shows an overview of the router configuration process.

Figure 12-2 Router Configuration Process Flowchart

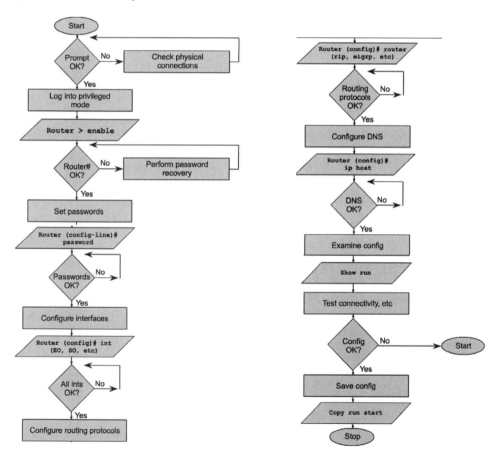

Password Recovery

This section explains several password-recovery techniques for Cisco routers and Catalyst switches. You can perform password recovery on most of the platforms without changing hardware jumpers, but all platforms require that the router be rebooted. Password recovery can be done only from the console port (physically attached to the router).

Overview of Password Recovery

Three ways exist for restoring access to a router when the password is lost. You can view the password, change the password, or erase the configuration and start over as if the box were new.

Each procedure follows these basic steps:

Step 1   Configure the router to start up without reading the configuration memory (NVRAM). This is done from what sometimes is called test system mode, ROM mode, or boot mode.

Step 2   Reboot the system.

Step 3   Access enable mode (which can be done without a password if you set the configuration register correctly in Step 1).

Step 4   View or change the password, or erase the configuration.

Step 5   Reconfigure the router to boot up and read the NVRAM as it normally does.

Step 6   Reboot the system.

Some password recovery requires a terminal to issue a BREAK signal; you must be familiar with how your terminal or PC terminal emulator issues this signal. In Pro-Comm, for example, the keys Alt-B generate the BREAK signal by default; in Windows HyperTerminal, you press Break or Ctrl-Break. Windows HyperTerminal also enables you to define a function key as BREAK. From the terminal window, select Function Keys and define one as Break by filling in the characters ^$B (Shift-6, Shift-4, and uppercase B). Several free terminal-emulation packages also are available for download on the Internet, which you might find preferable.

The following sections contain detailed instructions for specific Cisco routers. Locate your product at the beginning of each section to determine which technique to use.

Password Recovery Technique 1

The following are the relevant devices for this technique:

- Cisco 2500 series
- Cisco 3000 series
- Cisco 7000 series running Cisco IOS Software Release 10.0 or later in ROMs

This technique can be used on the Cisco 7000 and Cisco 7010 series only if the router has Cisco IOS Software Release 10.0 ROMs installed on the Route Processor (RP) card. It might be booting Flash Cisco IOS Software Release 10.0, but it needs the actual ROMs on the processor card as well. The following steps outline password recovery technique 1:

Step 1 Attach a terminal or PC with terminal emulation to the console port of the router. To connect a PC to the console port, attach a null modem adapter (Tandy Null Modem Adapter No. 26-1496 has been tested) to the console port, and then attach a straight-through modem cable to the null modem adapter.

Step 2 Type **show version** and record the setting of the configuration register. It is usually 0x2102 or 0x102. If you do not get the router prompt to do a **show version**, look on a similar router to obtain the configuration register number, or try using 0x2102.

Step 3 Power-cycle the router.

Step 4 Press the Break key on the terminal within 60 seconds of the power-up. You should see the > prompt with no router name. If you don't see this, the terminal is not sending the correct BREAK signal. In that case, check the terminal or terminal emulation setup.

Step 5 Type **o/r 0x42** at the > prompt to boot from Flash memory, or type **o/r 0x41** to boot from the boot ROMs. (Note that this is the letter *o*, not the numeral zero.) If you have Flash memory and it is intact, 0x42 is the best setting because it is the default. Use 0x41 only if the Flash memory is erased or is not installed. If you use 0x41, you can either view or erase the configuration. You cannot change the password.

Step 6 Type **i** at the > prompt. The router reboots but ignores its saved configuration.

Step 7 Answer **no** to all the setup questions, or press Ctrl-C.

Step 8 Type **enable** at the Router> prompt. You're then in enable mode and can see the Router# prompt.

Step 9   Choose one of the following three options:

- To view the password, type **show start**.
- To change the password (in case it is encrypted, for example), do the following:

     a. Type **copy start run** to copy the NVRAM into memory.

     b. Type **show run**.

     c. If you have the enable secret password set, perform the following:

     Type **config term** and make the changes.

     Type **enable secret** *new_password*.

     Press Ctrl-Z.

     d. If you do not have **enable secret xxxx**, type **enable password** *new_password* and press Ctrl-Z.

     e. Type **copy run start** to commit the changes.

- To erase the config, type **erase start**.

Step 10   Type **config term** at the prompt.

Step 11   Type **config-register 0x2102**, or whatever value you recorded in Step 2.

Step 12   Press Ctrl-Z to return to privileged EXEC mode.

Step 13   Type **reload** at the prompt. You do not need to write memory.

Password Recovery Technique 2

Use this procedure to recover lost passwords on the following routers:

- Cisco 1003
- Cisco 1600 series
- Cisco 2600 series
- Cisco 3600 series
- Cisco 4500 series
- Cisco 7100 series
- Cisco 7200 series
- Cisco 7500 series
- IDT Orion-based routers
- AS5200 and AS5300 platforms

To recover a password using procedure 2, perform the following steps:

Step 1   Attach a terminal or PC with terminal-emulation software to the console port of the router.

Step 2   Enter **show version** and record the setting of the configuration register. It is usually 0x2102 or 0x102.

The configuration register value is on the last line of the display. Note whether the configuration register is set to enable Break or disable Break.

The factory-default configuration register value is 0x2102. Notice that the third digit from the left in this value is 1, which disables Break. If the third digit is *not* 1, Break is enabled.

Step 3   Turn off the router and then turn it on again.

Step 4   Press the Break key on the terminal within 60 seconds of turning on the router. The rommon> prompt appears. If it does not appear, the terminal is not sending the correct Break signal.

If the prompt does not appear, check the terminal or terminal emulation setup.

Step 5   Enter **confreg** at the rommon> prompt.

The following prompt appears:

```
Do you wish to change configuration [y/n]?
```

Step 6   Enter **yes** and press Return.

Step 7   Enter **no** to subsequent questions until the following prompt appears:

```
ignore system config info [y/n]?
```

Step 8   Enter **yes**.

Step 9   Enter **no** to subsequent questions until the following prompt appears:

```
change boot characteristics [y/n]?
```

Step 10   Enter **yes**.

The following prompt appears:

```
enter to boot:
```

Step 11   At this prompt, either enter **2** and press Return if booting from Flash memory, or if Flash memory is erased, enter **1**.

If Flash memory is erased, the Cisco 4500 must be returned to Cisco for service. If you enter **1**, you can only view or erase the configuration; you cannot change the password.

A configuration summary and the following prompt appears:

```
Do you wish to change configuration [y/n]?
```

Step 12   Enter **no** and press Return.

The following prompt appears:

```
rommon>
```

Step 13   Enter **reset** at the privileged EXEC prompt or, for Cisco 4500 series and Cisco 7500 series routers, power-cycle the router.

Step 14   As the router boots, enter **no** to all the setup questions until the following prompt appears:

```
Router>
```

Step 15   Enter **enable** to enter enable mode.

The Router# prompt appears.

Step 16   Choose one of the following options:

- To view the password, if it is not encrypted, enter **more nvram:startup-config**.

- To change the password (if it is encrypted, for example), enter the following commands:

```
Router# configure memory
Router# configure terminal
Router(config)# enable secret 1234abcd
Router(config)# ctrl-z
Router# write memory
```

The **enable secret** command provides increased security by storing the enable secret password using a nonreversible cryptographic function; however, you cannot recover a lost password that has been encrypted.

Step 17   Enter **configure terminal** at the prompt.

Step 18   Type **config-register** and whatever value you recorded in Step 2.

Step 19   Press Ctrl-Z to quit the configuration editor.

Step 20   Enter **reload** at the prompt and enter **write memory** to save the configuration.

e-Lab Activity   Router Password Recovery

In this activity, you practice the recovery of the password for a router where it is not known.

Lab Activity   Password-Recovery Procedures

In this lab, you gain access to a router when the password is unknown.

Summary

This chapter summarized the key points in configuring a router.

The router has several modes:

- User mode
- Privileged mode
- Global configuration mode
- Other configuration modes

The command-line interface (CLI) is used to change configurations, including doing the following:

- Setting the host name
- Setting passwords
- Configuring interfaces
- Modifying configurations
- Showing configurations

Interface descriptions include important information to help network administrators understand and troubleshoot their networks.

Login banners and messages of the day provide users with information upon login to the router.

Host name resolutions translate names to IP addresses to allow the router to quickly convert names to addresses.

Three ways exist for restoring access to a router when the password is lost:

- You can view the password.
- You can change the password.
- You can erase the configuration and start over as if the box was new.
- Configuration standards are key elements in the success of any organization in maintaining an efficient network. Configuration backup and documentation is extremely important to keep a network operating smoothly.

Key Terms

CLI (command-line interface)   An interface that enables the user to interact with the operating system by entering commands and optional arguments.

global configuration mode   Used for one-line commands and commands that make global changes to the router configuration.

interface   Connection between two systems or devices. In routing terminology, a network connection.

NVRAM (Nonvolatile RAM)   RAM that retains its contents when a unit is powered off.

privileged mode   Used for copying and managing entire configuration files.

TFTP (Trivial File Transfer Protocol)   Simplified version of FTP that allows files to be transferred from one computer to another over a network, usually without the use of client authentication (for example, username and password).

Check Your Understanding

Complete all the review questions to test your understanding of the topics and concepts in this chapter. Answers are listed in Appendix B, "Answers to Check Your Understanding Review Questions."

1. What is a standard?

   A. A formal description of a set of rules and conventions that govern how devices on a network exchange information

   B. A set of rules or procedures that are either widely used or officially specified

   C. A way in which network devices access the network medium

2. A description on an interface does what?

   A. Welcomes users to the router

   B. Warns users not to enter the router

   C. Displays a comment about the interface

3. A good example of a login banner is what?

   A. Welcome everyone

   B. Everyone please log in

   C. Authorized access only

4. What is host name resolution?

   A. The process of associating a name with a network location

   B. The process of displaying a login message

   C. The process of displaying a description on a router

5. Configuration backup and documentation is necessary to an organization to maintain an efficient network. True or false?

   A. True

   B. False

6. Backing up configuration files is not necessary. True or false?

   A. True

   B. False

7. A TFTP server is the only location where backup files can be stored. True or false?

   A. True

   B. False

8. If you are planning to configure an interface, what prompt should be on the router?

   A. router(config)#

   B. router(config-in)#

   C. router(config-intf)#

   D. router(config-if)#

9. Which of the following is the correct order for the process of configuring a router? (Assume that you have already made router changes in configuration mode.)

   A. Save changes to backup, decide whether the changes are your intended results, examine the results, and examine the backup file.

   B. Examine the results, decide whether the changes are your intended results, save the changes to backup, and examine the backup file.

   C. Decide whether the changes are your intended results, examine the backup file, save the changes to backup, and examine the results.

   D. Examine the results, save the changes to backup, decide whether the changes are your intended results, and examine the backup file.

10. Which of the following is a command that can be used to save router configuration changes to a backup?

    A. Router# **copy running-config tftp**

    B. Router# **show running-config**

    C. Router# **config mem**

    D. Router# **copy tftp running-config**

11. Which of the following correctly describes password configuration on routers?

    A. All passwords are established in user EXEC mode.

    B. All passwords alter the password character string.

    C. A password can be established on all incoming Telnet sessions.

    D. The **enable password** command restricts access to user EXEC mode.

12. Which of the following does not describe password configuration on routers?

    A. Passwords can be established in every configuration mode.

    B. A password can be established on any console terminal.

    C. The enable secret password uses an encryption process to alter the password character string.

    D. All password establishment begins in global configuration mode.

13. What is used for one-line commands that change the entire router?

    A. Global configuration mode

    B. Privileged mode

    C. User EXEC mode

    D. Interface mode

14. What does the **exit** command do in a configuration mode with the prompt Router(config-if)#?

    A. It quits the current configuration interface mode.

    B. It reaches the privileged EXEC prompt.

    C. It exits the router.

    D. It switches to the user EXEC prompt.

15. What are the major elements of a typical router configuration?

   A. Passwords, interfaces, routing protocols, DNS

   B. Boot sequence, interfaces, TFTP server, NVRAM

   C. NVRAM, ROM, DRAM, interfaces

   D. Interfaces, routing protocols, configuration register, Flash memory

16. In a password-recovery procedure, immediately after pressing Ctrl-Z on router startup, what should be the config register setting?

   A. 0x2102

   B. 0x2142

   C. 0x0000

   D. 0x10F

17. In a password-recovery procedure, just before saving the running config and after you have enabled a new secret password, what should be the config register setting?

   A. 0x2102

   B. 0x2142

   C. 0x0000

   D. 0x10F

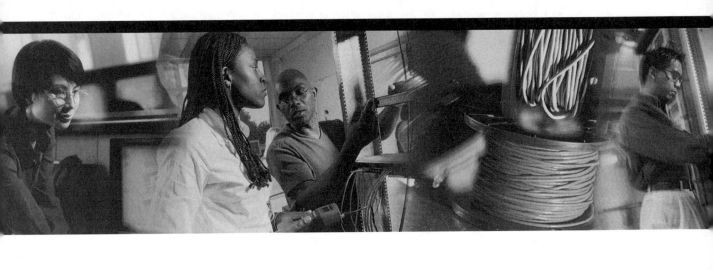

Router Configuration

The following table maps the numbering scheme used in this chapter's labs to the Target Identifiers (TIs) used in the online curriculum.

Lab Companion Numbering	Online Curriculum TI
Lab 12-1	3.1.2
Lab 12-2	3.1.3
Lab 12-3	3.1.4
Lab 12-4	3.1.5
Lab 12-5	3.1.7
Lab 12-6	3.1.6
Lab 12-7	3.2.3
Lab 12-8	3.2.5
Lab 12-9	3.2.7
Lab 12-10	5.2.7

Lab 12-1: Command Modes and Router Identification

Figure 12-1.1   Topology for Lab 12-1.1

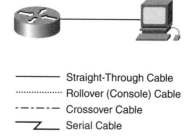

————— Straight-Through Cable
················ Rollover (Console) Cable
– – – – – Crossover Cable
⎯⎯Z⎯⎯ Serial Cable

Objectives

- Identify basic router modes of user EXEC and privileged EXEC
- Use commands to enter specific modes
- Become familiar with the router prompt for each mode
- Assign a name to the router.

Background / Preparation

Cable a network similar to the topology in Figure 12-1.1. Any router that meets the interface requirements displayed in Figure 12-1.1 (that is, 800, 1600, 1700, 2500 and 2600 routers or a combination) can be used. Please refer to the information in the "Router Interface Summary Chart" immediately preceding Chapter 1 to correctly specify the interface identifiers to be used based on the equipment in your lab. The configuration output used in this lab is produced from 1721 series routers. Any other router used might produce slightly different output. The following steps are intended to be executed on each router unless specifically instructed otherwise. Start a Hyper-Terminal session as performed in the "Establishing a Hyperterminal" session lab.

Please refer to and implement the procedure documented in "Erasing and Reloading the Router" immediately preceding Chapter 1 before continuing with this lab.

Step 1 Login to the router in user mode.

    A. Connect to the router and login.

    B. What prompt did the router display?_____

    C. What does this prompt mean?_____

Step 2 Login to the router in privilege mode.

    A. Enter **enable** at the user mode prompt.

```
Router>enable
```

    B. If prompted for a password, enter the password **class**.

    C. What prompt did the router display?

    _____

    D. What does this prompt mean?_____

Step 3 Enter global configuration mode.

    A. Enter **configure terminal** at the privilege mode prompt.

```
Router#configure terminal
```

    B. What prompt did the router display? _____

    C. What does this prompt mean?_____

Step 4 Enter router configuration mode

A. Enter **router rip** at the global configuration mode.

`Router(config)#router rip`

B. What prompt did the router display? _____

C. What does this prompt mean? _____

Step 5 Exit from router mode and go into interface configuration mode.

A. Enter **exit** at the prompt to return to global configuration mode.

`Router(config-router)#exit`

B. Enter **interface serial 0** (see chart for your interface identifier) at the global configuration mode prompt.

`Router(config)#interface serial 0`

C. What prompt did the router display? _____

D. What does this prompt mean?_____

E. Enter **exit** at the prompt to return to global configuration mode.

`Router(config-if)#exit`

Step 6 Assign a name to the router.

`Router(config)#hostname GAD`

A. What prompt did the router display? _____

B. What does this prompt mean?

_____

C. What change has occurred in the prompt?

_____

Step 7 Exit the router.

Enter **exit** at the prompt to close out of the router.

`GAD(config)#exit`

Upon completion of the previous steps logoff (by typing exit) and turn the router off.

Lab 12-2: Configuring Router Passwords

Figure 12-2.1 Topology for Lab 12-2

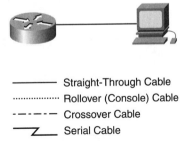

——————— Straight-Through Cable
················ Rollover (Console) Cable
– – – – – Crossover Cable
——ᴢ—— Serial Cable

Objectives

- Configure a password for console login to user mode
- Configure a password for virtual terminal (telnet) sessions
- Configure a secret password for privileged mode

Background / Preparation

Cable a network similar to the one in Figure 12-2.1. Any router that meets the interface requirements displayed in Figure 12-2.1 (that is, 800, 1600, 1700, 2500, and 2600 routers or a combination) can be used. Please refer to the information in the "Router Interface Summary Chart" immediately preceding Chapter 1 to correctly specify the interface identifiers to be used based on the equipment in your lab. The configuration output used in this lab is produced from 1721 series routers. Any other router used might produce slightly different output. The following steps are intended to be executed on each router unless specifically instructed otherwise.

Start a HyperTerminal session as performed in the "Establishing a HyperTerminal" session lab.

Please refer to and implement the procedure documented in "Erasing and Reloading the Router" immediately preceding Chapter 1 before continuing with this lab.

Step 1 Login to the router in user EXEC mode.

    A. Connect to the router and login.

    B. What prompt did the router display?

_____

    C. What does this prompt mean?

_____

Step 2   Login to the router in privileged EXEC mode

    A. Enter **enable** at the user mode prompt.

      `Router>enable`

    B. What prompt did the router display?

      _____

    C. What does this prompt mean?

      _____

Step 3   Enter global configuration mode.

    A. Enter configure terminal at the privilege mode prompt.

      `Router#configure terminal`

    B. What prompt did the router display? _____

    C. What does this prompt mean?

      _____

Step 4   Enter a hostname of GAD for this router.

    A. Enter **hostname GAD** at the prompt.

      `Router(config)#hostname GAD`

    B. What prompt did the router display? _____

    C. What does this prompt mean?

      _____

Step 5   Configure the console password on the router and exit line mode.

```
GAD(config)#line console 0
GAD(config-line)#password cisco
GAD(config-line)#login
GAD(config-line)#exit
GAD(config)#
```

Step 6   Configure the password on the virtual terminal lines and exit line mode.

```
GAD(config)#line vty 0 4
GAD(config-line)#password cisco
GAD(config-line)#login
GAD(config-line)#exit
GAD(config)#
```

Step 7   Configure the enable password.

```
GAD(config)#enable password cisco
GAD(config)#exit
```

Step 8   Return to the user EXEC mode by entering the **disable** command.

```
GAD#disable
```

Step 9   Enter the privileged EXEC mode again. This time a prompt for a password will show. Enter **cisco** but you will not see the characters on the line.

```
GAD>enable
Password:cisco
```

Step 10   Return to the configuration mode by entering **configure terminal.**

```
GAD#configure terminal
```

Step 11   Configure the enable secret password.

```
GAD(config)#enable secret class
GAD(config)#exit
```

NOTE

Remember the enable secret password is encrypted from the configuration view. Also do not type **enable secret password class,** or your secret password will be **password,** not **class.** The enable password is unencrypted and can be viewed from the configuration.

Step 12   Return to the user EXEC mode by entering the **disable** command.

```
GAD#disable
GAD>
```

Step 13   Enter the privileged EXEC mode again.

This time a prompt for a password will appear. Enter **cisco** but you will not see the characters on the line. If it fails keep trying until you see the % Bad secrets message.

```
GAD>enable
Password:cisco
Password:cisco
Password:cisco
% Bad secrets
```

Step 14   Enter the privileged EXEC mode again.

This time a prompt for a password will show. Enter **class** but you will not see the characters on the line.

```
GAD>enable
Password:class
GAD#
```

NOTE

The enable secret password takes precedence over the enable password. So once an enable secret password is entered the enable password no longer is accepted.

Step 15   Show the router's running configuration.

    A. Do you see an encrypted password? _____

    B. Do you see any other passwords? _____

    C. Are any others encrypted? _____

Once you have finished logoff (by typing **exit**) and turn the router off.

Lab 12-3: Using Router show Commands

Figure 12-3.1   Topology for Lab 12-3

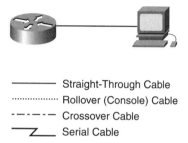

—————— Straight-Through Cable
················· Rollover (Console) Cable
-·—·-·— Crossover Cable
——Z—— Serial Cable

Objectives

- Become familiar with the basic router **show** commands
- Retrieve the current running configuration from RAM using **show running-config**
- View the backup configuration file in NVRAM using **show startup-config**
- View the IOS file information using **show flash** and **show version**
- View the current status of the router interfaces using **show interface**
- View the status of any configured Layer 3 protocol using **show protocol**

Background / Preparation

This lab helps you become familiar with the router **show** commands. The **show** commands are the most important information-gathering commands available for the router:

- **show running-config** (or **show run**) is probably the single most valuable command to help determine the current status of a router, because it displays the active configuration file running in RAM.
- **show startup-config** (or **show start**) displays the backup configuration file that is stored in non-volatile RAM (NVRAM). This is the file that will be used to configure the router when it is first started or rebooted with the **reload** command. All the detailed router interface settings are contained in this file.
- **show flash** is used to view the available flash memory and the amount used. Flash is where the Cisco IOS Software file or image is stored.
- **show arp** displays the router's IP to MAC to interface address mapping.
- **show interface** displays statistics for all interfaces configured on the router.
- **show protocol** displays global and interface-specific status of configured Layer 3 protocols (IP, IPX, etc.).

Cable a network similar to one of the diagram. Any router that meets the interface requirements displayed in Figure 12-3.1 (that is, 800, 1600, 1700, 2500, and 2600 routers or a combination) can be used. The configuration output used in this lab is produced from 1721 series routers. Any other router used might produce slightly different output. The following steps are intended to be executed on each router unless specifically instructed otherwise.

Start a HyperTerminal session as performed in the "Establishing a HyperTerminal" session lab.

Do not erase and reload the router prior to starting this lab.

Step 1 Log on to the router.

Connect to the router and log on. If prompted, enter the password cisco.

Step 2 Enter the help command.

A. Enter the help command by typing **?** at the router prompt. The router responds with all commands available in user mode.

B. What did the router reply with?

_____

C. Are all router commands available at the current prompt?

_____

D. Is **show** one of the options available?

_____

Step 3 Display help for the **show** command.

A. Enter **show ?**. The router responds with the **show** subcommands available in user mode.

B. List three user mode **show** subcommands.

show Subcommand	Description

Step 4 Display Cisco IOS Software version and other important information with the **show version** command.

A. Enter the **show version** command. The router will return information about the IOS that is running in RAM.

B. What is the Cisco IOS Software version?

_____

C. What is the name of the system image (IOS) file?

_____

D. Where was the router IOS image booted from?

_____

E. What type of processor (CPU) and how much RAM does this router have?

_____

F. How many Ethernet interfaces does this router have? _____
How many serial interfaces? _____

G. The router backup configuration file is stored in non-volatile random access memory (NVRAM). How much NVRAM does this router have?

_____

H. The router operating system (IOS) is stored in Flash memory. How much Flash memory does this router have?

_____

I. What is the configuration register set to?

_____

Step 5   Display the router's time and date.

Enter the **show clock** command. What information appears?

_____

Step 6   Display a cached list of host names and addresses.

Enter the **show hosts** command. What information is displayed with **show hosts**?

_____

Step 7   Display users who are connected to the router.

Enter the **show users** command. What information is displayed with **show users**?

_____

Step 8   Display the command buffer.

Enter the **show history** command. What information is displayed with **show history**?

_____

Step 9   Enter privileged mode.

   A. From user EXEC mode, enter privileged EXEC mode using the **enable** command.

   B. Enter the enable password **class**.

   C. What command did you use to enter privileged mode?

   _____

   D. How do you know if you are in privileged mode?

   _____

Step 10   Enter the help command.

   A. Enter **show ?** at the router prompt. What did the router reply with?

   _____

   B. How is this output different from the one you got in user mode in Step 3?

   _____

Step 11   Display the router ARP table.

   Enter the **show arp** command at the router prompt. What is the ARP table?

   _____

Step 12   Display information about the Flash memory device.

   A. Enter **show flash** at the router prompt.

   B. How much Flash memory is available and used?

   _____

   C. What is the file that is stored in Flash memory?

   _____

   D. What is the size in bytes of the Flash memory?

   _____

Step 13   Show information about the active configuration file.

   Enter **show running-config** (or **show run**) at the router prompt. What important information is displayed with **show run**?

   _____

   _____

   _____

Step 14   Display information about the backup configuration file.

Enter **show startup-config** (or **show start**) at the router prompt. What important information is displayed with **show start,** and where is this information kept?

_____

_____

_____

Step 15   Display statistics for all interfaces configured on the router.

A. Enter **show interface** at the router prompt.

B. Find the following information for interface Ethernet 0 or Fast Ethernet 0/0:

1. What is MTU?

_____

2. What is rely?

_____

3. What is load?

_____

C. Find the following information for interface Serial 0

1. What is the IP address and subnet mask?

_____

2. What data link layer encapsulation is being used?

_____

Step 3   Display the protocols configured on the router.

Enter **show protocol** at the router prompt. What important information is displayed?

_____

Once you have finished logoff (by typing **exit**) and turn the router off.

Lab 12-4: Configuring a Serial Interface

Figure 12-4.1 Topology for Lab 12-4

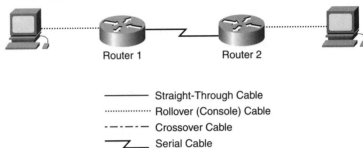

Router 1   Router 2

——————— Straight-Through Cable
················· Rollover (Console) Cable
− − − − − Crossover Cable
——z—— Serial Cable

Use the information in Table 12-4.1 to configure the equipment for this lab.

Table 12-4.1 Lab Equipment Configuration

Router Designation	Router Name	Interface Type	Serial 0 Address	Subnet Mask
Router 1	GAD	DCE	192.168.15.1	255.255.255.0
Router 2	BHM	DTE	192.168.15.2	255.255.255.0

Enable secret password is **class** for both routers.
Enable, VTY, and Console password is **cisco** for both routers.

Objective

Configure a serial interface on each of two routers so they can communicate.

Background / Preparation

Cable a network similar to the one in Figure 12-4.1. Any router that meets the interface requirements displayed on this diagram (that is, 800, 1600, 1700, 2500, and 2600 routers or a combination) can be used. Please refer to the information in the "Router Interface Summary Chart" immediately preceding Chapter 1 to correctly specify the interface identifiers to be used based on the equipment in your lab. The configuration output used in this lab is produced from 1721 series routers. Any other router used may produce slightly different output. The following steps are intended to be executed on each router unless specifically instructed otherwise. Start a HyperTerminal session as performed in Lab 11-2 in Chapter 11.

Please refer to and implement the procedure documented in "Erasing and Reloading the Router" immediately preceding Chapter 1 before continuing with this lab.

Step 1   Basic router configuration.

    A. Connect the routers as shown in Figure 12-4. This lab requires a null serial cable (a DTE and DCE cable connected together) and two roll-over (console) cables.

Step 2   Configure the name and passwords for Router 1.

    A. On Router 1, enter the global configuration mode and configure the hostname as shown in the chart in Table 12-4.1.

    B. Configure the console, virtual terminal, and enable passwords. If you have trouble doing this, refer to Lab 12-2.

Step 3   From the configure terminal mode, configure serial interface serial 0 (refer to the "Router Interface Summary Chart") on Router GAD.

```
GAD(config)#interface serial 0
GAD(config-if)#ip address 192.168.15.1 255.255.255.0
GAD(config-if)#clock rate 56000
GAD(config-if)#no shutdown
GAD(config-if)#exit
GAD(config)#exit
```

> **NOTE**
>
> Once you enter interface configuration mode, note that the IP address of the interface as well as the subnet mask must be entered. The clock rate needs to be entered only on the DCE interface side of the WAN link. The **no shutdown** command turns on the interface. Shutdown is when the interface is off.

Step 4   Save the running configuration to the startup configuration at the privileged EXEC mode.

```
GAD#copy running-config startup-config
```

Step 5   Display information about serial interface 0 on GAD.

    A. Enter the command **show interface serial** 0 (refer to the "Router Interface Summary Chart") on GAD.

```
GAD#show interface serial 0
```

    This will show the details of interface serial 0.

    B. List at least the following three details you discovered from issuing this command.

    Serial0/0 is _____; line protocol is_____.

    Internet address is _____.

    Encapsulation _____

    C. To what OSI layer is the "Encapsulation" referring?

    _____

    D. If the serial interface was configured, why did **show interface serial** 0 say that the interface is down?

    _____
    _____
    _____

> **NOTE**
>
> If the running configuration is not saved, the next time that the router is restarted, either by a software **reload** command or a power shutdown, the running configuration will be lost. The router uses the startup configuration when the router is started.

Step 6   Configure the name and passwords for Router 2.

On the BHM router, enter the global configuration mode and configure hostname, console, virtual terminal, and enable passwords as shown in the chart above.

Step 7   From the configure terminal mode, configure serial interface serial 0 (refer to "Router Interface Summary Chart") on Router BHM.

```
BHM(config)#interface serial 0
BHM(config-if)#ip address 192.168.15.1 255.255.255.0
BHM(config-if)#no shutdown
BHM(config-if)#exit
BHM(config)#exit
```

Step 8   Save the running configuration to the startup configuration at the privileged EXEC mode.

```
BHM#copy running-config startup-config
```

Step 9   Display information about serial interface 0 on BHM.

A. Enter the command **show interface serial** 0 (refer to the "Router Interface Summary Chart") on BHM.

```
BHM#show interface serial 0
```

This will show the details of interface serial 0.

B. List at least following three details you discovered from issuing this command.

Serial0/0 is _____; line protocol is_____.

Internet address is _____.

Encapsulation _____

C. What is the difference in the Line and Protocol status recorded on GAD earlier? Why?

_____

Step 10   Verify that the serial connection is functioning.

A. Ping the serial interface of the other router.

```
BHM#ping 192.168.15.1
GAD#ping 192.168.15.2
```

B. From GAD, can you ping the BHM router's serial interface?

_____

C. From BHM, can you ping the GAD router's serial interface?

_____

D. If the answer is no for either question, toubleshoot the router configurations to find the error. Then do the pings again until the answer to both questions is yes.

Upon completion of the previous steps, logoff (by typing **exit**) and turn the router off. Then remove and store the cables and adapter.

Lab 12-5: Configuring an Ethernet Interface

Figure 12-5.1   Topology for Lab 12-5

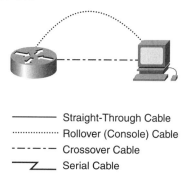

```
———————— Straight-Through Cable
················ Rollover (Console) Cable
-·-·-·- Crossover Cable
——Z—— Serial Cable
```

Table 12-5.1   Lab Equipment Configuration

Router Designation	Router Name	Router Type	FA0/0Address	Subnet Mask
Router 1	GAD		192.168.14.1	255.255.255.0

Enable secret password is **class** for both routers.
Enable, VTY, and Console password is **cisco** for both routers.

Objective

- Configure an Ethernet interface on the router with an IP address and a subnet mask.

Background / Preparation

Cable a network similar to the one in Figure 12-5.1. Any router that meets the interface requirements displayed in the diagram (that is, 800, 1600, 1700, 2500, and 2600 routers or a combination) can be used. Please refer to the information in the "Router Interface Summary Chart" immediately preceding Chapter 1 to correctly specify the interface identifiers to be used based on the equipment in your lab. The configuration output used in this lab is produced from 1721 series routers. Any other router used might produce slightly different output. The following steps are intended to be executed on each router unless specifically instructed otherwise.

Start a HyperTerminal session as performed in the "Establishing a Hyperterminal" session lab.

Please refer to and implement the procedure documented in "Erasing and Reloading the Router" immediately preceding Chapter 1 before continuing with this lab.

NOTE

Once interface configuration mode is entered, you must enter the IP address of the interface as well as the subnet mask. The command **no shutdown** turns on the interface. Shutdown is when the interface is off.

Step 1   Configure the hostname and passwords on the GAD router.

On the GAD router, enter the global configuration mode and configure the hostname as shown in the chart. Then configure the console, virtual terminal, and enable passwords.

Step 2   Configure the FastEthernet 0 interface.

```
GAD(config)#interface fastEthernet 0
GAD(config-if)#ip address 192.168.14.1 255.255.255.0
GAD(config-if)#no shutdown
GAD(config-if)#exit
GAD(config)#exit
```

Step 3   Save the configuration.

Save the configuration information from the privileged EXEC command mode .

```
GAD# copy running-config startup-config
```

NOTE

This will show the details of the Ethernet interface.

Step 4   Display FastEthernet 0s configuration information.

```
GAD#show interface fastethernet 0
```

A. List at least the following three details discovered from issuing this command:
FastEthernet0 is _____; line protocol is_____.

Internet address is _____.

Encapsulation _____

B. To what OSI layer is the "Encapsulation" referring?

Upon completion of the previous steps logoff (by typing **exit**) and turn the router off.

Lab 12-6: Making Configuration Changes

Figure 12-6.1   Topology for Lab 12-6

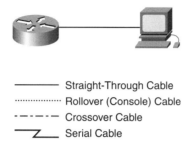

——————— Straight-Through Cable

··············· Rollover (Console) Cable

- - - - - Crossover Cable

⌐───⌐── Serial Cable

Table 12-6.1   Lab Equipment Configuration

Router Name	Router Type	Serial 0 Address	Subnet Mask
GAD		192.168.14.1	255.255.255.0

Enable secret password is **class** for both routers.
Enable, VTY, and Console password is **cisco** for both routers.

Objectives

- Configure some basic router settings
- Bring interfaces up and down
- Make changes to the router configuration

Background / Preparation

Cable a network similar to the one in Figure 12-6.1. Any router that meets the interface requirements displayed in the diagram (that is, 800, 1600, 1700, 2500, and 2600 routers or a combination) can be used. Please refer to the information in the "Router Interface Summary Chart" immediately preceding Chapter 1 to correctly specify the interface identifiers to be used based on the equipment in your lab. The configuration output used in this lab is produced from 1721 series routers. Any other router used may produce slightly different output. The following steps are intended to be executed on each router unless specifically instructed otherwise.

Start a HyperTerminal session as performed in Lab 11-2.

Please refer to and implement the procedure documented in "Erasing and Reloading the Router" immediately preceding Chapter 1 before continuing with this lab.

Step 1   Basic router configuration.

Connect the routers as shown in Figure 12-6.1. This lab requires a null serial cable (DTE and DCE together) and two rollover (console) cables.

Step 2   Configure hostname and passwords.

On the GAD router, enter global configuration mode and configure the hostname as shown in the chart. Then configure the console, virtual terminal, and enable passwords.

Step 3   Configure interface serial 0.

From the configure terminal mode, configure interface serial 0 (refer to the interface chart in Table 12-6.1) on Router GAD.

```
GAD(config)#interface Serial 0
GAD(config-if)#ip address 192.168.14.1 255.255.255.0
GAD(config-if)#no shutdown
GAD(config-if)#description Connection to the host
GAD(config-if)#exit
GAD(config)#exit
```

Step 4   Save the configuration.

Save the running configuration to the startup configuration at the privileged EXEC mode.

```
GAD#copy running-config startup-config
```

Step 5   Verify the configuration.

A. Issue the **show running-config** command from the privileged EXEC mode.

B. If the configuration is not correct, re-enter any incorrect commands.

Step 6   Modify the configuration.

A. Based on the information in Table 12-6.2, reconfigure the GAD router. This includes changing the router hostname, the enable, VTY, and console passwords and removing the secret password and interface description. The interface address and subnet mask will also need to be changed.

NOTE

Once interface configuration mode is entered, you must enter the IP address of the interface as well as the subnet mask. The command **no shutdown** turns on the interface. Shutdown is when the interface is off.

NOTE

If the running configuration is not saved, the next time that the router is restarted, either by a software **reload** command or a power shutdown, the running configuration will be lost. The router uses the startup configuration when the router is started.

NOTE

Before making changes to the interface IP address and subnet mask bring the interface down as shown in Step 7.

Table 12-6.1   Lab Equipment Configuration: Modified

Router Name	Serial 0 Address	Subnet Mask	Enable Secret Password	Enable, VTY, and Console Passwords
Gadsden	172.16.0.1	255.255.0.0		Cisco1

B. To change information, go to the proper command mode and retype the command with the new information. To remove an old command, go to the proper command mode and retype the command exactly as it was entered with the word **no** in front of it. For example,

```
Gadsden(config-if)#description Connection to the host
Gadsden(config-if)#no description Connection to the host
```

Step 7 Bring down serial interface 0 .

A. Bring the interface down for maintenance by entering:

```
GAD(config)# interface Serial 0
GAD(config-if)# shutdown
GAD(config-if)# exit
GAD(config)# exit
GAD#
```

B. Issue the **show interface Serial** 0 and note the interface status:

Serial 0 is _____ ; line protocol is _____ .

C. Make changes to the interface and then go to Step 8.

Step 8 Bring up serial interface 0.

A. To make the interface operational, enable the interface by entering:

```
GAD(config)# interface Serial 0
GAD(config-if)# no shutdown
GAD(config-if)#exit
GAD (config)# exit
```

B. Issue the **show interface Serial** 0 and note the interface status:

Serial 0 is _____ ; line protocol is _____ .

Step 9 Verify the configuration .

Issue a **show running-config** command from the privileged EXEC mode to see if the modifications were properly made. If the configuration is not correct, re-enter any incorrect commands and verify again.

Upon completion of the previous steps, logoff (by typing **exit**) and turn the router off.

Lab 12-7: Configuring Interface Descriptions

Figure 12-7.1 Topology for Lab 12-7

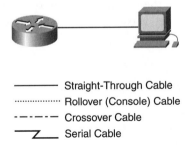

——————— Straight-Through Cable
················· Rollover (Console) Cable
- - - - - Crossover Cable
———Z——— Serial Cable

Table 12-7.1 Lab Equipment Configuration

Router Designation	Router Name	FastEthernet0 Address	Serial 0 Address	Subnet Mask for Both Interfaces
Router 1	GAD	192.168.14.1	192.168.15.1	255.255.255.0

Enable secret password is **class** for both routers.
Enable, VTY, and Console password is **cisco** for both routers.

Objective

- Choose a description for an interface and use interface configuration mode to enter that description.

Background / Preparation

Interface descriptions are an important part of network documentation. They are very helpful in understanding how a network is built and for troubleshooting purposes.

Cable a network similar to the one in Figure 12-7.1. You can use any router that meets the interface requirements displayed in the diagram (that is 800, 1600, 1700, 2500, and 2600 routers or a combination). Please refer to the information in the "Router Interface Summary Chart" immediately preceding Chapter 1 to correctly specify the interface identifiers to be used based on the equipment in your lab. The configuration output used in this lab is produced from 1721 series routers. Any other router used might produce slightly different output. The following steps are intended to be executed on each router unless specifically instructed otherwise.

Start a HyperTerminal session as performed in Lab 11-2.

Please refer to and implement the procedure documented in "Erasing and Reloading the Router" immediately preceding Chapter 1 before continuing with this lab.

Step 1 Configure the hostname and passwords on the Gadsden router.

   A. On the GAD router, enter the global configuration mode and configure the hostname as shown in Table 12-7.1. Then configure the console, virtual terminal, and enable passwords. If you have trouble doing this, refer to Lab 12-2.

   B. What is the router command to view the current running configuration?

   _____

   C. What command mode must be used to enter the command listed in the last question?

   _____

   D. Enter that command to verify the configuration that was just entered. If the configuration is not correct, fix the errors, and verify it again until correct.

Step 2 Enter global configuration mode.

   Enter **configure terminal** at the router prompt. Notice the change in the router prompt.

   What did the router prompt change to? _____

Step 3 Enter interface configuration mode.

   Enter **interface serial** 0 (refer to interface chart) at the global configuration prompt.

   What does the router prompt look like in interface configuration mode?

   _____

Step 4 Display help for the description command.

   Enter **description** ? at the router prompt.

   What is the maximum number of characters in an interface description?

   _____

Step 5 Choose a description for the interface.

   A. An interface description includes the purpose and location of the interface, other devices, or locations connected to the interface and circuit identifiers. Descriptions help the support personnel better understand the scope of problems related to an interface and allow for a faster resolution of problems.

B. Given the diagram in Figure 12-7.1 and the circuit information that follows, choose a description for the serial 0/0 interfaces for both GAD and BHM. Use the following form to document your choice.

Link	Carrier	Circuit ID	Speed
GAD to BHM	BellSouth	10DHDG551170	1.544 Mbps

NOTE

This would be the same as typing **exit** to leave the interface configuration mode and **exit** again to leave global configuration mode. This is a keyboard shortcut.

Step 6 Enter a description for interface serial 0.

From the interface configuration mode for serial 0, enter **description** *text*. Where *text* is the description from the previous step. Then enter Ctrl-z or type **end** to return to the privileged EXEC mode.

Step 7 Examine the active configuration file.

A. From the enable (another name for the privileged EXEC) mode, enter the command that will show the running configuration. The router will display information on how it is currently configured.

B. What command was entered?

_____

C. What is the description for interface serial 0?

_____

Step 8 Confirm interface description is correct.

From the enable mode, enter the **show interfaces serial** 0 command. The router displays information about the interface. Examine this output to confirm that the description you entered is the correct description.

Upon completion of the previous steps logoff (by typing **exit**) and turn the router off.

Lab 12-8: Configuring Message of the Day

Figure 12-8.1 Topology for Lab 12-8

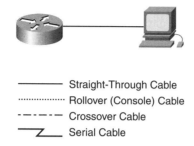

——————— Straight-Through Cable

················· Rollover (Console) Cable

‑ ‑ ‑ ‑ ‑ Crossover Cable

⎯⎯Z⎯ Serial Cable

Table 12-8.1 Lab Equipment Configuration

Router Name	FA0/0	S0/0 Address	Subnet Mask	Routing
GAD	172.16.0.1	192.168.15.1	255.255.255.0	RIP

Enable secret password is **class** for both routers.
Enable, VTY, and Console password is **cisco** for both routers.

Objective

- Enter a message of the day (MOTD) on the router that allows all users to view the message upon entering the router.

Background / Preparation

A message of the day or "login banner" can be useful as a warning to unauthorized users and assist with security measures.

Cable a network similar to the one in Figure 12-8.1. You can use any router that meets the interface requirements displayed in the diagram (that is, 800, 1600, 1700, 2500, and 2600 routers or a combination). Please refer to the information in the "Router Interface Summary Chart" immediately preceding Chapter 1 to correctly specify the interface identifiers to be used based on the equipment in your lab. The configuration output used in this lab is produced from 1721 series routers. Any other router used might produce slightly different output. The following steps are intended to be executed on each router unless specifically instructed otherwise.

Start a HyperTerminal session as performed in Lab 11-2.

Please refer to and implement the procedure documented in "Erasing and Reloading the Router" immediately preceding Chapter 1 before continuing with this lab.

Step 1   Configure basic router information.

   A. On the GAD router, enter the global configuration mode and configure the hostname as shown in the chart. Then configure the console, virtual terminal, and enable passwords. If you have trouble doing this, refer to Lab 12-2.

   B. Enter the **show running-config** command to verify the configuration that was just entered.

   C. Save the configuration information from the privileged EXEC command mode.

```
GAD#copy running-config startup-config
```

Step 2   Enter global configuration mode.

   Enter **configure terminal** at the router prompt. Notice the change in the router prompt.

Step 3   Display help for the **banner motd** command.

   Enter **banner motd ?** at the router prompt.

   What is the character that is used to indicate the beginning and end of the banner called?

   _____

Step 4   Choose a description for the interface.

   The login banner should be a warning not to attempt login unless authorized. In the space below, enter an appropriate warning banner. The message can contain any printable character as well as spaces and carriage returns.

   _____

   _____

Step 5   Enter the desired banner message.

   From the global configuration mode enter **banner motd #** *message* **#** where the # are used as delimiters and *message* is the banner message from the previous step.

Step 6   Test the MOTD display.

   Exit the console session. Re-enter the router to display the message of the day. This is done by pressing the **Enter** key. This will display the message entered into the configuration.

Step 7   Verify the MOTD by looking at the router configuration.

   A. Enter the **show running-config** command.

   B. How does the banner MOTD show in the configuration listing?

   _____

   C. Save the configuration information from the privileged EXEC command mode.

Upon completion of the previous steps logoff (by typing **exit**) and turn the router off.

Lab 12-9: Configuring Host Tables

Figure 12-9.1   Topology for Lab 12-9

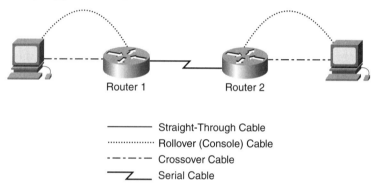

Router 1   Router 2

——————— Straight-Through Cable
············· Rollover (Console) Cable
- — - — - Crossover Cable
——Z—— Serial Cable

Table 12-9.1   Lab Equipment Configuration

Router Designation	Router Name	FastEthernet 0 Address	Interface Type	Serial 0 Address	Subnet Mask for Both Interfaces
Router 1	GAD	172.16.0.1	DCE	172.17.0.1	255.255.0.0
Router 2	BHM	172.18.0.1	DTE	172.17.0.2	255.255.0.0

Enable secret password is **class** for both routers.
Enable, VTY, and Console password is **cisco** for both routers.

Objective

■ Create IP host tables associating router names with IP addresses

Background / Preparation

IP host tables allow a router to use names to identify all of the attached interfaces on that router. These names can be used in place of an IP addresses in commands that use IP addresses to identify a location such as ping or telnet.

Cable a network similar to the one in Figure 12-9.1. You can use any router that meets the interface requirements displayed in the diagram (that is, 800, 1600, 1700, 2500, and 2600 routers or a combination). Please refer to the information in the "Router Interface Summary Chart" immediately preceding Chapter 1 to correctly specify the interface identifiers to be used based on the equipment in your lab. The configuration output used in this lab is produced from 1721 series routers. Any other router used might produce slightly different output. The following steps are intended to be executed on each router unless specifically instructed otherwise.

Start a HyperTerminal session as performed in Lab 11-2.

Please refer to and implement the procedure documented in "Erasing and Reloading the Router" immediately preceding Chapter 1 before continuing with this lab.

Step 1   Configure the hostname and passwords on the GAD router.

On the GAD router, enter the global configuration mode and configure the hostname as shown in Table 12-9.1. Then configure the console, virtual terminal, and enable passwords. If you have trouble doing this, refer to Lab 12-2.

Step 2   Configure the interfaces and routing protocol on the GAD router.

Go to the proper command mode and enter the following:

```
GAD(config)#interface fastethernet 0
GAD(config-if)#ip address 172.16.0.1 255.255.0.0
GAD(config-if)#no shutdown
GAD(config-if)#exit
GADconfig)#interface serial 0
GAD(config-if)#ip address 172.17.0.1 255.255.0.0
GAD(config-if)#clock rate 56000
GAD(config-if)#no shutdown
GAD(config-if)#exit
GAD(config)#router rip
GAD(config-router)#network 172.16.0.0
GAD(config-router)#network 172.17.0.0
GAD(config-router)#exit
GAD(config)#exit
```

Step 3   Save the GAD router configuration.

```
GAD# copy running-config startup-config
```

Step 4   Configure the hostname and passwords on the Birmingham router.

On the BHM router, enter the global configuration mode and configure the hostname as shown in the chart. Then configure the console, virtual terminal, and enable passwords. If you have trouble doing this, refer to the "Configuring Router Passwords" lab.

Step 5   Configure the interfaces and routing protocol on the BHM router.

Go to the proper command mode and enter the following:

```
BHM(config)# interface fastethernet 0
BHM(config-if)# ip address 172.18.0.1 255.255.0.0
BHM(config-if)# no shutdown
BHM(config-if)# exit
BHMconfig)# interface serial 0
BHM(config-if)# ip address 172.17.0.2 255.255.0.0
BHM(config-if)# no shutdown
BHM(config-if)# exit
BHM(config)# router rip
BHM(config-router)# network 172.17.0.0
BHM(config-router)# network 172.18.0.0
BHM(config-router)# exit
BHM(config)# exit
```

Step 6   Save the BHM router configuration.

```
BHM# copy running-config startup-config
```

Step 7   Verify that the internetwork is functioning by pinging the FastEthernet interface of the other router.

   A. From GAD, can you ping the BHM router's FastEthernet interface?

   _____

   B. From BHM, can you ping the GAD router's FastEthernet interface?

   _____

   C. If the answer is no for either question troubleshoot the router configurations to find the error. Then do the pings again until the answer to both questions is yes.

Step 8   Configure the IP host table for the network.

   A. Create a name for each router in the network lab. Enter that name along with the IP addresses of the routers interfaces in the table that follows. This is a local name and can be anything that is comfortable to you. Although the name does not have to match the configured hostname of the router, that would be the normal procedure.

Router Name	IP Address Fa0	Interface S0

B. From the global configuration mode, enter the command **ip host** followed by the name of each router in the network as well as all of the IP addresses of the interfaces on each of the routers.

For example to name the GAD router accessible from BHM by the name "G," enter

```
BHM(conf)#ip host G 172.16.0.1 172.17.0.1
```

C. What commands did you enter on GAD?

_____

_____

D. What commands did you enter on BHM?

_____

_____

Step 9 Exit configuration mode and test

A. From the enable (privileged EXEC) mode, examine the host table entries, using command **show ip hosts** command on each router.

B. Do you see the host entries that were configured in the previous steps?

GAD _____   BHM _____

C. If there are no IP host entries go back and repeat Step 6.

D. Now try to ping the other router by host name. From the enable prompt type **ping** *host*, where *host* is the IP host name that was configured in the previous steps. For example for a hostname of "G," enter

```
BHM#ping G
```

E. Was the ping successful? _____

F. If not check the accuracy of the IP host table entries.

G. Now from the enable prompt, enter the hostname and press **Enter.** For example for a host name of "G," enter

```
BHM#G
```

H. What happened?

_____

Upon completion of the previous steps logoff (by typing **exit**) and turn the router off.

Lab 12-10: Password Recovery Procedures

Figure 12-10.1   Topology for Lab 12-10

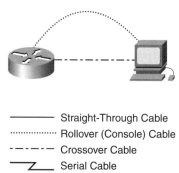

——————   Straight-Through Cable
·················   Rollover (Console) Cable
– – – – –   Crossover Cable
⎯⎯Z⎯⎯   Serial Cable

Table 12-10.1   Lab Equipment Configuration

Router Designation	Router Name	Enable Secret Password	Enable, VTY, Console Passwords
Router 1	GAD	class	cisco

Objective

- Gain access to a router with an unknown privileged mode (enable) password

Background / Preparation

This lab demonstrates gaining access to a router with an unknown privileged mode (enable) password. One point to be made here is that anyone with this procedure and access to a console port on a router can change the password and take control of the router. That is why it is of critical importance that routers also have physical security to prevent unauthorized access.

Cable a network similar to the one in Figure 12-10. You can use any router that meets the interface requirements displayed in the diagram (that is, 800, 1600, 1700, 2500, and 2600 routers or a combination) may be used. Please refer to the information in the "Router Interface Summary Chart" immediately preceding Chapter 1 to correctly specify the interface identifiers to be used based on the equipment in your lab. The configuration output used in this lab is produced from 1721 series routers. Any other router used might produce slightly different output. The following steps are intended to be executed on each router unless specifically instructed otherwise.

Start a HyperTerminal session as performed in Lab 11-2.

NOTE

Configure the hostname and passwords on the router and have an instructor, lab assistant, or other student configure a basic configuration with an enable secret password and perform **copy running-config startup-config** and reload the router.

Step 1   Attempt login to the router.

Make the necessary console connections and establish a Hyperterminal session with the router. Attempt to logon the router using the privileged mode password **class**. Your output should look something like

```
Router>enable
Password:
Password:
Password:
% Bad secrets

Router>
```

Step 2   Document the current config register setting.

A. At the user EXEC prompt type **show ver.**

B. Record the value displayed for configuration register _____ (for example, 0x2102).

Step 3   Enter the ROM monitor mode.

Turn the router off, wait a few seconds and turn it back on. When the router starts displaying "System Bootstrap, Version ..." on the HyperTerminal screen, press the **Ctrl** key and the **Break** key together. The router will boot in ROM monitor mode. Depending on the router hardware you may get one of several prompts such as: rommon 1 > or simply >.

NOTE

The version of Hyper-Terminal provided with Windows 95, 98, NT, and 2000 was developed for Microsoft by Hilgraeve and some versions may not issue a "break" sequence as required for the Cisco router password recovery technique. If this is the case, upgrade to Hyper-Terminal Private Edition (PE), which is free of charge for personal and educational use. The program can be down-loaded at

Step 4   Examine the ROM monitor mode help.

Type ? at the prompt. The output should be similar to the following:

```
rommon 1 >?
alias           set and display aliases command
boot            boot up an external process
break           set/show/clear the breakpoint
confreg         configuration register utility
context         display the context of a loaded image
dev             list the device table
dir             list files in file system
dis             display instruction stream
help            monitor builtin command help
history         monitor command history
meminfo         main memory information
repeat          repeat a monitor command
reset           system reset
set             display the monitor variables
sysret          print out info from last system return
tftpdnld        tftp image download
xmodem          x/ymodem image download
```

Step 5   Change the configuration register setting to boot without loading configuration file.

From the ROM Monitor mode, type **confreg 0x2142** to change the config-register

```
rommon 2 > confreg 0x2142
```

Step 6   Restart the router.

A. From the ROM Monitor mode, type **reset** or power cycle the router
```
rommon 2 > reset
```

B. Due to the new configuration register setting, the router will not load the configuration file. When the system prompts:"Would you like to enter the initial configuration dialog? [yes]:" enter **no** and press **Enter**.

Step 7   Enter privilege EXEC mode and change password.

A. Now at the user mode prompt Router>, type **enable** and press **Enter** to go to the privileged mode without a password.

B. Use the command **copy startup-config running-config** to restore the existing configuration. Since the user is already in privileged EXEC no password is needed.

C. Type **configure terminal** to enter the global configuration mode.

D. In the global configuration mode type **enable secret class** to change the secret password.

E. While still in the global configuration mode, type **config-register** *xxxxxxx* (where *xxxxxxx* is the original configuration register value recorded in Step 2) and press **Enter**.

F. Use the Ctrl-z combination to return to the privileged EXEC mode and

G. Use the **copy running-config startup-config** command to save the new configuration.

H. Before restarting the router verify the new configuration setting. From the privileged EXEC prompt, enter the **show version** command and press **Enter**.

I. Looking at the last line of output verify that it reads
```
Configuration register is 0x2142 (will be 0x2102 at next reload)
```

J. Use the **reload** command to restart the router.

Step 8   Verify new password and configuration.

When the router reloads the password should be **class**.

Upon completion of the previous steps logoff (by typing **exit**) and turn the router off.

Objectives

Upon completing this chapter, you will be able to

- Understand the purpose of ACLs
- Describe how ACLs work
- Determine which wildcard mask should be used
- Describe and use standard ACLs, extended ACLs, and named ACLs
- Describe a simple firewall architecture

Chapter 20

Access Control Lists

In this chapter, you learn about using standard and extended access control lists (ACLs) as a means to control network traffic and how ACLs are used as part of a security solution.

In addition, this chapter includes tips, considerations, recommendations, and general guidelines on how to use ACLs, and includes the commands and configurations needed to create ACLs. Finally, this chapter provides examples of standard and extended ACLs and shows how to apply ACLs to router interfaces.

Please be sure to look at this chapter's associated e-labs, movies, and photozooms that you will find on the CD-ROM accompanying the full text of this title. These CD elements are designed to supplement the material and reinforce the concepts introduced in this chapter.

ACL Overview

Network administrators must be capable of denying unwanted access to the network while allowing appropriate access. Although security tools such as passwords, callback equipment, and physical security devices are helpful, they often lack the flexibility of basic traffic filtering and the specific controls that most administrators prefer. For example, a network administrator might want to allow users access to the Internet but might not want external users telnetting into the LAN.

Routers provide basic traffic-filtering capabilities, such as blocking Internet traffic, with *access control lists (ACLs)*. An ACL is a sequential collection of permit or deny statements that apply to addresses or upper-layer protocols.

It is important to configure ACLs correctly and to know where to place ACLs on the network. ACLs serve multiple purposes in a network. Common ACL functions include

- Filtering packets internally
- Protecting the internal network from illegal Internet access
- Restricting access to virtual terminal ports

NOTE

ACLs consume CPU resources in the router because every packet has to be punted to the CPU.

ACLs are lists of instructions that you apply to a router's interface. These lists tell the router what kinds of packets to accept and what kinds of packets to deny. Acceptance and denial can be based on certain specifications, such as source address, destination address, and TCP/UDP port number.

ACLs enable you to manage traffic and scan specific packets by applying the ACL to a router interface. Any traffic going through the interface is tested against certain conditions that are part of the ACL.

You can create ACLs for all routed network protocols, such as Internet Protocol (IP) and Internetwork Packet Exchange (IPX), to filter packets as the packets pass through a router. ACLs can be configured at the router to control access to a network or subnet.

ACLs filter network traffic by controlling whether routed packets are forwarded or blocked at the router's interfaces. The router examines each packet to determine whether to forward or drop it, based on the conditions specified in the ACL. ACL conditions could be the source address of the traffic, the destination address of the traffic, the upper-layer protocol, the port, or applications.

You must define ACLs on a per-protocol basis. In other words, you must define an ACL for every protocol enabled on an interface if you want to control traffic flow for *that* protocol on *that* interface. (Note that some protocols refer to ACLs as *filters*.) For example, if your router interface were configured for IP, AppleTalk, and IPX, you would need to define at least three ACLs. As shown in Figure 20-1, ACLs can be used as a tool for network control by adding the flexibility to filter the packets that flow in or out of router interfaces. This is accomplished by establishing a numbering range or scheme for each protocol's ACL. You learn more about the ACL numbers later in this chapter.

Figure 20-1 ACL Example

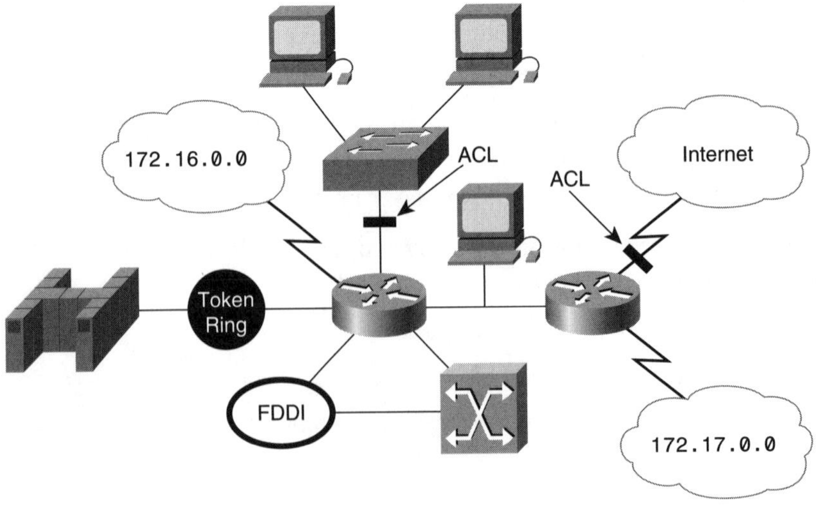

Why Create ACLs?

Many reasons exist for creating ACLs. ACLs can be used to do the following:

- Limit network traffic and increase network performance. For example, ACLs can designate certain packets to be processed by a router before other traffic, on the basis of a protocol. This is referred to as *queuing*. Queuing ensures that routers will not process packets that are not needed. As a result, queuing limits network traffic and reduces network congestion.

- Provide traffic flow control. For example, ACLs can restrict or reduce the contents of routing updates. These restrictions are used to limit information about specific networks from propagating through the network.

- Provide a basic level of security for network access. ACLs can allow one host to access a part of your network and prevent another host from accessing the same area. In Figure 20-2, Host A is allowed to access the Human Resources network, and Host B is prevented from accessing the Human Resources network. If you do not configure ACLs on your router, all packets passing through the router could be allowed onto all parts of the network.

- Decide which type of traffic is forwarded or blocked at the router interface. For example, you can permit e-mail traffic to be routed, but at the same time block all telnet traffic.

NOTE

The rule of thumb is one ACL per interface per direction.

Figure 20-2 Limiting Network Traffic

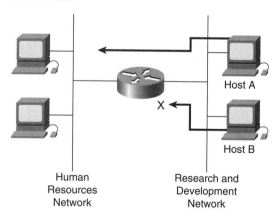

Human Resources Network

Research and Development Network

Host A

Host B

Creating an ACL: Why Order Matters

Order matters when creating an ACL. As traffic enters or exits a router's interface, where an ACL is applied, Cisco IOS Software compares the packet against the rules defined in the ACL. Statements are evaluated in the order they were entered into the

NOTE

When an ACL is created, new lines are added to the end of the ACL. Individual lines cannot be deleted. Only entire ACLs can be deleted.

ACL by the network administrator. The packet is compared, one at a time in sequence, until a match is found. After a match is found, the action specified in the line matching the traffic in question is taken. No more conditions are checked.

For example, if a condition statement permitting all traffic is created, statements added later will never be checked. If additional statements are required or if statements must be changed, you must delete the ACL and re-create it with the new statements. It is a good idea to use a PC text editor to create and modify ACLs and then send them to the router via Trivial File Transfer Protocol (TFTP) or HyperTerminal text file transfer.

Using ACLs

You can create an ACL for each protocol that you want to filter for each router interface. For some protocols, you create one ACL to filter inbound traffic and one ACL to filter outbound traffic.

After an ACL statement checks a packet for a match, the packet can be denied or permitted to use an interface in the access group. Cisco IOS Software ACLs check the packet and upper-layer headers, as shown in Figure 20-3.

Figure 20-3 Checking the Packet and Upper-Layer Headers

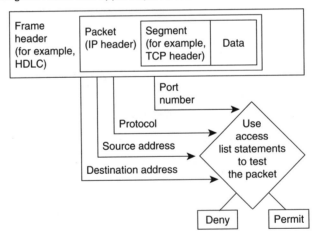

How ACLs Work

An ACL is a group of statements that define how packets do the following:

- Enter inbound router interfaces
- Relay through the router
- Exit outbound router interfaces

As shown in Figure 20-4, the beginning of the communication process is the same, whether ACLs are used or not. As a packet enters an interface, the router checks to see whether the packet is routable or bridgeable. Now the router checks whether the inbound interface has an ACL. If one exists, the packet is tested against the conditions in the list. If the packet is allowed, it then is checked against routing table entries to determine the destination interface. ACLs filter not packets that originate in the router itself, but packets from other sources.

Next, the router checks whether the destination interface has an ACL. If it does not, the packet can be sent to the destination interface directly; for example, if it will use E0, which has no ACLs, the packet uses E0 directly.

Figure 20-4 How ACLs Work

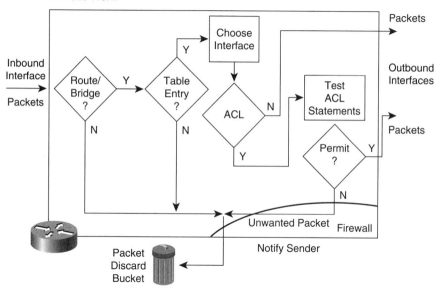

ACL statements operate in a sequential, logical order. If a condition match is true, the packet is permitted or denied and the rest of the ACL statements are not checked. If all the ACL statements are unmatched, an implicit **deny any** statement is imposed. Even though you will not see the **deny any** as the last line of an ACL, it is there by default. In Figure 20-5, if by matching the first test a packet is denied access to the destination, it is discarded and dropped into the *bit bucket.* It is not exposed to any ACL tests that follow. If the packet does not match the conditions of the first test, it drops to the next statement in the ACL.

Figure 20-5 ACL Test Matching and Implicit deny any

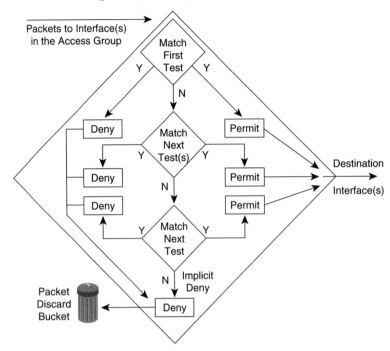

ACLs enable you to control what clients can access on your network. Conditions in an ACL file can do the following:

- Screen out certain hosts to either allow or deny access to part of your network
- Grant or deny users permission to access only certain types of applications, such as FTP or HTTP

ACL Configuration Tasks

In practice, ACL commands can be lengthy character strings. Key tasks covered in this section for creating ACLs include the following:

- You create ACLs by using global configuration mode.
- Specifying an ACL number from 1 to 99 defines a standard ACL for IP and instructs the router to accept standard ACL statements.
- Specifying an ACL number from 100 to 199 defines an extended ACL for IP and instructs the router to accept extended ACL statements.

- You must carefully select and logically order the ACL. Permitted IP protocols must be specified; all other protocols should be denied unless required.
- You need to select which protocols to check; any other protocols are not checked. Later in the procedure, you can specify an optional destination port for more precision.
- You apply an ACL to an interface.

Although each protocol has its own set of specific tasks and rules that are required to provide traffic filtering, in general most protocols require two basic steps:

Step 1   Create an ACL definition.

Step 2   Apply the ACL to an interface.

ACLs are assigned to one or more interfaces and can filter inbound traffic or outbound traffic, depending on the configuration and how they are applied. Outbound ACLs generally are more efficient than inbound and, therefore, are preferred. A router with an inbound ACL must check every packet to see whether it matches the ACL condition before switching the packet to an outbound interface.

Assigning a Unique Number to Each ACL

When configuring ACLs on a router, you must identify each ACL uniquely by assigning a number to the protocol's ACL. When you use a number to identify an ACL, the number must be within the specific range of numbers that is valid for the protocol. Example 20-1 defines ACLs 1 and 2 and applies the ACLs to interface Ethernet 0.

Example 20-1 *Assigning ACLs to an Interface*

```
access-list 1 permit 5.6.0.0 0.0.255.255
access-list 1 deny 7.9.0.0 0.0.255.255
!
access-list 2 permit 1.2.3.4
access-list 2 deny 1.2.0.0 0.0.255.255
!
interface ethernet 0
ip address 1.1.1.1 255.0.0.0
!
ip access-group 1 in
ip access-group 2 out
```

Table 20-1 lists valid protocol ACL numbers.

Table 20-1 Protocols, ACLs, and Their Corresponding Numbers

Protocol	Range
IP	1 to 99
Extended IP	100 to 199
AppleTalk	600 to 699
IPX	800 to 899
Extended IPX	900 to 999
IPX Service Advertising Protocol	1000 to 1099

Using Wildcard Mask Bits

A *wildcard mask* is a 32-bit quantity that is divided into four octets, with each octet containing 8 bits. A wildcard mask bit of 0 means "Check the corresponding bit value," and a wildcard mask bit of 1 means "Do not check (ignore) that corresponding bit value" (see Figure 20-6).

Figure 20-6 Wildcard Mask Bit Matching

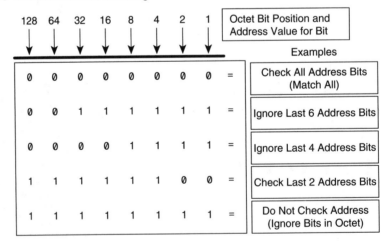

A wildcard mask is paired with an IP address, similar to how a subnet mask is paired with an IP address. Wildcard mask bits use the numbers 1 and 0 to identify how to treat the corresponding IP address bits.

ACLs use wildcard masking to identify a single address or multiple addresses for permit or deny tests. The term *wildcard masking* is a nickname for the ACL mask bit–matching process and comes from of an analogy of a wildcard that matches any other card in a poker game.

Although both are 32-bit quantities, wildcard masks and IP subnet masks operate differently. Recall that the 0s and 1s in a subnet mask determine the network, subnet, and host portions of the corresponding IP address. The 0s and 1s in a wildcard, as just noted, determine whether the corresponding bits in the IP address should be checked or ignored for ACL purposes.

As you have learned, the 0 and 1 bits in an ACL wildcard mask cause the ACL to either check or ignore the corresponding bits in the IP address. Figure 20-7 demonstrates how this wildcard masking process is applied.

Suppose that you want to test an IP address for subnets that will be permitted or denied. Assume that the IP address is a Class B address (that is, the first two octets are the network number) with 8 bits of subnetting (the third octet is for subnets).

You want to use IP wildcard mask bits to permit all packets from any host in the 172.30.16.0 to 172.30.31.0 subnets. Figure 20-7 shows an example of how to use the wildcard mask to do this.

Figure 20-7 Wildcard Mask Example

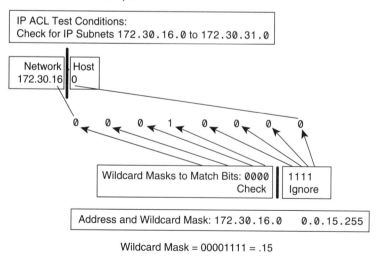

To begin, the wildcard mask checks the first two octets (172.30), using corresponding 0 bits in the wildcard mask.

Because there is no interest in individual host addresses (a valid host ID does not have .0 at the end of the address), the wildcard mask ignores the final octet, using corresponding 1 bits in the wildcard mask.

In the third octet, the wildcard mask is 15 (00001111), and the IP address is 16 (00010000). The first four 0s in the wildcard mask tell the router to match the first 4 bits of the IP address (0001). Because the last 4 bits are ignored, all numbers in the range of 16 (00010000) to 31 (00011111) will match because they begin in the pattern 0001.

For the final (least-significant) 4 bits in this octet, the wildcard mask ignores the value because in these positions, the address value can be binary 0 or binary 1, and the corresponding wildcard bits are 1s. In this example, the wildcard mask tells the router to match the first 4 bits of the IP address. The remaining 4 bits are ignored altogether. Therefore, the address 172.30.16.0 with the wildcard mask 0.0.15.255 matches subnets 172.30.16.0 to 172.30.31.0. The wildcard mask does not match any other subnets.

Using the Wildcard any

Working with decimal representations of binary wildcard mask bits can be tedious. For the most common uses of wildcard masking, you can use abbreviations. These abbreviations reduce the amount of typing you need to do when configuring address test conditions. One such example is the wildcard **any**. For example, assume that you want to specify that any destination address will be permitted in an ACL test. To indicate any IP address, you would enter **0.0.0.0**, as shown in Figure 20-8; then to indicate that the ACL should ignore (that is, allow without checking) any value, the corresponding wildcard mask bits for this address would be all 1s (that is, 255.255.255.255).

Figure 20-8 Wildcard **any**

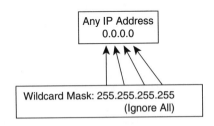

You can use the abbreviation of **any** to communicate this same test condition on Cisco IOS Software. Instead of typing **0.0.0.0 255.255.255.255**, you can use the word **any** by itself as the keyword.

For example, instead of using this

```
Router(config)#access-list 1 permit 0.0.0.0 255.255.255.255
```

you can use this

```
Router(config)#access-list 1 permit any
```

Using the Wildcard host

A second common condition in which Cisco IOS Software permits an abbreviation in the ACL wildcard mask arises when you want to match all the bits of an entire IP host address. For example, suppose that you want to specify that a unique host IP address will be permitted in an ACL test. To indicate a host IP address, you would enter the full address (for example, 172.30.16.29, as shown in Figure 20-9). Then to indicate that the ACL should check all the bits in the address, the corresponding wildcard mask bits for this address would be all 0s (that is, 0.0.0.0).

Figure 20-9 Wildcard **host**

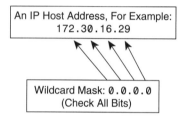

You can use the abbreviation of **host** to communicate this same test condition on Cisco IOS Software. In the example, instead of typing **172.30.16.29 0.0.0.0**, you can use the word **host** in front of the address.

For example, instead of using this

```
Router(config)#access-list 1 permit 172.30.16.29 0.0.0.0
```

you can use this

```
Router(config)#access-list 1 permit host 172.30.16.29
```

Standard ACLs

Standard ACLs check the source address of routed IP packets and compare it against the statements defining the ACL, as demonstrated in Figure 20-10.

Figure 20-10 Standard ACL Operations

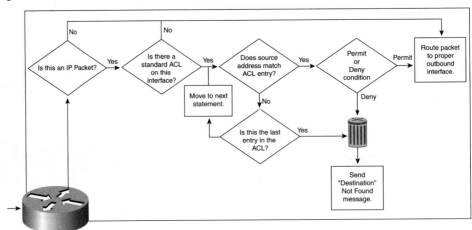

Standard ACLs either permit or deny access for an entire protocol suite (such as IP), based on the network, subnet, and host addresses. For example, packets coming in interface E0 or Fa0/0 are checked for their source addresses and protocols and then are compared against the ACL. When a match is found, that action (**permit** or **deny**) is performed. Packets matching **permit** statements in the ACL then are routed through the router to an output interface. Packets matching **deny** statements in the ACL are discarded (dropped) at the incoming interface.

The following is the full syntax of the standard ACL command:

```
Router(config)# access-list access-list-number {deny | permit} source [source-wildcard]
   [log]
```

The **no** form of this command is used to remove a standard ACL. This following is the syntax for the **no** form of this command:

```
Router(config)# no access-list access-list-number
```

Table 20-2 shows descriptions of the parameters used in this syntax.

Table 20-2 Standard ACL Parameters

Parameter	Description
access-list-number	Number of an access list. This is a decimal number from 1 to 99 or from 1300 to 1999.
deny	Denies access if the conditions are matched.
permit	Permits access if the conditions are matched.

Table 20-2 Standard ACL Parameters (Continued)

Parameter	Description
source	Number of the network or host from which the packet is being sent. There are two alternative ways to specify the source: ■ Use a 32-bit quantity in four-part dotted-decimal format. ■ Use the any keyword as an abbreviation for a *source* and *source-wildcard* of 0.0.0.0 255.255.255.255.
source-wildcard	(Optional) Wildcard bits to be applied to the source. There are two alternative ways to specify the source wildcard: Use a 32-bit quantity in four-part dotted-decimal format. Place 1s in the bit positions you want to ignore. Use the **any** keyword as an abbreviation for a *source* and *source-wildcard* value of 0.0.0.0 255.255.255.255.
log	(Optional) Causes an informational logging message about the packet that matches the entry to be sent to the console. (The level of messages logged to the console is controlled by the **logging console** command.) The message includes the access list number, whether the packet was permitted or denied, the source address, and the number of packets. The message is generated for the first packet that matches and then at five-minute intervals, including the number of packets permitted or denied in the previous five-minute interval. Use the **ip access-list log-update** command to generate the logging messages to appear when the number of matches reaches a configurable threshold (instead of waiting for a five-minute interval). To learn more about the **ip access-list log-update** command, you can check the following resource at Cisco for more information: www.cisco.com/univercd/cc/td/doc/product/software/ios120/12cgcr/cbkixol.htm. The logging facility might drop some logging message packets if there are too many to be handled or if there is more than one logging message to be handled in one second. This behavior prevents the router from crashing because of too many logging packets. Therefore, the logging facility should not be used as a billing tool or an accurate source of the number of matches to an access list.

The standard version of the **access-list** global configuration command defines a standard ACL with a number ranging from 1 to 99. Example 20-2 shows four ACL statements, all of which belong to access list 2, although this combination is not likely it illustrates how several different statements can work. Also remember that if a packet does not match any of these tests, there is an implicit (unseen) **deny any** at end of the ACL.

Example 20-2 *Standard ACL Statements*

```
access-list 2 deny 172.16.1.1
access-list 2 permit 172.16.1.0 0.0.0.255
access-list 2 deny 172.16.1.1 0.0.255.255
access-list 2 permit 172.16.1.1 0.255.255.255
```

In the first ACL statement, notice that there is no wildcard mask. In situations like this, when no wildcard mask is shown, the default mask is used, which is 0.0.0.0. This statement denies the IP address 172.16.1.1.

The second statement permits the specific host 172.16.1.0 or any host from the 172.16.1.0 subnet.

The third statement denies any host from the 172.16.0.0 network, and the fourth statement permits any host from any network starting with 172.

The **ip access-group** command links an existing ACL to an interface. It is necessary to enter interface configuration mode first to access the desired interface (for example, s0/0). The format of the command is as follows:

```
Router(config-if)# ip access-group access-list number {in | out}
```

e-Lab Activity   Standard IP Access List

In this activity, you demonstrate how to use the **access-list** command to define a standard IP ACL.

e-Lab Activity   Working with Standard ACLs

In this activity, you work through several tasks for configuring standard ACLs.

Lab Activity   Standard ACLs

In this lab, you plan, configure, and apply a standard ACL to permit or deny specific traffic and test the ACL to determine whether the desired results were achieved.

Extended ACLs

Extended ACLs are used more often than standard ACLs because they provide a greater range of flexibility and control. Extended ACLs check the source and destination IP addresses and also can check for protocols and TCP or UDP port numbers. Figure 20-11 illustrates the decision process that a router uses to evaluate packets against extended ACLs.

Figure 20-11 Extended ACL Operations

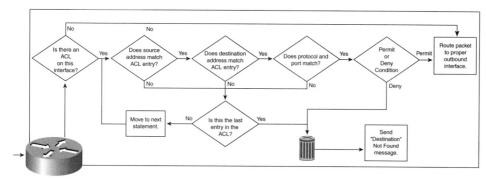

Access can be permitted or denied based on where a packet originated, its destination, the protocol type, the port addresses, and application. An extended ACL can allow e-mail traffic from Fa0/0 to specific S0/0 destinations while denying file transfers and web browsing. When packets are discarded, some protocols send an echo packet to the sender, which states that the destination was unreachable.

Extended ACLs have more granularity in terms of control and packet manipulation than standard ACLs. Whereas standard ACLs can prevent or deny only an entire protocol suite, extended ACLs give you the capability to "nitpick" which protocol in the suite you want to deny or allow—for example, allow HTTP but not FTP.

The following is the full syntax of the extended ACL command:

```
Router(config)# access-list access-list-number [dynamic dynamic-name [timeout
   minutes]] {deny | permit} protocol source source-wildcard destination
   destination-wildcard [precedence precedence] [tos tos] [log | log-input]
   [time-range time-range-name] [fragments]
```

The **no** form of this command is used to remove a extended ACL. The following is the syntax for the **no** form of this command:

```
Router(config)# no access-list access-list-number
```

The syntax for extended ACL statements can get very long and often wraps in the terminal window. Many additional options are available in extended ACLs as documented in Table 20-3.

Table 20-3 Extended ACL Parameters

Parameter	Description
access-list-number	Number of an access list. This is a decimal number from 100 to 199 or from 2000 to 2699.
dynamic *dynamic-name*	(Optional) Identifies this ACL as a dynamic ACL. Refer to lock-and-key access documented in the "Configuring Lock-and-Key Security (Dynamic Access Lists)" chapter in the *Cisco IOS Security Configuration Guide*.
timeout *minutes*	(Optional) Specifies the absolute length of time, in minutes, that a temporary access list entry can remain in a dynamic access list. The default is an infinite length of time and allows an entry to remain permanently. Refer to lock-and-key access documented in the "Configuring Lock-and-Key Security (Dynamic Access Lists)" chapter in the *Cisco IOS Security Configuration Guide*.
deny	Denies access if the conditions are matched.
permit	Permits access if the conditions are matched.
protocol	Name or number of an Internet protocol. It can be one of the keywords **eigrp, gre, icmp, igmp, igrp, ip, ipinip, nos, ospf, pim, tcp,** or **udp,** or an integer in the range from 0 to 255 representing an Internet protocol number. To match any Internet protocol (including ICMP, TCP, and UDP), use the **ip** keyword. Some protocols allow further qualifiers.
source	Number of the network or host from which the packet is being sent. There are three alternative ways to specify the source: Use a 32-bit quantity in four-part dotted-decimal format. Use the **any** keyword as an abbreviation for a *source* and *source-wildcard* of 0.0.0.0 255.255.255.255. Use **host source** as an abbreviation for a **source** and *source-wildcard* of *source* 0.0.0.0.

Table 20-3 Extended ACL Parameters (Continued)

Parameter	Description
source-wildcard	Wildcard bits to be applied to the source. Each wildcard bit set to 0 indicates the corresponding bit position in the source. Each wildcard bit set to 1 indicates that both a 0 bit and a 1 bit in the corresponding position of the IP address of the packet will be considered a match to this access list entry.
	There are three alternative ways to specify the source wildcard:
	Use a 32-bit quantity in four-part dotted-decimal format. Place 1s in the bit positions that you want to ignore.
	Use the any keyword as an abbreviation for a *source* and *source-wildcard* of 0.0.0.0 255.255.255.255.
	Use host source as an abbreviation for a *source* and *source-wildcard* of source 0.0.0.0.
	Wildcard bits set to 1 need not be contiguous in the *source* wildcard. For example, a *source* wildcard of 0.255.0.64 would be valid.
destination	Number of the network or host to which the packet is being sent. There are three alternative ways to specify the destination:
	Use a 32-bit quantity in four-part dotted-decimal format.
	Use the **any** keyword as an abbreviation for the *destination* and *destination-wildcard* of 0.0.0.0 255.255.255.255.
	Use **host destination** as an abbreviation for a *destination* and *destination-wildcard* of destination 0.0.0.0.
destination-wildcard	Wildcard bits to be applied to the *destination*. There are three alternative ways to specify the destination wildcard:
	Use a 32-bit quantity in four-part dotted-decimal format. Place 1s in the bit positions that you want to ignore.
	Use the **any** keyword as an abbreviation for a *destination* and *destination-wildcard* of 0.0.0.0 255.255.255.255.
	Use **host destination** as an abbreviation for a *destination* and *destination-wildcard* of destination 0.0.0.0.

continues

Table 20-3 Extended ACL Parameters (Continued)

Parameter	Description
precedence *precedence*	(Optional) Packets can be filtered by precedence level, as specified by a number from 0 to 7. This is used by the quality of service (QoS) mechanism.
tos *tos*	(Optional) Packets can be filtered by type of service level, as specified by a number from 0 to 15. This is used by the QoS mechanism.
log	(Optional) Causes an informational logging message about the packet that matches the entry to be sent to the console. (The level of messages logged to the console is controlled by the **logging console** command.)
	The message includes the access list number, whether the packet was permitted or denied; the protocol, whether it was TCP, UDP, ICMP, or a number; and, if appropriate, the source and destination addresses and source and destination port numbers. By default, the message is generated for the first packet that matches and then at five-minute intervals, including the number of packets permitted or denied in the previous five-minute interval.
	Use the **ip access-list log-update** command to generate logging messages when the number of matches reaches a configurable threshold (instead of waiting for a five-minute interval). See the **ip access-list log-update command** for more information.
	The logging facility might drop some logging message packets if there are too many to be handled or if there is more than one logging message to be handled in one second. This behavior prevents the router from crashing because of too many logging packets. Therefore, the logging facility should not be used as a billing tool or an accurate source of the number of matches to an access list.
log-input	(Optional) Includes the input interface and source MAC address or VC in the logging output.
time-range *time-range-name*	(Optional) Name of the time range that applies to this statement. The name of the time range and its restrictions are specified by the **time-range** command.
icmp-type	(Optional) ICMP packets can be filtered by ICMP message type. The type is a number from 0 to 255.

Table 20-3 Extended ACL Parameters (Continued)

Parameter	Description
icmp-code	(Optional) ICMP packets that are filtered by ICMP message type also can be filtered by the ICMP message code. The code is a number from 0 to 255.
icmp-message	(Optional) ICMP packets can be filtered by an ICMP message type name or ICMP message type and code name.
igmp-type	(Optional) IGMP packets can be filtered by IGMP message type or message name. A message type is a number from 0 to 15.
operator	(Optional) Compares source or destination ports. Possible operands include **lt** (less than), **gt** (greater than), **eq** (equal), **neq** (not equal), and **range** (inclusive range). If the operator is positioned after the *source* and *source-wildcard*, it must match the source port. If the operator is positioned after the *destination* and *destination-wildcard*, it must match the destination port. The range operator requires two port numbers. All other operators require one port number.
port	(Optional) Indicates the decimal number or name of a TCP or UDP port. A port number is a number from 0 to 65,535. TCP port names can be used only when filtering TCP. UDP port names can be used only when filtering UDP. TCP port names can be used only when filtering TCP. UDP port names can be used only when filtering UDP.
established	(Optional) For the TCP protocol only: Indicates an established connection. A match occurs if the TCP datagram has the ACK, FIN, PSH, RST, SYN, or URG control bits set. The nonmatching case is that of the initial TCP datagram to form a connection.
fragments	(Optional) This ACL entry applies to noninitial fragments of packets; the fragment is either permitted or denied accordingly.

For a single ACL, multiple statements can be configured. Each of these statements should contain the same *access-list-number* to relate the statements to the same ACL, as in Example 20-2. There can be as many condition statements as necessary. These condition statements are limited only by the available router memory. The more statements there are, the more difficult it will be to comprehend and manage the ACL. The three statements in Example 20-3 combine to permit telnet, ftp, and ftp-data from any host on the 172.16.6.0 subnetwork to any other network.

Example 20-3 *Extended ACL Statements*

```
access-list 114 permit tcp 172.16.6.0 0.0.0.255 any eq telnet
access-list 114 permit tcp 172.16.6.0 0.0.0.255 any eq ftp
access-list 114 permit tcp 172.16.6.0 0.0.0.255 any eq ftp-data
```

Extended ACLs are very versatile and, as such, provide different options and arguments based on the protocol used. Therefore, syntax will differ based on which of these protocols are in use. These protocols are listed here:

- Internet Control Message Protocol (ICMP)
- Internet Group Message Protocol (IGMP)
- Transmission Control Protocol (TCP)
- User Datagram Protocol (UDP)

The sections that follow describe the syntax variation of extended ACLs based on the protocol used.

e-Lab Activity   Extended IP ACLs

In this activity, you demonstrate how to use the **access-list** command to define an extended IP ACL.

Configuring Extended ACLs for ICMP

ACLs for ICMP use the following syntax:

```
access-list access-list-number [dynamic dynamic-name [timeout minutes]] {deny |
   permit} icmp source source-wildcard destination destination-wildcard [icmp-type
   [icmp-code] | icmp-message] [precedence precedence] [tos tos] [log | log-input]
   [time-range time-range-name] [fragments]
```

Configuring Extended ACLs for IGMP

ACLs for IGMP use the following syntax:

```
access-list access-list-number [dynamic dynamic-name [timeout minutes]] {deny |
   permit} igmp source source-wildcard destination destination-wildcard
   [igmp-type] [precedence precedence] [tos tos] [log | log-input] [time-range time-
   range-name] [fragments]
```

Configuring Extended ACLs for TCP

ACLs for TCP use the following syntax:

```
access-list access-list-number [dynamic dynamic-name [timeout minutes]] {deny |
    permit} tcp source source-wildcard [operator [port]] destination destination-
    wildcard [operator [port]] [established] [precedence precedence] [tos tos]
    [log | log-input] [time-range time-range-name] [fragments]
```

Configuring Extended ACLs for UDP

ACLs for UDP use the following syntax:

```
access-list access-list-number [dynamic dynamic-name [timeout minutes]] {deny |
    permit} udp source source-wildcard [operator [port]] destination destination-
    wildcard [operator [port]] [precedence precedence] [tos tos] [log | log-input]
    [time-range time-range-name] [fragments]
```

Extended ACL Defaults

An extended ACL defaults to a list that denies everything. An extended ACL is terminated by an implicit **deny** statement.

At the end of the extended ACL statement, additional precision is gained from a field
that specifies the optional TCP or UDP port number. Figure 20-12 illustrates this concept.

Figure 20-12 Transport/Application Port Numbers

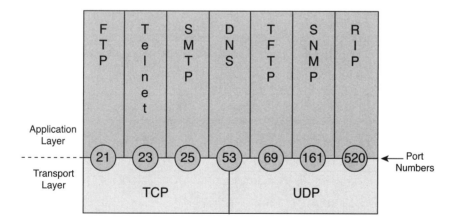

Table 20-4 lists some of the more common reserved UDP and TCP port numbers.

Table 20-4 Some Reserved TCP/UDP Numbers

Decimal	Keyword	Description
0		Reserved
1 to 4		Unassigned
5	RJE	Remote job entry
7	ECHO	Echo
9	DISCARD	Discard
11	USERS	Active users
13	DAYTIME	Daytime
15	NETSTAT	Who is up or NETSTAT
17	QUOTE	Quote of the day
19	CHARGEN	Character generator
20	FTP-DATA	File Transfer Protocol (data)
21	FTP	File Transfer Protocol
23	TELNET	Terminal connection
25	SMTP	Simple Mail Transfer Protocol
53	DOMAIN	Domain Name Server (DNS)
69	TFTP	Trivial File Transfer Protocol
80	HTTP	Hypertext Transfer Protocol (WWW)

The **ip access-group** command links an existing extended ACL to an interface. Only one ACL per interface, per direction, per protocol is allowed, as emphasized in Figure 20-13. The format of the command is as follows:

```
Router(config-if)# ip access-group access-list number {in | out}
```

Figure 20-13 ACL Rules

One List, Per Port, Per Direction, Per Protocol

Named ACLs

IP *named ACLs* were introduced in Cisco IOS Software Release 11.2, which allowed standard and extended ACLs to be given names instead of numbers. The advantages that a named access list provides are as follows:

- Intuitively identifies an ACL using an alpha or alphanumeric name
- Eliminates the limit of 99 simple and 100 extended ACLs
- Enables administrators to modifies ACLs without having to delete and then reconfigure them

A named ACL is created with the **ip access-list** command. The named ACL syntax is as follows:

```
ip access-list {extended | standard} name
```

This places the user in ACL configuration mode. In this mode, you can specify one or more conditions for permitting or denying access to a packet. The available options are as follows:

```
Router(config-ext-nacl)#permit | deny protocol source source-wildcard [operator
    [port]] destination destination-wildcard [operator [port]] [established]
    [precedence precedence] [tos tos] [log] [time-range time-range-name]
```

The **permit** or **deny** operand tells the router what action to take when a packet has met the other criteria specified in the ACL—that is, whether to forward or drop the packet.

Example 20-4 demonstrates applying a named ACL.

Example 20-4 *Named ACL Statements*

```
! Named ACL created:
Rt(config)#ip access-list extended server-access
Rt(config-ext-nacl)#permit tcp any host 131.108.101.99 eq smtp
Rt(config-ext-nacl)#permit tcp any host 131.108.101.99 eq domain
Rt(config-ext-nacl)#deny ip any any log
Rt(config-ext-nacl)#^Z
! Named ACL Applied:
Rt(config)#interface fastethernet0/0
Rt(config-if)#ip access-group server-access out
Rt(config-if)#^Z
```

In Example 20-4, the access list is given the name server-access. This access list then is applied to interface Fast Ethernet 0/0. This access list enables users to access the mail and DNS server only; all other requests are denied.

A named ACL allows for the deletion of statements, but statements can be inserted only at the end of a list, as demonstrated in Example 20-5.

Example 20-5 *Named ACL Statements*

```
router#configure terminal
 Enter configuration commands, one per line.
 router(config)#ip access-list extended test
 router(config-ext-nacl)#permit ip host 2.2.2.2 host 3.3.3.3
 router(config-ext-nacl)#permit tcp host 1.1.1.1 host 5.5.5.5 eq www
 router(config-ext-nacl)#permit icmp any any
 router(config-ext-nacl)#permit udp host 6.6.6.6 10.10.10.0 0.0.0.255 eq domain
 router(config-ext-nacl)#^Z
 1d00h: %SYS-5-CONFIG_I: Configured from console by consoles-1
 router#show access-list
 Extended IP access list test
     permit ip host 2.2.2.2 host 3.3.3.3
     permit tcp host 1.1.1.1 host 5.5.5.5 eq www
     permit icmp any any
     permit udp host 6.6.6.6 10.10.10.0 0.0.0.255 eq domain


 router#configure terminal
 Enter configuration commands, one per line. End with CNTL/Z.
 router(config)#ip access-list extended test
 !--- The following command deletes a named ACL entry.
 router(config-ext-nacl)#no permit icmp any any
 !--- The following command adds a named ACL entry.
 router(config-ext-nacl)#permit gre host 4.4.4.4 host 8.8.8.8
 router(config-ext-nacl)#^Z
 1d00h: %SYS-5-CONFIG_I: Configured from console by consoles-1


 router#show access-list
 Extended IP access list test
     permit ip host 2.2.2.2 host 3.3.3.3
     permit tcp host 1.1.1.1 host 5.5.5.5 eq www
     permit udp host 6.6.6.6 10.10.10.0 0.0.0.255 eq domain
     permit gre host 4.4.4.4 host 8.8.8.8
```

Consider the following before implementing named ACLs:

- Named ACLs are not compatible with Cisco IOS Software releases prior to Release 11.2.
- The same name cannot be used for multiple ACLs. For example, it is not permissible to specify both a standard and an extended ACL named George.

The series of commands shown in Example 20-6 first create a standard ACL named Internetfilter and an extended ACL named marketing_group. The commands then access interface e0/5, assign an IP address, and then apply both ACLs to an interface (Ethernet 0/5).

Example 20-6 *Named ACL Creation*

```
. . .
ip access-list standard Internetfilter
permit 1.2.3.4
deny any
ip access-list extended marketing_group
permit tcp any 171.69.0.0 0.255.255.255 eq telnet
deny tcp any any
deny udp any 171.69.0.0 0.255.255.255 lt 1024
deny ip any log
ip interface Ethernet0/5
ip address 2.0.5.1 255.255.255.0
ip access-group Internetfilter out
ip access-group marketing_group in
```

e-Lab Activity   Naming an ACL

In this activity, you demonstrate how to use the **ip access-list** command to name an ACL.

e-Lab Activity   Using **deny** with Named ACLs

In this activity, you demonstrate how to use the **deny** command to set conditions for a named ACL.

Lab Activity Named ACLs

In this lab, you create a Named ACL to permit or deny specific traffic and test the ACL to determine if the desired results were achieved.

Placing ACLs

ACLs control traffic by filtering packets and eliminating unwanted traffic on a network. An important consideration when implementing ACLs is where the access list is placed. When placed in the proper location, ACLs not only filter traffic, but they also can make the entire network operate more efficiently. For filtering traffic, the ACL should be placed where it has the greatest impact on increasing network efficiency.

Refer to Figure 20-14. Suppose that the enterprise policy wants to deny telnet or FTP traffic on Router A access to the switched Ethernet LAN on the Fa0/0 port of Router D. At the same time, other traffic must be permitted. This policy can be implemented several ways. The recommended approach uses an extended ACL, specifying both source and destination addresses. If this extended ACL is placed in Router A, packets will not cross the Ethernet of Router A or the serial interfaces of Routers B and C, and will not enter Router D. This will reduce traffic on the network links between Routers A and D. Traffic with different source and destination addresses still will be permitted.

Figure 20-14 Placing ACLs

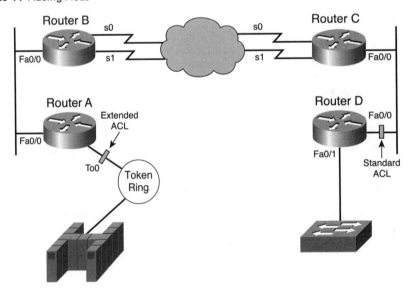

The general rule is to put the extended ACLs as close to the source of the denied traffic as possible. Standard ACLs do not specify destination addresses, so they should be placed as close to the destination as possible. For example, a standard ACL would be placed on Fa0/0 of Router D to prevent traffic from Router A.

In the advanced configuration, a feature called Turbo ACL compiles the ACL, making the process a lot faster. The Turbo ACL feature allows for a more efficient searching algorithm and also allows the list to be parsed in a more efficient manner.

e-Lab Activity   Placing Extended ACLs

In this activity, you use extended ACL parameters to block traffic.

Lab Activity   Extended ACLs

In this lab, you plan, configure, and apply an Extended ACL to permit or deny specific traffic and test the ACL to determine whether the desired results were achieved.

CAUTION

ACL operation can slow the router in peforming its routing tasks. The router has to read more of the packet and compare more prameters before it even gets to the routing operations.

Firewalls

A *firewall* is a computer or networking device that exists between the user and the outside world to protect the internal network from intruders. In most circumstances, intruders come from the global Internet and the thousands of remote networks that it interconnects. Typically, a network firewall consists of several different machines that work together to prevent unwanted and illegal access. Figure 20-15 shows a simple firewall architecture.

Figure 20-15 Firewall Architecture

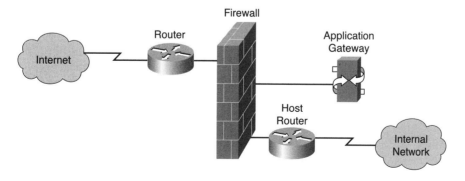

In firewall architecture, the router that is connected to the Internet is referred to as the *exterior router.* It forces all incoming traffic to pass through the application gateway. The router that is connected to the internal network is the **interior router.** The interior router accepts packets only from the application gateway. The gateway controls the delivery of network-based services both to and from the internal network. For example, the firewall might allow only certain users to communicate with the Internet, or permit only certain applications to establish connections between an interior and exterior host. If the only application that is permitted is mail, then only mail packets will be allowed through the router. This protects the application gateway and avoids overwhelming it with unauthorized packets.

Using ACLs with Firewalls

ACLs should be used in *firewall routers,* which often are positioned between the internal network and an external network, such as the Internet. The firewall router provides a point of isolation so that the rest of the internal network structure is not affected. You also can use ACLs on a router positioned between two parts of the network, to control traffic entering or exiting a specific part of the internal network.

To provide the security benefits of ACLs, you should, at a minimum, configure ACLs on **border routers**, which are routers situated on the boundaries of the network, and are also known as firewall routers. This provides basic security from the outside network, or from a less controlled area of the network, into a more private area of the network.

On these border routers, ACLs can be created for each network protocol configured on the router interfaces. You can configure ACLs so that inbound traffic, outbound traffic, or both are filtered on an interface.

Restricting Virtual Terminal Access

Standard and extended ACLs apply to packets traveling through a router. They are not designed to block packets that originate within the router. By default, an outbound telnet-extended ACL does not prevent router-initiated telnet sessions.

In addition to physical ports or interfaces on the router, such as Fa0/0 and S0/0, there are virtual ports. These virtual ports are called vty lines. There are five vty lines, which are numbered zero through four, as shown in Figure 20-16. For security purposes, users can be denied or permitted virtual terminal access to the router but denied access to destinations from that router. For example, an administrator can configure the ACL to allow terminal access to the router for management or troubleshooting purposes, while at the same time restricting access beyond this router.

Figure 20-16 Restricting vty Access with ACLs

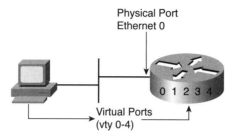

Restricting vty access is not commonly used as a traffic control mechanism; instead, it is for increasing network security. vty access is accomplished using the telnet protocol to make a nonphysical connection to the router. As a result, there is only one type of vty ACL. Identical restrictions should be placed on all vty lines because it is impossible to control which line a user will connect on.

Whereas a vty ACL is created the same way as on an interface, applying the vty ACL to a terminal line requires using the **access-class** command instead of the **access-group** command. Example 20-7 demonstrates creating and applying a virtual terminal access list.

Example 20-7 *Restricting vty Access with ACLs*

```
! Creating the standard list:
Rt1(config)#access-list 2 permit 172.16.1.0 0.0.0.255
Rt1(config)#access-list 2 permit 172.16.2.0 0.0.0.255
Rt1(config)#access-list 2 deny any
! Applying the access list:
Rt1(config)#line vty 0 4
Rt1(config)#login
Rt1(config)#password secret
Rt1(config)#access-class 2 in
```

Keep the following considerations in mind when configuring access lists on vty lines:

- A name or number can be used when controlling access to an interface.
- Only numbered access lists can be applied to virtual lines.
- Identical restrictions should be set on all the virtual terminal lines because a user can attempt to connect to any of them.

Verifying ACLs

The **show ip interface** command displays IP interface information and indicates whether any ACLs are set. Example 20-8 shows the output of the **show ip interface** command. As you can see in rows 9 and 10 in Example 20-8, ACL 10 is set to the outgoing traffic on interface Ethernet 0. There is no ACL set to inbound traffic.

Example 20-8 show ip interface *Command*

```
Router> show ip interface
Ethernet0 is up, line protocol is up
Internet address is 192.54.22.2, subnet mask is 255.255.255.0
Broadcast address is 255.255.255.255
Address determined by nonvolatile memory
MTU is 1500 bytes
Helper address is 192.52.71.4
Secondary address 131.192.115.2, subnet mask 255.255.255.0
Outgoing ACL 10 is set
Inbound ACL is not set
Proxy ARP is enabled
Security level is default
Split horizon is enabled
ICMP redirects are always sent
ICMP unreachables are never sent
ICMP mask replies are never sent
IP fast switching is enabled
Gateway Discovery is disabled
IP accounting is disabled
TCP/IP header compression is disabled
Probe proxy name replies are disabled
Router>
```

The **show access-lists** command displays the contents of all ACLs. By entering the ACL name or number as an option for this command, you can see a specific list.

e-Lab Activity   Using show ip interface

In this activity, you demonstrate how to use the **show ip interface** command to display IP interface information.

e-Lab Activity   Using show access-lists

In this activity, you demonstrate how to use the **show access-lists** command to display the contents of all current ACLs.

e-Lab Activity   Working with Extended ACLs

In this activity, you work through several tasks for configuring extended ACLs.

Summary

This chapter presented an overview of the following key points:

- The two main types of ACLs are standard and extended.
- Named ACLs allow access lists to be identified by name instead of number.
- ACLs can be configured for all routed network protocols
- ACLs typically are used in firewall routers, which often are positioned between the internal network and an external network such as the Internet.
- ACLs also can restrict virtual terminal access to the router.
- ACLs perform several functions within a Cisco router, including implementing security/access procedures.
- ACLs are used to control and manage traffic.
- For some protocols, you can apply up to two ACLs to an interface: one inbound ACL and one outbound ACL.
- With ACLs, after a packet is checked for a match with the ACL statement, it can be denied or permitted the use of an associated interface.
- Wildcard mask bits use the numbers 1 and 0 to determine how to treat the corresponding IP address bits.

Key Terms

ACL (access control list)   A means of controlling or limiting network traffic that compares different criteria to a defined rule set.

bit bucket   The destination of discarded bits (dropped packets), as determined by the router.

border router   A router situated at the edges or end of the network boundary, which provides basic security from the outside network or from a less controlled area of the network into a more private area of the network.

extended ACL   Compares source IP address, destination IP address, TCP/UDP port number, and other criteria to the rules defining an extended ACL.

exterior router   In firewall architecture, the router that is connected to the Internet is referred to as the exterior router. It forces all incoming traffic to pass through the application gateway.

firewall   One or more network devices, such as routers or access servers, designated as a buffer between any connected public networks and a private network. A firewall router uses access control lists and other methods to ensure the security of the private network.

interior router   The router that is connected to the internal network. The interior router accepts packets only from the application gateway. The gateway controls the delivery of network-based services both to and from the internal network.

named ACL   ACL that allows standard and extended ACLs to be given names.

queuing   A process by which ACLs can designate certain packets to be processed by a router before other traffic, on the basis of some configurable parameter such as specifying a protocol.

standard ACL   ACL that compares source IP addresses to the rules defining a standard ACL.

Check Your Understanding

Complete all the review questions to test your understanding of the topics and concepts in this chapter. Answers are listed in Appendix B, "Answers to Check Your Understanding Review Questions."

1. Common ACL functions include filtering packets internally, protecting the internal network from illegal Internet access, and restricting access to virtual terminal ports. True or false?

   A. True

   B. False

2. ACL is an acronym for

   A. Accessibility control list

   B. Accountability control list

   C. Assessment control list

   D. Access control list

3. A(n) _____ ACL works by comparing the source IP address against the ACL rules.

   A. Extended

   B. Named

   C. Standard

   D. Router

4. A(n) _____ ACL works by comparing the source IP address, destination IP address, or other parameters against the ACL rules.

   A. Extended

   B. Named

   C. Standard

   D. Router

5. A(n) _____ ACL uses names instead of numbers to distinguish ACLs.

   A. Extended

   B. Named

   C. Standard

   D. Router

6. As a general rule, ACLs should be placed where in the network?

   A. In the Internet

   B. In the core

   C. Closest to the traffic to be controlled

   D. None of the above

7. In a firewall architecture, which router most likely will be configured with an ACL?

   A. The most powerful router

   B. The interior router

   C. The exterior router

   D. All of the above

8. Named ACLs were introduced in Cisco IOS 11.2. True or false?

   A. True

   B. False

9. What command is used to apply an ACL to a VTY port?

   A. **ip access-list**

   B. **ip access-class**

   C. **ip access-group**

10. Which of the following commands would you use to find out whether any ACLs are set on an interface?

    A. **show running-config**

    B. **show ip protocols**

    C. **show ip interface**

    D. **show ip network**

11. What do you call the additional 32 bits of information in the access-list statement?

    A. Wildcard bits

    B. Access bits

    C. 0 bits

    D. 1 bits

12. If you want to permit traffic based on its addressing or protocol type, you would use which of the following commands?

    A. Router #**access-list** *access-list number* {**permit** | **deny**} {*test conditions*}

    B. Router (config)#**access-list** *access-list number* {**permit** | **deny**} {*test conditions*}

    C. Router (config-if)#**access-list** *access-list number* {**permit** | **deny**} {*test conditions*}

    D. None of the above

13. Standard IP access lists permit or deny routing of a packet based on the IP address that it originates from and the protocol suite that it is destined for. True or false?

    A. True

    B. False

14. Access lists impact network security based on which of the following factors?

    A. The data content of the packets

    B. The destination subnet/host/network for the packets

    C. The source subnet/host/network of the packets

    D. The type of the network they are routed through

15. What type of networking device would be needed to implement access lists to increase network security?

    A. Hub

    B. Router

    C. Bridge

    D. Switch

16. What does the following access list allow? **access-list 1 permit 204.211.19.162 0.0.0.0**

    A. "Deny my network only."

    B. "Permit a specific host."

    C. "Permit only my network."

    D. None of the above.

Access Control Lists

The following table maps the numbering scheme used in this chapter's labs to the Target Identifiers (TIs) used in the online curriculum.

Lab Companion Numbering	Online Curriculum TI
Lab 20-1	11.2.1
Lab 20-2	11.2.3
Lab 20-3	11.2.2

Lab 20-1.1: Configuring Standard ACLs

Figure 20-1.1 Topology for Lab 20-1

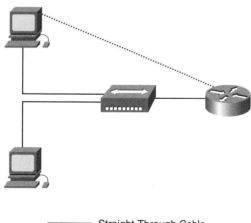

—————— Straight-Through Cable
················· Rollover (Console) Cable
– – – – – Crossover Cable
⎯Z⎯ Serial Cable

Table 20-1.1 Lab Equipment Configuration

Router Designation	Router Name	Router Type	FA0/0 Address	Subnet Mask
Router 1	GAD		192.168.14.1	255.255.255.0

Enable secret password is **class** for both routers.
Enable, VTY, and Console password is **cisco** for both routers.

Objectives

- Configure and apply a standard ACL to permit or deny specific traffic
- Test the ACL to determine if the desired results were achieved

Background / Preparation

Cable a network similar to the one in Figure 20-1.1. You can use any router that meets the interface requirements displayed in the diagram (that is, 800, 1600, 1700, 2500, and 2600 routers or a combination). Please refer to the information in the "Router Interface Summary Chart" immediately preceding Chapter 1 to correctly specify the interface identifiers to be used based on the equipment in your lab. The configuration output used in this lab is produced from 1721 series routers. Any other router used may produce slightly different output. The following steps are intended to be executed on each router unless specifically instructed otherwise. Start a HyperTerminal session as performed in Lab 11-2 in Chapter 11.

Please refer to and implement the procedure documented in "Erasing and Reloading the Router" immediately preceding Chapter 1 before continuing with this lab.

Step 1   Configure the hostname and passwords on the GAD router.

On the GAD router, enter the global configuration mode and configure the hostname as shown in the chart. Then configure the console, virtual terminal, and enable passwords. Configure the FastEthernet interface on the router according to the chart in Table 20-1.1.

Step 2   Configure the hosts on the Ethernet segment.

A. Host 1
```
IP address 192.168.14.2
Subnet mask 255.255.255.0
Default gateway 192.168.14.1
```

B. Host 2
```
IP address 192.168.14.3
Subnet mask 255.255.255.0
Default gateway 192.168.14.1
```

Step 3   Save the configuration information from the privileged EXEC command mode.

```
GAD# copy running-config startup-config
```

Step 4   Confirm connectivity by pinging the default gateway from both hosts.

If the pings are not successful, correct your configuration and repeat until they are successful.

Step 5   Prevent access to the Ethernet interface from the hosts.

A. Create an access list that will prevent access to FastEthernet 0 from the 192.168.14.0 network.

B. At the router configuration prompt type the following command.
```
GAD(config)#access-list 1 deny 192.168.14.0  0.0.0.255
GAD(config)#access-list 1 permit any
```

C. Why is the second statement needed?

_____

Step 6   Ping the router from the hosts.

A. Were these pings successful? _____

B. If they were, why? _____

Step 7   Apply the access list to the interface.

At the FastEthernet 0 interface mode prompt type:

```
GAD(config-if)#ip access-group 1 in
```

Step 8   Ping the router from the hosts.

A. Were these pings successful? _____

B. If they were, why? _____

Step 9   Create a new access list.

A. Now create an access list that will prevent the even numbered hosts from pinging but permit the odd numbered one.

B. What will that access list look like? Finish this command with an appropriate comparison IP address (*aaa.aaa.aaa.aaa*) and wildcard mask (*www.www.www.www*):

```
ip access-list 2 permit aaa.aaa.aaa.aaa   www.www.www.www
```

C. Why wasn't the **permit any** statement needed at the end this time?

_____

_____

Step 10   Apply the access list to the proper router interface.

    A. First remove the old access list application by typing **no ip access-group 1** in at the interface configuration mode.

    B. Apply the new access list by typing **ip access-group 2 in.**

Step 11   Ping the router from each hosts.

    A. Was the ping from host 1 successful? _____

    B. Why or why not? _____

    C. Was the ping from host 2 successful? _____

    D. Why or why not?

Upon completion of the previous steps logoff (by typing **exit**) and turn the router off.

Lab 20-2: Configuring Named ACLs

Figure 20-2.2   Topology for Lab 20-2

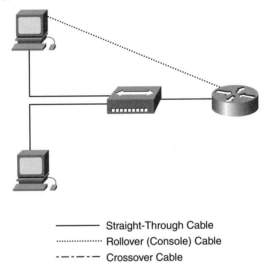

——————— Straight-Through Cable
················ Rollover (Console) Cable
– – – – – Crossover Cable
⎯Z⎯ Serial Cable

Table 20-2.1   Lab Equipment Configuration

Router Designation	Router Name	Router Type	FA0/0 Address	Subnet Mask
Router 1	GAD		192.168.14.1	255.255.255.0

Enable secret password is **class** for both routers.
Enable, VTY, and Console password is **cisco** for both routers.

Objectives

- Create a named ACL to permit or deny specific traffic
- Test the ACL to determine if the desired results were achieved

Background / Preparation

Cable a network similar to the one in Figure 20-2.2. You can use any router that meets the interface requirements displayed in the diagram (that is, 800, 1600, 1700, 2500, and 2600 routers or a combination). Please refer to the information in the "Router Interface Summary Chart" immediately preceding Chapter 1 to correctly specify the interface identifiers to be used based on the equipment in your lab. The configuration output used in this lab is produced from 1721 series routers. Any other router used may produce slightly different output. The following steps are intended to be executed on each router unless specifically instructed otherwise. Start a HyperTerminal session as performed in Lab 11-2 in Chapter 11.

Please refer to and implement the procedure documented in "Erasing and Reloading the Router" immediately preceding Chapter 1 before continuing with this lab.

Step 1   Configure the hostname and passwords on the GAD router.

On the GAD router, enter the global configuration mode and configure the hostname as shown in the chart. Then configure the console, virtual terminal, and enable passwords. Configure the FastEthernet interface on the router according to the chart in Table 20-2.1.

Step 2   Configure the hosts on the Ethernet segment.

A. Host 1
```
IP address 192.168.14.2
Subnet mask 255.255.255.0
Default gateway 192.168.14.1
```

B. Host 2
```
IP address 192.168.14.3
Subnet mask 255.255.255.0
Default gateway 192.168.14.1
```

Step 3   Save the configuration information from the privileged EXEC command mode.
```
GAD# copy running-config startup-config
```

Step 4   Confirm connectivity by pinging the default gateway from both hosts.

If the pings are not successful, correct your configuration and repeat until they are successful.

Step 5   Prevent access to the Ethernet interface from the hosts.

    A. Create a named access list that will prevent access to FastEthernet 0 from the 192.168.14.0 network.

    B. At the configuration prompt type the following command.

```
GAD(config)#ip access-list standard no_access
GAD(config)#deny 192.168.14.0 0.0.0.255
GAD(config)#permit any
```

    C. Why is the third statement needed?

    _____

Step 6   Ping the router from the hosts.

    A. Were these pings successful? _____

    B. If they were, why? _____

Step 7   Apply the access list to the interface.

At the FastEthernet interface mode prompt type

```
GAD(config-if)#ip access-group no_access in
```

Step 8   Ping the router from the hosts.

    A. Were these pings successful? _____

    B. Why or why not? _____

Upon completion of the previous steps, logoff (by typing **exit**) and turn the router off.

Lab 20-3: Configuring Extended ACLs

Figure 20-3.1   Topology for Lab 20-3

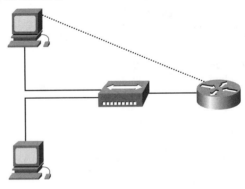

—————— Straight-Through Cable

················ Rollover (Console) Cable

– – – – – Crossover Cable

————Z———— Serial Cable

Table 20-3.1 Lab Equipment Configuration

Router Designation	Router Name	Router Type	FA0/0 Address	Subnet Mask
Router 1	GAD		192.168.14.1	255.255.255.0

Enable secret password is **class** for both routers.
Enable, VTY, and Console password is **cisco** for both routers.

Objectives

- Configure and apply an extended ACL to permit or deny specific traffic
- Test the ACL to determine if the desired results were achieved

Background / Preparation

Cable a network similar to the one in Figure 20-3.1. You can use any router that meets the interface requirements displayed in the diagram (that is, 800, 1600, 1700, 2500, and 2600 routers or a combination). Please refer to the information in the "Router Interface Summary Chart" immediately preceding Chapter 1 to correctly specify the interface identifiers to be used based on the equipment in your lab. The configuration output used in this lab is produced from 1721 series routers. Any other router used may produce slightly different output. The following steps are intended to be executed on each router unless specifically instructed otherwise. Start a HyperTerminal session as performed in Lab 11-2 in Chapter 11.

Please refer to and implement the procedure documented in "Erasing and Reloading the Router" immediately preceding Chapter 1 before continuing with this lab.

Step 1   Configure the hostname and passwords on the GAD router.

    A. On the GAD router, enter the global configuration mode and configure the hostname as shown in the chart. Then configure the console, virtual terminal, and enable passwords. Configure the FastEthernet interface on the router according to the chart.

    B. Allow HTTP access by issuing the **ip http server** command in global configuration mode

Step 2   Configure the hosts on the Ethernet segment.

    A. Host 1
```
IP address 192.168.14.2
Subnet mask 255.255.255.0
Default gateway 192.168.14.1
```

B. Host 2

```
IP address 192.168.14.3
Subnet mask 255.255.255.0
Default gateway 192.168.14.1
```

Step 3   Save the configuration information from the privileged EXEC command mode.

```
GAD# copy running-config startup-config
```

Step 4   Confirm connectivity by pinging the default gateway from both hosts.

If the pings are not successful, correct your configuration and repeat until they are successful.

Step 5   Connect to the router using the web browser.

Connect to the router using a web browser to ensure that the web server function is active.

Step 6   Prevent access to HTTP (port 80) the Ethernet interface from the hosts.

A. Create an access list that will prevent web browsing access to FastEthernet 0 from the 192.168.14.0 network.

B. At the router configuration prompt type the following command:

```
GAD(config)#access-list 101 deny tcp 192.168.14.0 0.0.0.255
  any eq 80
GAD(config)#access-list 101 permit ip any any
```

C. Why is the second statement needed?

_____

Step 7   Apply the access list to the interface.

At the FastEthernet 0 interface mode prompt type

```
GAD(config-if)#ip access-group 101 in
```

Step 8   Ping the router from the hosts.

A. Were these pings successful? _____

B. If they were, why? _____

Step 9   Connect to the router using the web browser.

Was the browser able to connect? _____

Step 10 Telnet to the router from the hosts.

A. Were you able to telnet successful? _____

B. Why or why not? _____

Upon completion of the previous steps logoff (by typing **exit**) and turn the router off.

Objectives

After reading this chapter, you will be able to

- Understand trunking
- Understand the fundamentals of the VTP and VTP configuration
- Understand inter-VLAN routing
- Configure basic inter-VLAN routing

Chapter 10

VLAN Trunking Protocol

In this chapter, you will learn the origins of trunking and its operation. You will also discover how the VLAN Trunking Protocol (VTP) can solve some of the problems that are related to managing and implementing virtual LANs (VLANs) in a large LAN network environment. Finally, you will be introduced to inter-VLAN routing.

Please be sure to look at this chapter's associated e-labs, movies, and photozooms that you will find on the CD-ROM accompanying the full text of this title. These CD elements are designed to supplement the material and reinforce the concepts introduced in this chapter.

Trunking

The history of *trunking* goes back to the origins of radio and telephony technologies. In radio technologies, a trunk is a single communications line that carries multiple channels of radio signals.

In the telephony industry, the trunking concept is associated with the telephone communication path or channel between two points (one usually being a central office). An example is shown in Figure 10-1.

Figure 10-1 Trunk Link

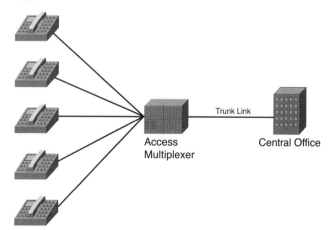

Shared trunks can also be created for redundancy between central offices (COs) (see Figure 10-2).

Figure 10-2 Trunk Shared Link

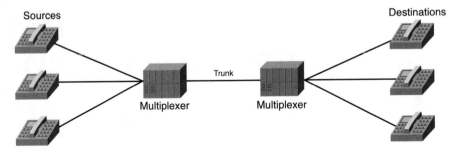

The same concept that the telephone and radio industries used was also the first one that the default hardware of telecommunications used. An example on this line is the segment of a communications network in which many lines come together, as shown in Figure 10-3. A backbone is composed of a number of trunks.

Figure 10-3 Trunks Using Frame Division Multiplexing (FDM)

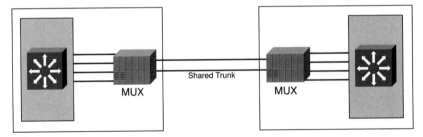

At present, the same principle of trunking has been applied to network switching technologies, whereby a trunk is a physical and logical connection between two switches across which network traffic travels.

Trunking Concepts

A *trunk* is a single transmission channel between two points that are usually switching centers. The trunk is a physical connection that carries (or enables) logical links.

In the context of a VLAN switching environment, a trunk is a point-to-point link that supports several VLANs. The purpose of a trunk is to save ports when creating a link between two devices that are implementing VLANs—typically two switches. Figure 10-4 shows two VLANs that are available on two switches: Sa and Sb.

Figure 10-4 Why Trunking?

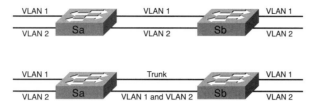

The first method shown in Figure 10-4 creates two physical links between the devices, each one carrying the traffic for a separate VLAN. This first solution does not scale well. If a third VLAN were added, two additional ports would be sacrificed. This design is also inefficient in terms of load sharing; the traffic on some VLANs might not justify a dedicated link. A trunk bundles multiple virtual (logical) links over one physical link.

An analogy for trunking is a Highway Distributor (trunk) in which roads with different starting and ending points share a main national highway for a few kilometers and then divide again to reach their particular destinations. This method is more cost effective than building an entire road from start to finish for every existing or new destination. An example is shown in Figure 10-5.

Figure 10-5 Analogy of a Highway Distributor

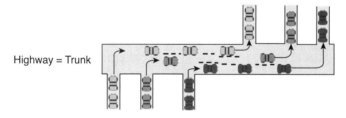

Trunking Operation

The use of the existing switching tables at both ends of a trunk to make port delivery decisions, based on the destination MAC addresses of the frames, becomes slow and difficult to manage as the number of VLANs traveling across the trunk increases. The larger the tables that a switch has to store, the slower the decision process when switching frames to their respective ports.

To effectively manage the transmission of frames from different VLANs on a single physical line or link between two networking devices, a type of communication/language between these two devices is needed. This communication or protocol is used so that the devices can "agree" on the travel and distribution of the frames onto their associated ports at both ends of the trunk. Trunking protocols were created for this purpose.

Trunking protocols allow the traveling of frames from different VLANs through a single physical channel; they manage the distribution of the frames accordingly to their associated VLAN ports. At present, two types of trunking mechanisms exist: frame filtering and frame tagging. This chapter uses frame tagging because this method is the standard trunking mechanism recommended by IEEE. Figure 10-6 shows an example of trunk links.

Figure 10-6 Trunk Links

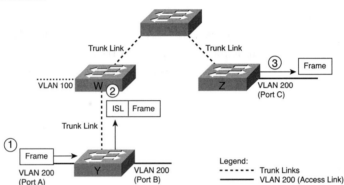

Trunking protocols that use a frame tagging mechanism assign an identifier to the frames to make their management easier, which in turn achieves a faster delivery of the frames. These tags are added on the way out of a trunk link and removed at the other end. They are not broadcast.

The unique physical link between the two switches is able to carry traffic for any VLAN. To achieve this, each frame that is sent on the link is tagged to identify which VLAN it belongs to. Different tagging schemes exist. The most common schemes for Ethernet segments are as follows:

- *Inter-Switch Link (ISL)*—This is the original Cisco proprietary Inter-Switch Link protocol.
- *802.1Q*—This is an IEEE standard method for inserting VLAN membership information into Ethernet frames.

VLANs and Trunking

You need certain rules or protocols to achieve trunking. Trunking mechanisms aid in the expansion of VLAN-switched networks. A *VLAN* is a group of devices on one or more LANs that are configured (using management software) so that they can communicate as if they were attached to the same wire, when in fact they are located on a number of different LAN segments. Trunking provides an effective method to distribute VLAN ID information to other switches and for communication between switches in the network, as shown in Figure 10-7.

Figure 10-7 VLANs and Trunking

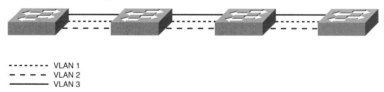

```
-------- VLAN 1
- - - -  VLAN 2
———————— VLAN 3
```

Frame tagging is the standard trunking mechanism; compared to frame filtering, frame tagging provides a more scalable solution to VLAN deployment that can be implemented campus wide. IEEE 802.1Q states that frame tagging is the way to implement VLANs. An example is shown in Figure 10-8.

VLAN frame tagging is an approach that has been specifically developed for switched communications. Frame tagging places a unique identifier in the header of each frame as it is forwarded throughout the network backbone. Each switch understands and examines the identifier before any broadcasts or transmissions to other switches, routers, or end-station devices. When the frame exits the network backbone, the switch removes the identifier before the frame is transmitted to the target end station. Frame identification functions at Layer 2 and requires little processing or administrative overhead.

A trunk link does not belong to a specific VLAN. The responsibility of a trunk link is to act as a conduit for VLANs between switches and routers.

Figure 10-8 Frame Tagging

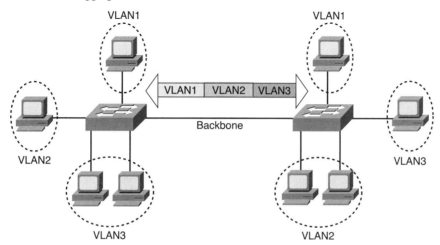

The switches in Figure 10-6 communicate with each other using ISL, which is a protocol that maintains VLAN information as traffic flows between the switches. With ISL, an Ethernet frame is encapsulated with a header that contains a VLAN ID.

Switch Command-Line Interfaces

Depending on the switch model you are working with, you can encounter two different types of command entry. The command-line interface (CLI) for Cisco switches is either IOS command based or set command based. The first uses IOS commands that are similar to those used with Cisco routers. The second uses set commands to configure the switch. Commands can vary between the two types of CLIs. Both types of commands are provided in the following configuration examples. Switches such as the 2900 Series use IOS-based commands. Switches such as the 4500 and 6500 Series use set-based commands. Older base model switches such as the 1900 Series utilize IOS commands and also have a menu-driven interface. All models of switches provide a graphic web-based management interface that you can access with a browser.

The following is an IOS command-based switch privileged mode prompt and command example:

```
Switch#show trunk
```

The following is a set command-based switch privileged mode prompt and command example:

```
Switch>(enable)set vtp v2 enable
```

Trunking Implementation

To create or configure a VLAN trunk on a Cisco IOS command-based switch, configure the port first as a trunk and then specify the trunk encapsulation. Trunk encapsulation must be the same on both ends. To do this, issue the commands shown in Example 10-1.

Example 10-1 *Configuring VLAN Trunk Commands*

```
Switch(config-if)#switchport mode trunk ?
allowed        Set allowed VLAN characteristics when interface is in trunking
               mode
encapsulation  Set trunking encapsulation when interface is in trunking mode
native         Set trunking native characteristics when interface is in trunking
               mode
pruning        Set pruning VLAN characteristics when interface is in trunking mode
```

Example 10-1 *Configuring VLAN Trunk Commands (Continued)*

```
Switch(config-if)#switchport trunk encapsulation ?
dot1q        Interface uses only 802.1q trunking encapsulation when trunking
isl          Interface uses only ISL trunking encapsulation when trunking


Switch(config-if)#switchport trunk encapsulation isl
```

 Lab Activity   Trunking Using ISL Encapsulation

In this lab, you will configure ISL trunking encapsulation between two Catalyst 2900 switches.

Before you attempt to configure a VLAN trunk on a port, determine what encapsulation the port can support. You can do this by using the **show port capabilities** command on a set command-based switch, as shown in Example 10-2. Notice that Port 2/1 supports only the IEEE 802.1Q encapsulation.

Example 10-2 *show port capabilities Command*

```
Console>(enable) show port capabilities 2/1
Model             WS-X4232-GB-RJ
Port              2/1
Type              No GBIC
Speed             1000
Duplex            full
Trunk encap type  802.1Q
Trunk mode        on,off,desirable,auto,nonegotiate
Channel           2/1-2
Flow control      receive-(off,on,desired),send-(off,on,desired)
Security          yes
Membership        static,dynamic
Fast start        yes
QOS scheduling    rx-(none), tx-(2q1t)
CoS rewrite       no
ToS rewrite       no
Rewrite           no
UDLD              yes
SPAN              source,destination
```

To create or configure a VLAN trunk on a set command-based switch, enter the **set trunk** command to configure the port on each end of the link as a trunk port and to specify the VLANs to be transported on this trunk link:

```
Switch> (enable) set trunk mod_num/port_num [on | off | desirable | auto |
    nonegotiate] vlan_range [isl | dot1q | dot10 | lane | negotiate]
```

You can also use the **set trunk** command to change the mode of a trunk, as shown in Example 10 3.

Example 10-3 *set trunk Command*

```
Console>(enable)

Console>(enable)set trunk 2/1 on dot1q

Port(s) 2/1 trunk mode set to on.

Port(s) 2/1 trunk type set to dot1q
```

Fast Ethernet and Gigabit Ethernet trunking modes by keyword are as follows:

- **on**—This mode puts the port into permanent trunking. The port becomes a trunk port even if the neighboring port does not agree to the change. The on state does not allow for the negotiation of an encapsulation type; therefore, you must specify the encapsulation in the configuration.

- **off**—This mode puts the port into permanent nontrunking mode and negotiates to convert the link into a nontrunk link. The port becomes a nontrunk port even if the neighboring port does not agree to the change.

- **desirable**—This mode makes the port actively attempt to convert the link to a trunk link. The port becomes a trunk port if the neighboring port is set to on, desirable, or auto mode.

- **auto**—This mode makes the port willing to convert the link to a trunk link. The port becomes a trunk port if the neighboring port is set to on or desirable mode. This is the default mode for Fast and Gigabit Ethernet ports. Notice that if the default setting is left on both sides of the trunk link, it will not become a trunk; neither side will be the first to ask to convert to a trunk.

- **nonegotiate**—This mode puts the port into permanent trunking mode but prevents the port from generating Dynamic Trunking Protocol (DTP) frames. You must configure the neighboring port manually as a trunk port to establish a trunk link.

Verify that trunking has been configured and verify the settings by using the **show trunk** [*mod_num/port_num*] command from privileged mode on the switch.

The VLAN Trunking Protocol (VTP)

This section explains the concept and operation of the *VLAN Trunking Protocol (VTP)* as well as its implementation in a VLAN-switched LAN environment.

History of the VTP

The VTP was created to solve potential operational problems in a VLAN's network-switched environment.

For example, consider a domain that has several interconnected switches that support several VLANs. To maintain connectivity within VLANs, each VLAN must be manually configured on each switch. As the organization grows and additional switches are added to the network, each new switch must be manually configured with VLAN information. A single incorrect VLAN assignment could cause two potential problems:

- Cross-connected VLANs due to VLAN configuration inconsistencies
- VLAN configuration conciliations across mixed-media environments such as Ethernet and Fiber Distributed Data Interface (FDDI)

With VTP, VLAN configuration consistency is maintained across a common administration domain. Additionally, VTP reduces the complexity of managing and monitoring VLAN networks.

VTP Concepts

The role of VTP is to maintain VLAN configuration consistency across a common network administration domain. VTP is a messaging protocol that uses OSI Layer 2 trunk frames to manage the addition, deletion, and renaming of VLANs on a single domain. Further, VTP allows for centralized changes that are communicated to all other switches in the network.

VTP messages are encapsulated in either Cisco proprietary ISL or IEEE 802.1Q protocol frames and then passed across trunk links to other devices. In IEEE 802.1Q frames, a four-byte field is added that tags the frame. Both formats carry the VLAN ID.

Whereas switch ports are normally assigned to only a single VLAN, trunk ports by default carry frames from all VLANs.

VTP Benefits

VTP minimizes the possible configuration inconsistencies that arise when changes are made. These inconsistencies can result in security violations because VLANs cross-connect when duplicate names are used; they also can become internally disconnected when they are mapped from one LAN type to another (such as from Ethernet to ATM or FDDI). VTP provides the following benefits:

- VLAN configuration consistency across the network
- Mapping scheme that allows a VLAN to be trunked over mixed media, such as mapping Ethernet VLANs to a high-speed backbone VLAN like ATM LANE or FDDI
- Accurate tracking and monitoring of VLANs
- Dynamic reporting of added VLANs across the network
- Plug-and-play configuration when adding new VLANs

Before creating VLANs on the switch, you must first set up a VTP management domain within which you can verify the current VLANs on the network. All switches in the same management domain share their VLAN information with each other, and a switch can participate in only one VTP management domain. Switches in different domains do not share VTP information.

Using VTP, each Catalyst Family Switch advertises the following on its trunk ports:

- Management domain
- Configuration revision number
- Known VLANs and their specific parameters

VTP Domain

A VTP domain is made up of one or more interconnected devices that share the same VTP domain name. A switch can be in one VTP domain only.

When transmitting VTP messages to other switches in the network, the VTP message is encapsulated in a trunking protocol frame such as ISL or IEEE 802.1Q. Domain names must match (case sensitive) exactly for information to be passed. Figure 10-9 shows the generic encapsulation for VTP within an ISL frame.

Figure 10-9 VTP Encapsulation with ISL Frame

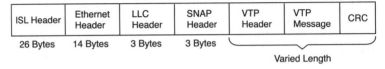

The VTP header varies depending on the type of VTP message, but generally, four items are found in all VTP messages:

- **VTP protocol version**—Will be either Version 1 or 2
- **VTP message type**—Indicates one of four types

- **Management domain name length**—Indicates the size of the name that follows
- **Management domain name**—Indicates the name configured for the management domain

VTP Modes

VTP switches operate in one of three modes:

- Server
- Client
- Transparent

VTP Server (Default Mode)

If a switch is configured for server mode, you can create, modify, and delete VLANs and specify other configuration parameters (such as VTP version and VTP pruning) for the entire VTP domain. VTP servers save VLAN configuration information in Catalyst nonvolatile random-access memory (NVRAM). VTP servers send VTP messages out all trunk ports.

VTP servers advertise their VLAN configuration to other switches in the same VTP domain and synchronize the VLAN configuration with other switches based on advertisements received over trunk links. This is the default mode on the switch.

VTP Client

A switch that is configured as a VTP client cannot create, modify, or delete VLAN information. In addition, clients cannot save VLAN information. This mode is useful for switches that lack sufficient memory to store large tables of VLAN information, as required by VTP servers. VTP clients process VLAN changes, as servers do, and they send VTP messages out all trunk ports.

VTP Transparent Mode

Switches configured for transparent mode do not participate in VTP. A VTP transparent switch does not advertise its VLAN configuration and does not synchronize its VLAN configuration based on received advertisements. They forward VTP advertisements (Version 2) received on their trunk ports but ignore information contained in the message. A transparent switch neither modifies its database when updates are received nor sends an update indicating a change in its VLAN status. Except for forwarding VTP advertisements, VTP is disabled on a transparent switch.

VTP Operation

Detecting the addition of VLANs within the advertisements serves as a notification to the switches (servers and clients) that they should be prepared to receive traffic on their trunk ports with the newly defined VLAN IDs, emulated LAN names, or 802.10 security association identifiers (SAIDs).

In Figure 10-10, C5000-3 transmits a VTP database entry with additions or deletions to C5000-1 and C5000-2. The configuration database has a revision number that is notification +1. A higher configuration revision number indicates that the VLAN information that is being sent is more current then the stored copy. When a switch receives an update that has a higher configuration revision number, the switch overwrites the stored information with the new information being sent in the VTP update. C5000-6 does not process the update because it is in a different domain.

By default, management domains are set to a nonsecure mode, which means that the switches interact without using a password. Adding a password automatically sets the management domain to secure mode. The same password must be configured on every switch in the management domain to use secure mode.

Figure 10-10 VTP Operation

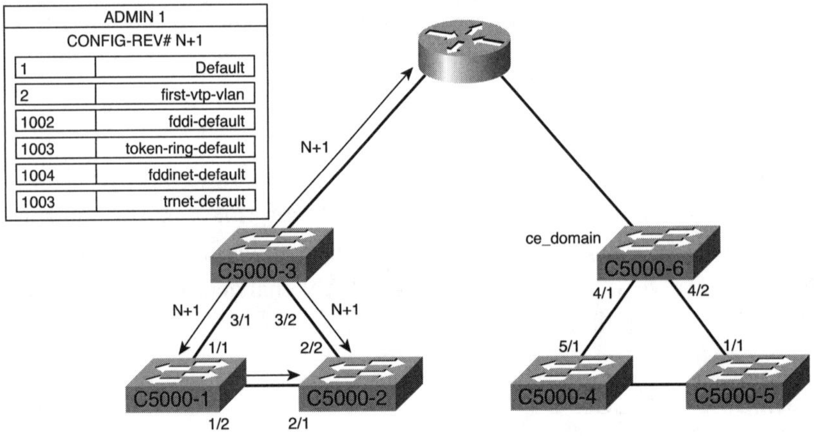

VTP Implementation

With VTP, each switch advertises on its trunk ports its management domain, configuration revision number, the VLANs that it knows about, and certain parameters for each known VLAN. These advertisement frames are sent to a multicast address so that all neighboring devices can receive the frames; however, the frames are not forwarded by normal bridging procedures. All devices in the same management domain learn about any new VLANs that are now configured in the transmitting device. A new

VLAN must be created and configured on one device only in the management domain. All the other devices in the same management domain automatically learn this information.

Advertisements on factory-default VLANs are based on media types. User ports should not be configured as VTP trunks. Each advertisement starts as configuration revision number 0. As changes are made, the configuration revision number increments by one (n + 1). The revision number in the management domain continues to increment until it reaches 2,147,483,648, at which point the counter resets back to 0.

Two types of VTP advertisements exist:

- Requests from clients that want information at bootup
- Responses from servers

VTP messages are one of three types:

- **Advertisement request**—Client requests VLAN information
- **Summary advertisement**—Server responds with summary
- **Subset advertisement**—Server responds with subset

These three types of VTP messages are displayed in Figure 10-11.

Figure 10-11 Advertisement Requests

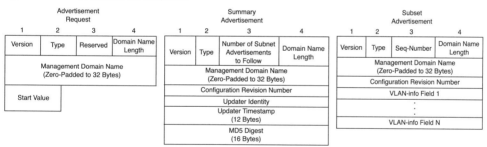

By default, server and client Catalyst switches issue summary advertisements every five minutes. They inform neighbor switches what they believe to be the current VTP revision number. Assuming the domain names match, the receiving server or client compares the configuration revision number. If the revision number in the advertisement is higher than the current revision number in the receiving switch, the receiving switch then issues an advertisement request for new VLAN information. See Figure 10-12 for an example of the summary advertisement format.

Figure 10-12 Summary Advertisement Format

Version	Type	Number of Subnet Advertisements to Follow	Domain Name Length
Management Domain Name (Zero-Padded to 32 Bytes)			
Configuration Revision Number			
Updater Identity			
Updater Timestamp (12 Bytes)			
MD5 Digest (16 Bytes)			

Subset advertisements contain detailed information about VLANs, such as VTP version type, domain name and related fields, and configuration revision number. Creating or deleting a VLAN, suspending or activating a VLAN, changing the name of a VLAN, and changing the maximum transmission unit (MTU) of a VLAN can trigger these advertisements. See Figure 10-13 for an example of the subset advertisement format.

Figure 10-13 Subset Advertisement Format

Version	Type	Seq-Number	Domain Name Length
Management Domain Name (Zero-Padded to 32 Bytes)			
Configuration Revision Number			
VLAN-info Field 1			
. . .			
VLAN-info Field N			

The VLAN-info Field contains information for each VLAN
and is formatted as follows:

Info Length	Status	VLAN-Type	VLAN-name Len
ISL VLAN-id		MTU Size	
802.10 Index			
VLAN-name (Padded with Zeros to Multiple of 4 Bytes)			

Advertisements might contain some or all of the following information:

■ **Management domain name**—Advertisements that have different names are ignored.

- **Configuration revision number**—The higher number indicates a more recent configuration.
- **Message Digest 5 (MD5)**—MD5 is the key that is sent with the VTP when a password has been assigned. If the key does not match, the update is ignored.
- **Updater identity**—The updater identity is the identity of the switch that is sending the VTP summary advertisement.

VTP Configuration

Following are the basic tasks to considered before configuring VTP and VLANs on the network:

Step 1   Determine the version number of VTP that will be utilized.

Step 2   Decide if this switch is to be a member of an existing management domain or if a new domain should be created. If a management domain does exist, determine the name and password of the domain.

Step 3   Choose a VTP mode for the switch.

Configuring the VTP Version

Two different versions of VTP can run in your management domain: VTP Version 1 and VTP Version 2. The two versions are not interoperable. If you choose to configure a switch in a domain for VTP Version 2, you must configure all switches in the management domain to be in VTP Version 2. VTP Version 1 is the default. You might need to implement VTP Version 2 if you require some of the specific features that VTP Version 2 offers that are not offered in VTP Version 1. The most common feature that is needed is Token Ring VLAN support.

To configure the VTP version on a Cisco IOS command-based switch, first enter VLAN database mode. Use the following command to change the VTP version number on a set command-based switch:

```
Switch#vlan database
Switch(vlan)#vtp v2-mode
```

Use the following command to change the VTP version number on a set command-based switch.

```
Switch(enable) set vtp v2 enable
```

VTP Version 2 supports the following features that are unsupported in Version 1:

- **Token Ring support**—VTP Version 2 supports Token Ring LAN switching and VLANs.

- **Unrecognized type/length/value (TLV) support**—A VTP server or client propagates configuration changes to its other trunks—even for TLVs it is not able to parse. The unrecognized TLV is saved in NVRAM.

- **Version-dependent transparent mode**—In VTP Version 1, a VTP transparent switch inspects VTP messages for the domain name and version and forwards a message only if the version and domain name match. Because only one domain is supported in the supervisor engine software, VTP Version 2 forwards VTP messages in transparent mode without checking the version.

- **Consistency checks**—In VTP Version 2, VLAN consistency checks (such as VLAN names and values) are performed only when you enter new information through the CLI or Simple Network Management Protocol (SNMP). Consistency checks are not performed when new information is obtained from a VTP message or when information is read from NVRAM. If the digest on a received VTP message is correct, its information is accepted without consistency checks. A switch that is capable of running VTP Version 2 can operate in the same domain as a switch that is running VTP Version 1 if VTP Version 2 remains disabled on the VTP Version 2-capable switch.

If all switches in a domain are capable of running VTP Version 2, you need to enable VTP Version 2 on only one switch (using the **set vtp v2 enable** command). The version number is propagated to the other VTP Version 2-capable switches in the VTP domain.

Configuring the VTP Domain

If the switch being installed is the first switch in the network, create the management domain. Otherwise, verify the name of the management domain to join. If the management domain has been secured, configure the password for the domain.

To create a management domain, use the following command:

```
Switch(vlan)#vtp domain Cisco
```

The domain name can be between 1 and 32 characters and is case sensitive. The password must be between 8 and 64 characters long.

To add a VTP client to an existing VTP domain, always verify that its VTP configuration revision number is lower than the configuration revision number of the other switches in the VTP domain. Use the **show vtp status** command. Switches in a VTP domain use the VLAN configuration of the switch with the highest VTP configuration revision number. If a switch is added that has a revision number higher than the revision number in the VTP domain, it can erase all VLAN information from the VTP server and VTP domain.

To create a management domain or to add your switch to a management domain on a set command-based switch, use the following command:

```
Switch(enable)set vtp domain domain_name
```

Configuring the VTP Mode

Choose one of the three available VTP modes for the switch. Following are some general guidelines for choosing the switch mode.

If this is the first switch in your management domain and you intend to add additional switches, set the mode to server. The additional switches can learn VLAN information from this switch. You should have at least one server.

If other switches are in the management domain, set your switch mode to client to prevent the new switch from accidentally propagating the incorrect information to your existing network. If you would like this switch to end up as a VTP server, change the mode of the switch to server after it has learned the correct VLAN information from the network.

If the switch is not going to share VLAN information with any other switch on the network, set the switch to transparent mode. In transparent mode, you can create, delete, and rename VLANs at will without the switch propagating changes to other switches. If a large number of people are configuring devices within your network, you run the risk of overlapping VLANs with two different meanings in the network but the same VLAN identification.

To set the correct mode of the Cisco IOS command-based switch, use the following command:

```
Switch(vlan)#vtp client | server | transparent
```

To set the correct mode of your set command-based switch, use this command:

```
Switch>(enable) set vtp mode server | client | transparent
```

Verifying VTP Configuration

Example 10-4 shows the output of the **show vtp status** command. This command verifies VTP configuration settings on a Cisco IOS command-based switch.

Example 10-4 *show vtp status Command*

```
Switch#show vtp status
VTP Version                    : 2
Configuration Revision         : 2
Maximum VLANs supported locally : 68
```

Example 10-4 *show vtp status Command (Continued)*

```
Number of existing VLANs          : 6

VTP Operating Mode                : Client

VTP Domain Name                   : Cisco

VTP Pruning Mode                  : Disabled

VTP V2 Mode                       : Enabled

VTP Traps Generation              : Disabled

MD5 Digest                        : 0x35  0x84  0x7B  0x04  0x3D

                                    0x55  0x3B  0xDA

Configuration last modified by 0.0.0.0 at 12-23-02 20:24:33
```

Example 10-5 displays the results of the **show vtp statistics** command on a set command-based switch. This command shows a summary of VTP advertisement messages sent and received, as well as configuration errors detected. Use this command to assist you in troubleshooting VTP.

Example 10-5 *show vtp statistics Command*

```
Switch>(enable) show vtp statistics

VTP statistics:

summary advts received           0

subset advts received            0

request advts received           0

summary advts transmitted        0

subset advts transmitted         0

request advts transmitted        0

No of config revision errors     0

No of config digest errors       0
```

Lab Activity   VTP Domain Configuration

In this lab, you will configure a VTP domain with a server and a client between two Catalyst 2900 switches.

Lab Activity   Trunk/VLAN Troubleshooting

In this lab, you will work with VTP mode and domain issues that can cause lack of information sharing or confusion among switches.

VTP Pruning

The default behavior of a switch is to propagate broadcast and unknown packets across the network. This behavior results in unnecessary traffic crossing the network.

VTP pruning enhances network bandwidth use by reducing unnecessary flooding of traffic, such as broadcast, multicast, unknown, and flooded unicast packets. VTP pruning increases available bandwidth by restricting flooded traffic to those trunk links that the traffic must use to access the appropriate network devices. By default, VTP pruning is disabled. If no device from VLAN 3 is available on a remote switch, pruning can keep the switch from sending VLAN 3 traffic out the trunk and wasting bandwidth.

Enabling VTP pruning on a VTP server enables pruning for the entire management domain. VTP pruning takes effect several seconds after you enable it. By default, VLANs 2 through 1000 are pruning eligible. VTP pruning does not prune traffic from VLANs that are pruning ineligible. VLAN 1 is always pruning ineligible; therefore, traffic from VLAN 1 cannot be pruned. You have the option to make specific VLANs pruning eligible or pruning ineligible on the device. To make VLANs pruning eligible on a Cisco IOS command-based switch, enter the following:

```
Switch(vlan)#vtp pruning
```

To make specific VLANs pruning ineligible on a Cisco IOS command-based switch, enter this:

```
Switch(config)#interface fastethernet 0/3
Switch(config-if)#switchport trunk pruning vlan remove vlan-id
```

To make specific VLANs pruning eligible on a set command-based switch, enter the following:

```
Console> (enable) set vtp pruneeligible vlan_range
```

To make specific VLANs pruning ineligible on a set command-based switch, enter the following:

```
Console> (enable) clear vtp pruneeligible vlan_range
```

Inter-VLAN Routing

When a host in one broadcast domain wants to communicate with another host, a router must be involved. The same situation exists with VLANS. An example is shown in Figure 10-14.

Port 1 on a switch is part of VLAN 1, and port 2 is part of VLAN 200. If all of the switch's ports were part of VLAN 1, the hosts that were connected to these ports could communicate. In this case, however, the ports are part of different VLANs: VLAN 1 and VLAN 200. A router must be involved if hosts from the different VLANs need to communicate, as shown in Figure 10-15.

Figure 10-14 Routers and VLANs

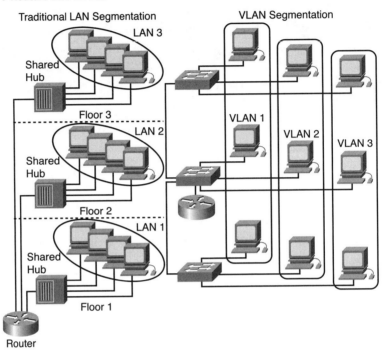

Figure 10-15 Removing Physical Boundaries

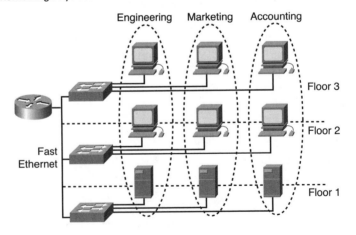

The most important benefit of routing is its proven history of facilitating networks, particularly networks that are large. Although the Internet serves as the obvious example, this point is true for any type of network, such as a large campus backbone. Because routers prevent broadcast propagation and use more intelligent forwarding algorithms than bridges and switches, routers provide much more efficient use of bandwidth. This simultaneously results in flexible and optimal path selection. For example, it is easy to implement load balancing across multiple paths in most networks when you are using routing. On the other hand, Layer 2 load balancing can be difficult to design, implement, and maintain.

If a VLAN spans across multiple devices, a trunk interconnects the devices. A trunk carries traffic for multiple VLANs. For example, a trunk can connect a switch to another switch, a switch to the inter-VLAN router, or a switch to a server that has a special network interface card (NIC) installed that supports trunking.

Remember that when a host on one VLAN wants to communicate with a host on another, a router is necessary.

Inter-VLAN Issues and Solutions

When VLANs are connected, several technical issues arise. Two of the most common in a multiple-VLAN environment are

- The need for end user devices to reach nonlocal hosts
- The need for hosts on different VLANs to communicate

When a device needs to make a connection to a remote host, it checks its routing table to determine if a known path exists. If the remote host falls into a subnet that it knows how to reach, then the system checks to see if it can connect along that interface. If all known paths fail, the system has one last option: the default route. This route is a special type of gateway route, and it is usually the only one present in the system. On a router, a default route is indicated by an asterisk (*) in the output of the **show ip route** command. For hosts on a local-area network (LAN), this gateway is set to whatever machine has a direct connection to the outside world, and it is the default gateway listed in the workstation's TCP/IP settings. If the default route is being configured for a router that is functioning as the gateway to the public Internet, the default route points to the gateway machine at an Internet service provider's (ISP) site. Default routes are implemented by using the **ip route** command, as shown in Example 10-6.

Example 10-6 *ip route Command*

```
Router(Config)#ip route 0.0.0.0 0.0.0.0 192.168.1.1
```

NOTE

In general, the router-on-a-stick approach to inter-VLAN routing is most appropriate when other options are unavailable. This is not to say that the router-on-a-stick design is a poor choice; it is only a reflection that other options tend to provide higher throughput and functionality. Also, because the router-on-a-stick technique functions as if the router were sitting on the edge of the network (at least as far as the Layer 2 network is concerned), it tends to be less tightly integrated with the rest of the campus network.

In Example 10-6, 192.168.1.1 is the gateway. Inter-VLAN connectivity can be achieved through either logical or physical connectivity. Logical connectivity involves a single connection, or trunk, from the switch to the router. That trunk can support multiple VLANs. This topology is called a "router on a stick" because there is a single connection to the router, but there are multiple logical connections between the router and the switch. An example is shown in Figure 10-16.

Figure 10-16 Router on a Stick

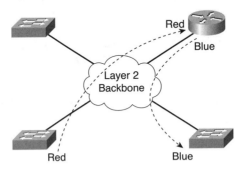

Isolated Broadcast Domains

In switched networks, route processors provide communications between VLANs. These processors provide VLAN access to shared resources and connect to other parts of the network that are either logically segmented with the more traditional subnet approach or require access to remote sites across wide-area links. Route processors are much like routers, but they can be built into a switch. They might lack physical interfaces, but they are configured with the same IOS commands as regular routers.

Before you can configure routing between VLANs, you must have defined the VLANs on the switches in your network. Issues that are related to network design and VLAN definition should be addressed during your network design phase. The following are issues that you need to consider:

- Sharing resources between VLANs
- Load balancing
- Redundant links
- Logical addressing
- Segmenting the network by using VLANs

Figure 10-17 shows isolated broadcast domains.

Figure 10-17 Isolated Broadcast Domains

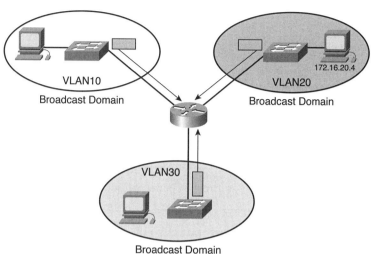

Finding the Route Between VLANs

The *route processor* contains most of the system memory components and the main system processor. A *default gateway* is simply a router interface that is normally referenced with an IP address. A *default router* is a router that has at least one interface serving as a default gateway. For DHCP, a default router is a router that provides a pool of IP addresses. A default gateway is shown in Figure 10-18.

Figure 10-18 Default Gateway

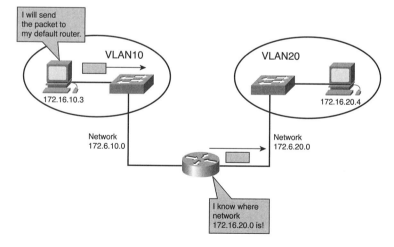

Connecting the separate subnets through a route processor introduces the issue of how end user devices can communicate with other devices through multiple LAN segments. Some network devices use routing tables to identify where to deliver packets outside of the local network segment. Even though it is not the responsibility of end user devices to route data, these devices still must be able to send data to addresses on subnets other than their own.

So that each end device does not have to manage its own routing tables, most devices are configured with the IP address of a designated route processor. This designated route processor is the default router to which all nonlocal network packets are sent. The route processor then forwards the packets toward the appropriate destination. A network device's default router IP address depends on which IP subnet contains that network device.

Early VLAN designs relied on external routers connected to VLAN-capable switches. In this approach, traditional routers are connected via one or more links to a switched network. The router-on-a-stick designs employ a single trunk link that connects the router to the rest of the campus network. Inter-VLAN traffic must cross the Layer 2 backbone to reach the router where it can move between VLANs. The traffic then travels back to the desired end station by using normal Layer 2 forwarding. This "out-to-the-router-and-back" flow is characteristic of router-on-a-stick designs.

Physical and Logical Interfaces

In a traditional situation, a network that had four VLANs required four physical connections between the switch and the external router. As technologies such as ISL became more common, network designers began to use trunk links to connect routers to switches. Although any trunking technology such as ISL, 802.1Q, 802.10, or LAN Emulation (LANE) can be used, Ethernet-based approaches are most common (ISL and 802.1Q). On Catalyst 2900 switches, the default is 802.1q, whereas 29xx switches default to ISL.

The Cisco Proprietary protocol ISL trunks VLANs over Fast Ethernet links.

As the number of VLANs increases on a network, the physical approach of having one router interface per VLAN quickly becomes unscalable. Networks that have many VLANs must use VLAN trunking to assign multiple VLANs to a single router interface.

The primary advantage of using a trunk link is a reduction in router and switch ports. Not only can this save money, but it can also reduce configuration complexity. Consequently, the trunk-connected router approach can scale to a much larger number of VLANs than a one-link-per-VLAN design.

Dividing Physical Interfaces into Subinterfaces

A *subinterface* is a logical interface on a physical interface such as the Fast Ethernet interface on a router. Multiple subinterfaces can exist on a single physical interface.

Each subinterface supports one VLAN and is assigned one IP address. For multiple devices on the same VLAN to communicate, the IP addresses of all devices must be on the same network or subnetwork. For example, if subinterface 2 has an IP address of 192.168.1.1, then 192.168.1.2, 192.168.1.3, and 192.1.1.4 are the IP addresses of devices that are attached to subinterface 2. To route between VLANs with subinterfaces, you must create a subinterface for each VLAN.

Supporting Multiple VLAN Traffic

As the number of VLANs increases in a network, network administrators must determine whether they want to have an individual router interface per VLAN, as shown in Figure 10-19, or if they want to use VLAN trunking to assign multiple VLANs to a single router interface, as shown in Figure 10-20.

Figure 10-19 Multiple Links

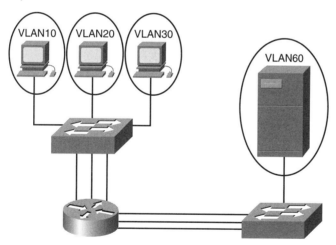

One solution is to dedicate one interface on the route processor for each VLAN that is supported. However, as the number of VLANs per switch increases, so does the requirement for the number of interfaces on the route processor. In addition, some VLANs might not require inter-VLAN routing on a regular basis, creating a situation in which interfaces on the route processor are underutilized.

Figure 10-20 Inter-Switch Link

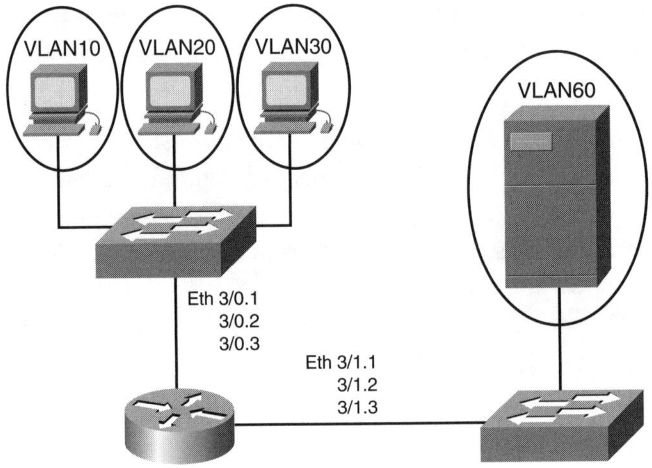

Another solution is to carry multiple VLAN traffic over a single link. To maintain integrity between VLAN traffic, a mechanism is required to identify the packet of each VLAN. The ISL protocol interconnects two VLAN-capable Fast Ethernet devices, such as a router and a switch. The ISL protocol is a proprietary frame-tagging protocol that contains a standard Ethernet frame and the VLAN information associated with that frame.

ISL is currently supported over Fast Ethernet links, but a single ISL link, or trunk, can carry traffic from multiple VLANs. The IEEE 802.1Q protocol interconnects VLANs; it is a standards-based protocol that multiple vendors support.

In Figure 10-20, the clients—on VLANs 10, 20, and 30—need to establish sessions with a server that is attached to a port in VLAN 60. Because the file server resides in a different VLAN than any of the requestors, you need to configure inter-VLAN routing. The route processor performs this function as follows:

1. The route processor accepts the packets from each VLAN because the route processor is configured to route VLAN 10, 20, and 30 traffic as well as VLAN 60 traffic to the server.

2. The route processor then classifies the packet based on the destination network address. The route processor prepends the packet with an ISL VLAN header—in this case ISL = 60—that is appropriate to the destination subnet. The prepending action is what differentiates this as a routing process rather than a switching process.

3. The router then routes the packets to the appropriate interface—in this case to FastEthernet 3/1.

Distribution Layer Topology

The distribution layer provides boundaries for different types of traffic, such as broadcast and multicast. This is also where inter-VLAN routing often occurs. An example is shown in Figure 10-21.

Figure 10-21 Distribution Layer Topology

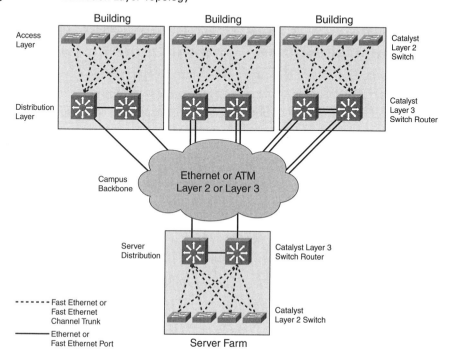

Configuring Inter-VLAN Routing

This section demonstrates the commands that are necessary to configure inter-VLAN routing between a router and a switch. Before any of these commands is implemented, check each router and switch to see which VLAN encapsulations they support. For example, Catalyst 2950 switches have supported 802.1Q trunking since the release of Cisco IOS release 12.0(5.2)WC(1), but they do not support ISL trunking. Cisco routers have supported ISL and 802.1Q trunking features since Cisco IOS release 12.0(T). For inter-VLAN routing to work properly, all the routers and switches involved must support the same encapsulation.

On a router, an interface can be logically divided into multiple, virtual subinterfaces. Subinterfaces provide a flexible solution for routing multiple data streams through a single physical interface. To define subinterfaces on a physical interface, perform the following tasks:

1. Identify the interface.

2. Define the VLAN encapsulation.

3. Assign an IP address to the interface.

To identify the interface, use the **interface** command in global configuration mode:

```
Router(config)#interface FastEthernet port-number subinterface-number
```

The *port-number* identifies the physical interface, and the *subinterface-number* identifies the virtual interface. The router must be able to talk to the switch by using a standardized trunking protocol. This means that both devices that are connected must understand each other. In the example, 802.1Q is used.

To define the VLAN encapsulation, enter the **encapsulation** command in interface configuration mode:

```
Router(config-if)#encapsulation dot1q vlan-number
```

The *vlan-number* identifies the VLAN for which the subinterface carries traffic. A VLAN ID is added to the frame only when the frame is destined for a nonlocal network. Each VLAN packet carries the VLAN ID within the packet header.

To assign the IP address to the interface, enter the following command in interface configuration mode:

```
Router(config-if)#ip address ip-address subnet-mask
```

The *ip-address* and *subnet-mask* are the 32-bit network address and mask of the specific interface.

 Lab Activity   Routing Inter-VLAN Traffic

In this lab, you will configure an external router to route traffic between multiple VLANs on a switch.

Summary

Trunking is implemented on a VLAN network environment to allow the extension of the VLANs across the network. Trunking is normally implemented among switches by setting at least one of the ports on each of the switches participating on the trunk link to trunking mode.

Two of the most common trunking protocols that allow and manage the flow of different VLANs frames are as follows:

- ISL
- 802.1Q

VLAN Trunking Protocol (VTP) was created to minimize some of the potential problems of a VLAN network environment by maintaining the consistency of the network. VTP provides the following benefits:

- VLAN configuration consistency across the network
- Mapping scheme that allows a VLAN to be trunked over mixed media
- Accurate tracking and monitoring of VLANs
- Dynamic reporting of added VLANs across the network
- Plug-and-play configuration when adding new VLANs

When an end station in one VLAN needs to communicate with an end station in another VLAN, inter-VLAN routing is required.

Key Terms

802.1Q   A trunking protocol that can carry the traffic of more than one subnet down a single cable. The IEEE 802.1Q committee defined this method of multiplexing VLANs in an effort to provide multivendor VLAN support.

default gateway   A router interface that is normally referenced with an IP address.

default router   A router that has at least one interface serving as a default gateway.

Inter-Switch Link (ISL)   A Cisco-specific, proprietary trunking protocol that interconnects multiple switches and maintains VLAN information as traffic travels between switches on trunk links.

route processor   Contains most of the system memory components and the main system processor.

trunk   A single transmission channel between two points that are usually switching centers.

trunking   A physical and logical connection between two switches across which network traffic travels. A backbone is composed of a number of trunks.

VLAN (virtual LAN)   A group of devices on one or more LANs that are configured (using management software) so that they can communicate as if they were attached to the same wire, when in fact they are located on a number of different LAN segments.

VLAN Trunking Protocol (VTP)   VTP is a messaging protocol that uses Layer 2 trunk frames to manage the addition, deletion, and renaming of VLANs on a network-wide basis.

Check Your Understanding

1. What is the primary advantage of using a trunk link?

    A. Provides more bandwidth for each trunk

    B. Efficient use of router and switch ports

    C. Allows for a single VLAN on each physical port

    D. Creates less overhead on the router

2. Which protocol carries multiple VLANs over a single trunk?

   A. 802.2

   B. 802.3

   C. 802.1Q

   D. 802.11B

3. Which protocol is Cisco proprietary and designed to carry traffic from multiple VLANs?

   A. 802.11A

   B. 802.1Q

   C. VNET

   D. ISL

4. To create or configure a VLAN trunk on a Cisco IOS command-based switch, configure the port first as a trunk and then specify the trunk encapsulation.

   A. True

   B. False

5. VTP messages are encapsulated in either Cisco proprietary Inter-Switch Link (ISL) or what type of frame?

   A. IEEE 802.1Q protocol frames

   B. IEEE 802.1R protocol frames

   C. 802.11D protocol frames

   D. 802.19 protocol frames

6. Using VTP, each Catalyst Family Switch advertises which of the following on its trunk ports?

   A. Management domain

   B. Configuration revision number

   C. Known VLANs and their specific parameters

   D. All of the above

7. VTP switches can operate in which modes?

   A. Server

   B. Client

   C. Transparent

   D. All of the above

8. Two different versions of VTP can run in your management domain: VTP Version 1 and VTP Version 2. The two versions are interoperable.

   A. True

   B. False

9. To create a management domain, use which command?

   A. Switch(vlan)#**domain Cisco**

   B. Switch(vtp)#**domain Cisco**

   C. Switch(vlan)#**vtp domain Cisco**

   D. Switch(vtp)#**vtp domain Cisco**

10. The default behavior of a switch is to propagate broadcasts and unknown _____ across the network.

    A. frames

    B. packets

    C. tags

    D. VLANs

11. Enabling VTP pruning on a VTP server enables pruning for the entire _____ domain.

    A. server

    B. transparent

    C. management

    D. user

12. In switched networks, _____ are used to provide communication between VLANs.

    A. route processors

    B. modulators

    C. VTPs

    D. subnets

VLAN Trunking Protocol

The following table maps the numbering scheme used in this chapter's labs to the Target Identifiers (TIs) used in the online curriculum.

Lab Companion Numbering	Online Curriculum TI
Lab 10-1	9.1.5.1
Lab 10-2	9.1.5.2
Lab 10-3	9.2.5
Lab 10-4	9.3.6

Lab 10-1: Trunking with ISL

Figure 10-1.1 Topology for Lab 10-1

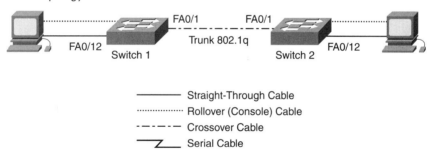

Table 10-1.1 Topology for Lab 10-1

Switch Designation	Switch Name	VLAN 1 IP Address	Subnet Mask	VLAN Names and Numbers	Switch Port Assignments
Switch 1	Switch_A	192.168.1.2	255.255.255.0	VLAN 1 Native VLAN 10 Accounting VLAN 20 Marketing VLAN 30 Engineering	fa 0/2 - 0/3 fa 0/4 - 0/6 fa 0/7 - 0/9 fa0/10 – 0/12
Switch 2	Switch_B	192.168.1.3	255.255.255.0	VLAN 1 Native VLAN 10 Accounting VLAN 20 Marketing VLAN 30 Engineering	fa 0/2 - 0/3 fa 0/4 - 0/6 fa 0/7 - 0/9 fa0/10 – 0/12

Enable secret password is **class** for both switches.
Enable, VTY, and Console password is **cisco** for both switches.

Objectives

- Create a basic switch configuration and verify it.
- Determine the switch firmware version.
- Create multiple VLANs, name them, and assign multiple member ports to them
- Create an ISL trunk line between the two switches to allow communication between paired VLANs.
- Test the VLANs functionality by moving a workstation from one VLAN to another.

Background / Preparation

Important Note: The use of Catalyst 2950 switches is not appropriate for this lab as they support only 802.1q trunking.

Trunking changes the formatting of the packets. The ports need to be in agreement as to which format is being used to transmit data on the trunk or no data will be passed. If there is different trunking encapsulation on the two ends of the link they will not be able to communicate. Similar situation will occur if one of your ports is configured in trunking mode (unconditionally) and the other one as in access mode (unconditionally).

When managing a switch, the Management Domain is always VLAN 1. The Network Administrator's workstation must have access to a port in the VLAN 1 Management Domain. All ports are assigned to VLAN 1 by default. This lab will also help demonstrate how VLANs can be used to separate traffic and reduce broadcast domains.

Cable a network similar to the one in Figure 10-1.1. The configuration output used in this lab is produced from a 2900 series switch. Any other switch used may produce different output. The following steps are intended to be executed on each switch unless specifically instructed otherwise.

Start a Hyperterminal session.

Please refer to and implement the procedure documented in Appendix B, "Erasing and Reloading the Switch," before continuing with this lab.

Step 1   Configure the switch.

Configure the hostname, access, and command mode passwords, as well as the management LAN settings. These values are shown in the chart. If problems occur while performing this configuration, refer to Lab 7-2, "Basic Switch Configuration" in Chapter 7.

Step 2   Configure the hosts attached to the switch.

Configure the host to use the same subnet for addresses, mask, and the default gateway as the switch.

Step 3   Verify connectivity

A. To verify the hosts and switch are correctly configured, **ping** the switch from the hosts.

B. Were the pings successful? _____

C. If the answer is no, troubleshoot the hosts and switch configurations.

Step 4   Look at the VLAN interface information.

On Switch_A, type the command **show vlan** at the privileged EXEC prompt.

```
Switch_A#show vlan
```

Step 5   Create and name three VLANs.

```
Switch_A#vlan database
Switch_A(vlan)#vlan 10 name Accounting
Switch_A(vlan)#vlan 20 name Marketing
Switch_A(vlan)#vlan 30 name Engineering
Switch_A(config)#exit
```

Step 6   Assign ports to a VLAN 10.

Assigning ports to VLANs must be done from the interface mode. Enter the following commands to add ports 0/4 to 0/6 to VLAN 10:

```
Switch_A#configure terminal
Switch_A(config)#interface fastethernet 0/4
Switch_A(config-if)#switchport mode access
```

```
Switch_A(config-if)#switchport access vlan 10
Switch_A(config-if)#interface fastethernet 0/5
Switch_A(config-if)#switchport mode access
Switch_A(config-if)#switchport access vlan 10
Switch_A(config-if)#interface fastethernet 0/6
Switch_A(config-if)#switchport mode access
Switch_A(config-if)#switchport access vlan 10
Switch_A(config-if)#end
```

Step 7 Assign ports to VLAN 20.

```
Switch_A# configure terminal
Switch_A(config)#interface fastethernet 0/7
Switch_A(config-if)#switchport mode access
Switch_A(config-if)#switchport access vlan 20
Switch_A(config-if)#interface fastethernet 0/8
Switch_A(config-if)#switchport mode access
Switch_A(config-if)#switchport access vlan 20
Switch_A(config-if)#interface fastethernet 0/9
Switch_A(config-if)#switchport mode access
Switch_A(config-if)#switchport access vlan 20
Switch_A(config-if)#end
```

Step 8 Assign ports to VLAN 30.

```
Switch_A# configure terminal
Switch_A(config)#interface fastethernet 0/10
Switch_A(config-if)#switchport mode access
Switch_A(config-if)#switchport access vlan 30
Switch_A(config-if)#interface fastethernet 0/11
Switch_A(config-if)#switchport mode access
Switch_A(config-if)#switchport access vlan 30
Switch_A(config-if)#interface fastethernet 0/12
Switch_A(config-if)#switchport mode access
Switch_A(config-if)#switchport access vlan 30
Switch_A(config-if)#end
```

Step 9 Create VLANs on Switch_B.

Repeat Steps 5 through 9 on Switch_B to create its VLANs.

Step 10 Look at the VLAN interface information.

A. On Switch_A, type the command **show vlan** at the privileged EXEC prompt.
```
Switch_A#show vlan
```

B. Are ports 0/10-0/12 assigned to VLAN 30? _____

Step 11 Test the VLANs.

A. Ping from the host in Switch_A port 0/12 to the host in Switch_B port 0/12.

B. Was the ping successful? _____

C. Why? _____

D. **Ping** from the host in Switch_A port 0/12 to the switch IP 192.168.1.2.

E. Was the ping successful? _____

F. Why? _____

Step 12 Create the ISL trunk.

On both switches, Switch_A and Switch_B, type the following command at the fastethernet 0/1 interface command prompt:

```
Switch_A(config)#interface fastethernet 0/1
Switch_A(config-if)#switchport mode trunk
Switch_A(config-if)#switchport trunk encapsulation isl
Switch_A(config-if)#end

Switch_B(config)#interface fastethernet 0/1
Switch_B(config-if)#switchport mode trunk
Switch_B(config-if)#switchport trunk encapsulation isl
Switch_B(config-if)#end
```

Step 13 Verify the ISL Trunk.

A. To verify that port fastethernet 0/1 has been established as a trunk port, type **show interface fastethernet 0/1 switchport** at the privileged EXEC mode prompt.

B. What type of trunking encapsulation is shown on the output results?

_____

C. According to the output with **show interface fastethernet 0/1 switchport** on Switch_B, is there a difference from the Administrative Trunking Encapsulation from the Operational Trunking Encapsulation?

_____

D. On the fragment "Trunking VLANs Enable" from the last output, what does the word "ALL" mean? _____

E. What would happen if the two ports of the trunk were using different encapsulation? _____

F. Explain _____

Step 14 Test the VLANS and the trunk.

A. To test the VLANS and the trunk, **ping** from the host in Switch_A port 0/12 to the host in Switch_B port 0/12.

B. Was the ping successful? _____

C. Why? _____

   D. **Ping** from the host in Switch_A port 0/12 to the switch IP 192.168.1.2.

   E. Was the ping successful? _____

   F. Why? _____

Step 15   Move hosts.

   Move the host in Switch_A from port 0/12 to port 0/8, wait until the port LED goes green and then go to the next step.

Step 16   Test the VLANS and the trunk.

   A. To test the VLANS and the trunk, **ping** from the host in Switch_A port 0/8 to the host in Switch_B port 0/12.

   B. Was the ping successful? _____

   C. Why? _____

   D. **Ping** from the host in Switch_A port 0/8 to the switch IP 192.168.1.2.

   E. Was the ping successful? _____

   F. Why? _____

Step 17   Move hosts.

   Move the host in Switch_B from port 0/12 to port 0/7, wait until the port LED goes green and then go to the next step.

Step 18   Test the VLANS and the trunk.

   A. To test the VLANS and the trunk, **ping** from the host in Switch_A port 0/8 to the host in Switch_B port 0/7.

   B. Was the ping successful? _____

   C. Why? _____

   D. **Ping** from the host in Switch_A port 0/8 to the switch IP 192.168.1.2.

   E. Was the ping successful? _____

   F. Why? _____

Step 19   Move hosts.

   Move the host in Switch_A from port 0/8 to port 0/2, wait until the port LED goes green and then go to the next step.

Step 20   Test the VLANS and the trunk.

  A. To test the VLANS and the trunk, **ping** from the host in Switch_A port 0/2 to the host in Switch_B port 0/7.

  B. Was the ping successful? _____

  C. **Ping** from the host in Switch_A port 0/2 to the switch IP 192.168.1.2.

  D. Was the ping successful? _____

  E. Why? _____

Step 21   Move hosts.

  Move the host in Switch_B from port 0/7 to port 0/3, wait until the port LED goes green and then go to the next step.

Step 22   Test the VLANS and the trunk.

  A. To test the VLANS and the trunk, **ping** from the host in Switch_A port 0/2 to the host in Switch_B port 0/3.

  B. Was the ping successful? _____

  C. Why? _____

  D. **Ping** from the host in Switch_B port 0/3 to the switch IP 192.168.1.2.

  E. Was the ping successful? _____

  F. Why? _____

  G. **Ping** from the host in Switch_B port 0/3 to the switch IP 192.168.1.3.

  H. Was the ping successful? _____

  I. Why? _____

  J. What conclusions can be drawn from the testing that was just performed in regards to VLAN membership and VLANs across a trunk.

  _____
  _____
  _____

Upon completion of the previous steps, logoff (by typing **exit**) and turn all the devices off. Then remove and store the cables and adapter.

Lab 10-2: Trunking with 802.1q

Figure 10-2.1 Topology for Lab 10-2

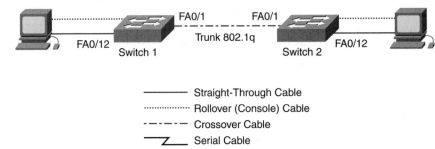

———— Straight-Through Cable

·············· Rollover (Console) Cable

– – – – – Crossover Cable

——⌇—— Serial Cable

Table 10-2.1 Lab Equipment Configuration

Switch Designation	Switch Name	VLAN 1 IP Address	Subnet Mask	VLAN Names and Numbers	Switch Port Assignments
Switch 1	Switch_A	192.168.1.2	255.255.255.0	VLAN 1 Native VLAN 10 Accounting VLAN 20 Marketing VLAN 30 Engineering	fa 0/2 - 0/3 fa 0/4 - 0/6 fa 0/7 - 0/9 fa0/10 – 0/12
Switch 2	Switch_B	192.168.1.3	255.255.255.0	VLAN 1 Native VLAN 10 Accounting VLAN 20 Marketing VLAN 30 Engineering	fa 0/2 - 0/3 fa 0/4 - 0/6 fa 0/7 - 0/9 fa0/10 – 0/12

Enable secret password is **class** for both switches.
Enable, VTY, and Console password is **cisco** for both switches.

Objective

- Create a basic switch configuration and verify it.
- Determine the switch firmware version.
- Create multiple VLANs, name them, and assign multiple member ports to them.
- Create an 802.1q trunk line between the two switches to allow communication between paired VLANs.
- Test the VLANs functionality by moving a workstation from one VLAN to another.

Background / Preparation

Trunking changes the formatting of the packets. The ports need to be in agreement as to which format is being used to transmit data on the trunk or no data will be passed. If there is different trunking encapsulation on the two ends of the link they will not be able to communicate. Similar situation will occur if one of your ports is configured in trunking mode (unconditionally) and the other one as in access mode (unconditionally).

When managing a switch, the Management Domain is always VLAN 1. The Network Administrator's workstation must have access to a port in the VLAN 1 Management Domain. All ports are assigned to VLAN 1 by default. This lab will also help demonstrate how VLANs can be used to separate traffic and reduce broadcast domains.

Cable a network similar to the one in Figure 10-2.1. The configuration output used in this lab is produced from the 2950 series switch. Any other switch used may produce different output. The following steps are intended to be executed on each switch unless specifically instructed otherwise.

Start a Hyperterminal session.

Please refer to and implement the procedure documented in Appendix B, "Erasing and Reloading the Switch," before continuing with this lab.

Step 1   Configure the switch

Configure the hostname, access, and command mode passwords, as well as the management LAN settings. These values are shown in the chart. If problems occur while performing this configuration, refer to the "Basic Switch Configuration" lab. **Do not** configure VLANs and trunking yet.

Step 2   Configure the hosts attached to the switch.

Configure the host to use the same subnet for addresses, mask, and the default gateway as the switch.

Step 3   Verify connectivity.

A. To verify the hosts and switch are correctly configured, **ping** the switch from the hosts.

B. Were the pings successful? _____

C. If the answer is no, troubleshoot the hosts and switch configurations.

Step 4   Look at the VLAN interface information.

On Switch_A, type the command **show vlan** at the privileged EXEC prompt.

```
Switch_A#show vlan
```

Step 5   Create and name three VLANs.

```
Switch_A#vlan database
Switch_A(vlan)#vlan 10 name Accounting
Switch_A(vlan)#vlan 20 name Marketing
Switch_A(vlan)#vlan 30 name Engineering
Switch_A(vlan)#exit
```

Step 6 Assign ports to VLAN 10.

Assigning ports to VLANs must be done from the interface mode. Enter the following commands to add ports 0/4 to 0/6 to VLAN 10:

```
Switch_A#configure terminal
Switch_A(config)#interface fastethernet 0/4
Switch_A(config-if)#switchport mode access
Switch_A(config-if)#switchport access vlan 10
Switch_A(config-if)#interface fastethernet 0/5
Switch_A(config-if)#switchport mode access
Switch_A(config-if)#switchport access vlan 10
Switch_A(config-if)#interface fastethernet 0/6
Switch_A(config-if)#switchport mode access
Switch_A(config-if)#switchport access vlan 10
Switch_A(config-if)#end
```

Step 7 Assign ports to VLAN 20.

```
Switch_A#configure terminal
Switch_A(config)#interface fastethernet 0/7
Switch_A(config-if)#switchport mode access
Switch_A(config-if)#switchport access vlan 20
Switch_A(config-if)#interface fastethernet 0/8
Switch_A(config-if)#switchport mode access
Switch_A(config-if)#switchport access vlan 20
Switch_A(config-if)#interface fastethernet 0/9
Switch_A(config-if)#switchport mode access
Switch_A(config-if)#switchport access vlan 20
Switch_A(config-if)#end
```

Step 8 Assign ports to VLAN 30.

```
Switch_A#configure terminal
Switch_A(config)#interface fastethernet 0/10
Switch_A(config-if)#switchport mode access
Switch_A(config-if)#switchport access vlan 30
Switch_A(config-if)#interface fastethernet 0/11
Switch_A(config-if)#switchport mode access
Switch_A(config-if)#switchport access vlan 30
Switch_A(config-if)#interface fastethernet 0/12
Switch_A(config-if)#switchport mode access
Switch_A(config-if)#switchport access vlan 30
Switch_A(config-if)#end
```

Step 9 Create VLANs on Switch_B.

Repeat Steps 5 through 8 on Switch_B to create its VLANs.

Step 10 Look at the VLAN interface information.

A. On both switches, type the command **show vlan** at the privileged EXEC prompt.
```
Switch_A#show vlan
```

B. Are ports 0/10-0/12 assigned to VLAN 30? _____

Step 11 Test the VLANs.

    A. **Ping** from the host in Switch_A port 0/12 to the host in Switch_B port 0/12.

    B. Was the ping successful? _____

    C. Why? _____

    D. **Ping** from the host in Switch_A port 0/12 to the switch IP 192.168.1.2.

    E. Was the ping successful? _____

    F. Why? _____

Step 12 Create the trunk.

On both switches, Switch_A and Switch_B, type the following command at the fastethernet 0/1 interface command prompt:

```
Switch_A(config)#interface fastethernet 0/1
Switch_A(config-if)#switchport mode trunk
Switch_A(config-if)#end
Switch_B(config)#interface fastethernet 0/1
Switch_B(config-if)#switchport mode trunk
Switch_B(config-if)#end
```

Step 13 Verify the Trunk.

    A. To verify that port Fast Ethernet 0/1 has been established as a trunk port, type **show interface fastethernet 0/1 switchport** at the privileged EXEC mode prompt.

    B. What type of trunking encapsulation is shown on the output results?

    _____

    C. According to the output with **show interface fastethernet 0/1 switchport** on Switch_B, is there a difference from the Administrative Trunking Encapsulation from the Operational Trunking Encapsulation?

    _____

    _____

    D. On the fragment "Trunking VLANs Enable" from the last output, what does the word "ALL" mean?

    _____

    E. What would happen if the two ports of the trunk were using different encapsulation? _____

    F. Explain _____

Step 14 Test the VLANS and the trunk.

    A. To test the VLANS and the trunk, **ping** from the host in Switch_A port 0/12 to the host in Switch_B port 0/12.

B. Was the ping successful? _____

C. Why? _____

D. **Ping** from the host in Switch_A port 0/12 to the switch IP 192.168.1.2.

E. Was the ping successful? _____

F. Why? _____

Step 15 Move hosts.

Move the host in Switch_A from port 0/12 to port 0/8, wait until the port LED goes green and then go to the next step.

Step 16 Test the VLANS and the trunk.

A. To test the VLANS and the trunk, **ping** from the host in Switch_A port 0/8 to the host in Switch_B port 0/12.

B. Was the ping successful? _____

C. Why? _____

D. **Ping** from the host in Switch_A port 0/8 to the switch IP 192.168.1.2.

E. Was the ping successful? _____

F. Why? _____

Step 17 Move hosts.

Move the host in Switch_B from port 0/12 to port 0/7, wait until the port LED goes green and then go to the next step.

Step 18 Test the VLANS and the trunk.

A. To test the VLANS and the trunk, **ping** from the host in Switch_A port 0/8 to the host in Switch_B port 0/7.

B. Was the ping successful? _____

C. Why? _____

D. **Ping** from the host in Switch_A port 0/8 to the switch IP 192.168.1.2.

E. Was the ping successful? _____

F. Why? _____

Step 19 Move hosts.

Move the host in Switch_A from port 0/8 to port 0/2, wait until the port LED goes green and then go to the next step.

Step 20 Test the VLANS and the trunk.

    A. To test the VLANS and the trunk, **ping** from the host in Switch_A port 0/2 to the host in Switch_B port 0/7.

    B. Was the ping successful? _____

    C. **Ping** from the host in Switch_A port 0/2 to the switch IP 192.168.1.2.

    D. Was the ping successful? _____

    E. Why? _____

Step 21 Move hosts.

Move the host in Switch_B from port 0/7 to port 0/3, wait until the port LED goes green and then go to the next step.

Step 22 Test the VLANS and the trunk.

    A. To test the VLANS and the trunk, **ping** from the host in Switch_A port 0/2 to the host in Switch_B port 0/3.

    B. Was the ping successful? _____

    C. Why? _____

    D. **Ping** from the host in Switch_B port 0/3 to the switch IP 192.168.1.2.

    E. Was the ping successful? _____

    F. Why? _____

    G. **Ping** from the host in Switch_B port 0/3 to the switch IP 192.168.1.3.

    H. Was the ping successful? _____

    I. Why? _____

    J. What conclusions can be drawn from the testing that was just performed in regards to VLAN membership and VLANs across a trunk.

       _____

       _____

       _____

Upon completion of the previous steps, logoff (by typing **exit**) and turn all the devices off. Then remove and store the cables and adapter.

Lab 10-3: VTP Client and Server Configurations

Figure 10-3.1   Topology for Lab 10-3

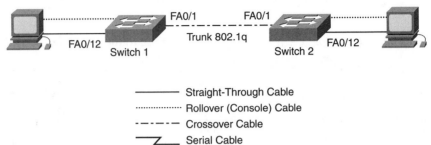

Straight-Through Cable
········· Rollover (Console) Cable
– – – – – Crossover Cable
⌐z̶ Serial Cable

Table 10-3.1   Lab Equipment Configuration

Switch Designation	Switch Name	VLAN 1 IP Address	Subnet Mask	VLAN Names and Numbers	Switch Port Assignments
Switch 1	Switch_A	192.168.1.2	255.255.255.0	VLAN 1 Native VLAN 10 Accounting VLAN 20 Marketing VLAN 30 Engineering	fa 0/2 - 0/3 fa 0/4 - 0/6 fa 0/7 - 0/9 fa0/10 – 0/12
Switch 2	Switch_B	192.168.1.3	255.255.255.0	VLAN 1 Native VLAN 10 Accounting VLAN 20 Marketing VLAN 30 Engineering	fa 0/2 - 0/3 fa 0/4 - 0/6 fa 0/7 - 0/9 fa0/10 – 0/12

Enable secret password is **class** for both switches.
Enable, VTY, and Console password is **cisco** for both switches.

Objective

- Create a basic switch configuration and verify it.
- Create multiple VLANs, name them, and assign multiple member ports to them.
- Configure the VTP protocol to establish Server and client switches
- Create an 802.1q trunk line between the two switches to allow communication between paired VLANs.
- Then test the VLANs functionality by moving a workstation from one VLAN to another.

Background / Preparation

When managing a switch, the Management Domain is always VLAN 1. The Network Administrator's workstation must have access to a port in the VLAN 1 Management Domain. All ports are assigned to VLAN 1 by default.

Cable a network similar to the one in Figure 10-3.1. The configuration output used in this lab is produced from a 2950 series switch. Any other switch used may produce different output. The following steps are intended to be executed on each switch unless specifically instructed otherwise.

Start a Hyperterminal session.

Please refer to and implement the procedure documented in Appendix B, "Erasing and Reloading the Switch," before continuing with this lab.

Step 1   Configure the switches.

Configure the hostname, access, and command mode passwords, as well as the management LAN settings. These values are shown in the chart. If problems occur while performing this configuration, refer to the "Basic Switch Configuration" lab.

Step 2   Configure the hosts attached to the switch.

Configure the host to use the same subnet for addresses, mask, and the default gateway as the switch.

Step 3   Verify connectivity.

A. To verify the hosts and switch are correctly configured, **ping** the switch from the hosts.

B. Were the pings successful? _____

C. If the answer is no, troubleshoot the hosts and switch configurations.

Step 4   Look at the VLAN interface information.

On Switch_A, type the command **show vlan** at the privileged EXEC prompt.

```
Switch_A#show vlan
```

Step 5   Configure VTP protocol.

A. VTP (VLAN Trunking Protocol) needs to be configured on both switches. VTP is the protocol that will communicate information about which VLANs exist from one switch to another. If VTP did not provide this information, VLANs would have to be created on all switches individually.

B. By default, the Catalyst switch series are configured as VTP servers. In the event that the sever services are turned off, use the following command to turn it back on.

```
Switch_A#vlan database
Switch_A(vlan)#vtp server
Switch_A(vlan)#exit
```

Step 6   Create and name three VLANs.

```
Switch_A#vlan database
Switch_A(vlan)#vlan 10 name Accounting
Switch_A(vlan)#vlan 20 name Marketing
Switch_A(vlan)#vlan 30 name Engineering
Switch_A(vlan)#exit
```

Step 7   Assign ports to VLAN 10.

Assigning ports to VLANs must be done from the interface mode. Enter the following commands to add ports 0/4 to 0/6 to VLAN 10

```
Switch_A#configure terminal
Switch_A(config)#interface fastethernet 0/4
Switch_A(config-if)#switchport mode access
Switch_A(config-if)#switchport access vlan 10
Switch_A(config-if)#interface fastethernet 0/5
Switch_A(config-if)#switchport mode access
Switch_A(config-if)#switchport access vlan 10
Switch_A(config-if)#interface fastethernet 0/6
Switch_A(config-if)#switchport mode access
Switch_A(config-if)#switchport access vlan 10
Switch_A(config-if)#end
```

Step 8   Assign ports to VLAN 20.

```
Switch_A# configure terminal
Switch_A(config)#interface fastethernet 0/7
Switch_A(config-if)#switchport mode access
Switch_A(config-if)#switchport access vlan 20
Switch_A(config-if)#interface fastethernet 0/8
Switch_A(config-if)#switchport mode access
Switch_A(config-if)#switchport access vlan 20
Switch_A(config-if)#interface fastethernet 0/9
Switch_A(config-if)#switchport mode access
Switch_A(config-if)#switchport access vlan 20
Switch_A(config-if)#end
```

Step 9   Assign ports to VLAN 30.

```
Switch_A# configure terminal
Switch_A(config)#interface fastethernet 0/10
Switch_A(config-if)#switchport mode access
Switch_A(config-if)#switchport access vlan 30
Switch_A(config-if)#interface fastethernet 0/11
Switch_A(config-if)#switchport mode access
Switch_A(config-if)#switchport access vlan 30
Switch_A(config-if)#interface fastethernet 0/12
Switch_A(config-if)#switchport mode access
Switch_A(config-if)#switchport access vlan 30
Switch_A(config-if)#end
```

Step 10   Look at the VLAN interface information.

   A. On Switch_A, type the command **show vlan** at the privileged EXEC prompt.
   ```
   Switch_A#show vlan
   ```

   B. Are ports 0/10-0/12 assigned to VLAN 30? _____

Step 11 Configure VTP Client.

Configure Switch_B to be a VTP client.

```
Switch_B#vlan database
Switch_B(vlan)#vtp client
Switch_B(vlan)#vtp domain group1
Switch_B(vlan)#exit
```

Step 12 Create the Trunk.

On both switches, Switch_A and Switch_B, type the following command at the fastethernet 0/1 interface command prompt:

```
Switch_A(config)#interface fastethernet 0/1
Switch_A(config-if)#switchport mode trunk
Switch_A(config-if)#end
Switch_B(config)#interface fastethernet 0/1
Switch_B(config-if)#switchport mode trunk
Switch_B(config-if)#end
```

Step 13 Verify the Trunk.

A. To verify that port fastethernet 0/1 has been established as a trunk port, type **show interface fastethernet 0/1 switchport** at the privileged EXEC mode prompt

B. What type of trunking encapsulation is shown on the output results?

_____

Step 14 Look at the VLAN interface information.

A. On Switch_A, type the command **show vlan** at the privileged EXEC prompt.
```
Switch_A#show vlan
```

B. Do VLANs 10, 20, and 30 show without having to type them in?

_____

C. Why did this happen?

_____

Step 15 Assign ports to VLAN 10.

Although the VLAN definitions have migrated to Switch_B using VTP, it is still necessary to assign ports to these VLANs on Switch_B. Assigning ports to VLANs must be done from the interface mode. Enter the following commands to add ports 0/4 to 0/6 to VLAN 10

```
Switch_B# configure terminal
Switch_B(config)#interface fastethernet 0/4
Switch_B(config-if)#switchport mode access
Switch_B(config-if)#switchport access vlan 10
Switch_B(config-if)#interface fastethernet 0/5
Switch_B(config-if)#switchport mode access
```

```
Switch_B(config-if)#switchport access vlan 10
Switch_B(config-if)#interface fastethernet 0/6
Switch_B(config-if)#switchport mode access
Switch_B(config-if)#switchport access vlan 10
Switch_B(config-if)#end
```

Step 16 Assign ports to VLAN 20.

```
Switch_B# configure terminal
Switch_B(config)#interface fastethernet 0/7
Switch_B(config-if)#switchport mode access
Switch_B(config-if)#switchport access vlan 20
Switch_B(config-if)#interface fastethernet 0/8
Switch_B(config-if)#switchport mode access
Switch_B(config-if)#switchport access vlan 20
Switch_B(config-if)#interface fastethernet 0/9
Switch_B(config-if)#switchport mode access
Switch_B(config-if)#switchport access vlan 20
Switch_B(config-if)#end
```

Step 17 Assign ports to VLAN 30.

```
Switch_B# configure terminal
Switch_B(config)#interface fastethernet 0/10
Switch_B(config-if)#switchport mode access
Switch_B(config-if)#switchport access vlan 30
Switch_B(config-if)#interface fastethernet 0/11
Switch_B(config-if)#switchport mode access
Switch_B(config-if)#switchport access vlan 30
Switch_B(config-if)#interface fastethernet 0/12
Switch_B(config-if)#switchport mode access
Switch_B(config-if)#switchport access vlan 30
Switch_B(config-if)#end
```

Step 18 Look at the VLAN interface information.

A. On Switch_B, type the command **show vlan** at the privileged EXEC prompt.

```
Switch_B#show vlan
```

B. Are ports 0/10-0/12 assigned to VLAN 30? _____

Step 19 Test the VLANS and the trunk.

A. To test the VLANS and the trunk, **ping** from the host in Switch_A port 0/12 to the host in Switch_B port 0/12.

B. Was the ping successful? _____

C. Why? _____

D. **Ping** from the host in Switch_A port 0/12 to the switch IP 192.168.1.2.

E. Was the ping successful? _____

F. Why? _____

Step 20 Move hosts.

Move the host in Switch_A from port 0/12 to port 0/8, wait until the port LED goes green and then go to the next step.

Step 21 Test the VLANS and the trunk.

A. To test the VLANS and the trunk, **ping** from the host in Switch_A port 0/8 to the host in Switch_B port 0/12.

B. Was the ping successful? _____

C. Why? _____

D. **Ping** from the host in Switch_A port 0/8 to the switch IP 192.168.1.2.

E. Was the ping successful? _____

F. Why? _____

Upon completion of the previous steps, logoff (by typing **exit**) and turn all the devices off. Then remove and store the cables and adapter.

Lab 10-4: Configuring Inter-VLAN Routing

Figure 10-4.1 Topology for Lab 10-4

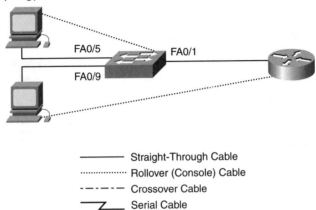

———————— Straight-Through Cable

················· Rollover (Console) Cable

– – – – – Crossover Cable

⌐Z⌐ Serial Cable

Table 10-4.1 Lab Equipment Configuration

Switch Designation	Switch Name	VLAN 1 IP Address	Subnet Mask	VLAN Names and Numbers	Switch Port Assignments
Switch 1	Switch_A	192.168.1.2	255.255.255.0	VLAN 1 Native VLAN 10 Sales VLAN 20 Support	fa 0/1 - 0/4 fa 0/5 - 0/8 fa 0/9 - 0/12

Enable secret password is **class** for both switches.
Enable, VTY, and Console password is **cisco** for both switches.

Objectives

- Create a basic switch configuration and verify it.
- Create multiple VLANs, name them, and assign multiple member ports to them.
- Create a basic configuration on a router.
- Create an 802.1q trunk line between the switch and router to allow communication between VLANs.
- Test the routing functionality.

Background / Preparation

When managing a switch, the Management Domain is always VLAN 1. The Network Administrator's workstation must have access to a port in the VLAN 1 Management Domain. All ports are assigned to VLAN 1 by default. This lab will also help demonstrate how VLANs can be used to separate traffic and reduce broadcast domains.

Cable a network similar to the one in Figure 10-4.1. The configuration output used in this lab is produced from a 2950 series switch. Any other switch used may produce different output. The following steps are intended to be executed on each switch unless specifically instructed otherwise.

Start a Hyperterminal session.

Please refer to and implement the procedure documented in Appendix B, "Erasing and Reloading the Switch," before continuing with this lab.

Step 1 Configure the switch.

Configure the hostname, access, and command mode passwords, as well as the management LAN settings. These values are shown in the chart. If problems occur while performing this configuration, refer to the "Basic Switch Configuration" lab.

Step 2 Configure the hosts attached to the switch.

Configure the hosts using the following information.

A. The host in port 0/5:

IP address 192.168.5.2

Subnet mask 255.255.255.0

Default gateway 192.168.5.1

B. The host in port 0/9:

IP address 192.168.7.2

Subnet mask 255.255.255.0

Default gateway 192.168.7.1

Step 3 Verify connectivity.

A. To verify the hosts and switch are correctly configured, **ping** the switch from the hosts.

B. Were the pings successful?

_____

Step 4 Create and name two VLANs.

```
Switch_A#vlan database
Switch_A(vlan)#vlan 10 name Sales
Switch_A(vlan)#vlan 20 name Support
Switch_A(vlan)#exit
```

Step 5 Assign ports to VLAN 10.

Assigning ports to VLANs must be done from the interface mode. Enter the following commands to add ports 0/4 to 0/6 to VLAN 10:

```
Switch_A#configure terminal
Switch_A(config)#interface fastethernet0/5
Switch_A(config-if)#switchport mode access
Switch_A(config-if)#switchport access vlan 10
Switch_A(config-if)#interface fastethernet0/6
```

```
Switch_A(config-if)#switchport mode access
Switch_A(config-if)#switchport access vlan 10
Switch_A(config-if)#interface fastethernet0/7
Switch_A(config-if)#switchport mode access
Switch_A(config-if)#switchport access vlan 10
Switch_A(config-if)#interface fastethernet0/8
Switch_A(config-if)#switchport mode access
Switch_A(config-if)#switchport access vlan 10
Switch_A(config-if)#end
```

Step 6   Assign ports to VLAN 20.

```
Switch_A#configure terminal
Switch_A(config)#interface fastethernet0/9
Switch_A(config-if)#switchport mode access
Switch_A(config-if)#switchport access vlan 20
Switch_A(config-if)#interface fastethernet0/10
Switch_A(config-if)#switchport mode access
Switch_A(config-if)#switchport access vlan 20
Switch_A(config-if)#interface fastethernet0/11
Switch_A(config-if)#switchport mode access
Switch_A(config-if)#switchport access vlan 20
Switch_A(config-if)#interface fastethernet0/12
Switch_A(config-if)#switchport mode access
Switch_A(config-if)#switchport access vlan 20
Switch_A(config-if)#end
```

Step 7   Look at the VLAN interface information.

A. On Switch_A, type the command **show VLAN** at the privileged EXEC prompt.
```
Switch_A#show vlan
```

B. Are ports assigned correctly? _____

Step 8   Create the trunk.

On Switch_A, type the following command at the Fast Ethernet 0/1 interface command prompt:

```
Switch_A(config)#interface fastethernet0/1
Switch_A(config-if)#switchport mode trunk
Switch_A(config-if)#end
```

Step 9   Configure the router.

A. Configure the router with the following data.

Hostname - Router_A

Console, VTY, and enable passwords - cisco

Enable secret password - class

B. Then configure the fastethernet interface using the following commands.

```
Router_A(config)#interface fastethernet 0/1
Router_A(config-if)#no shutdown
Router_A(config-if)#interface fastethernet 0/1.1
Router_A(config-subif)#encapsulation dot1q 1
Router_A(config-subif)#ip address 192.168.1.1 255.255.255.0
Router_A(config-if)#interface fastethernet 0/1.2
Router_A(config-subif)#encapsulation dot1q 10
Router_A(config-subif)#ip address 192.168.5.1 255.255.255.0
Router_A(config-if)#interface fastethernet 0/1.3
Router_A(config-subif)#encapsulation dot1q 20
Router_A(config-subif)#ip address 192.168.7.1 255.255.255.0
Router_A(config-subif)#end
```

Step 10 Save the router configuration.

Step 11 Look at the router routing table.

    A. Type **show ip route** at the privileged EXEC mode prompt.

    B. Are there entries in the routing table?

    _____

    C. What interface are they all pointing to?

    _____

    D. Why is not there a need to run a routing protocol?

    _____

Step 12 Step 12. Test the VLANS and the trunk.

    A. To test the VLANS and the trunk, **ping** from the host in Switch_A port 0/9 to the host in port 0/5.

    B. Was the ping successful? _____

    C. Why? _____

    D. **Ping** from the host in Switch_A port 0/5 to the switch IP 192.168.1.2.

    E. Was the ping successful? _____

Step 13 Move the hosts.

    A. Move the hosts to other VLANs and try pinging the management VLAN 1.

    B. Note the results.

    _____
    _____
    _____

Upon completion of the previous steps, logoff (by typing **exit**) and turn all the devices off. Then remove and store the cables and adapter.

Objectives

After reading this chapter, you will be able to

- Describe why scaling IP addresses is necessary
- Describe NAT terminology
- Describe NAT features
- Differentiate between static NAT, dynamic NAT, and PAT
- Configure and verify NAT and PAT
- Troubleshoot NAT and PAT
- Differentiate between BOOTP and DHCP
- Configure and verify DHCP
- Describe DHCP terminology and features
- Troubleshoot DHCP
- Identify and differentiate between public and private IP addresses

Chapter 11

Scaling IP Addresses

An IP address is required for any device that connects to the Internet. The number of devices requiring an IP address is increasing rapidly, yet the number of IP addresses available is limited. This chapter discusses the problem of IP address space depletion and the solutions that have been developed to help alleviate IP scaling problems. Solutions presented here include network address translation (NAT), port address translation (PAT), the Dynamic Host Configuration Protocol (DHCP), and the use of private IP addresses. You will learn how to configure, verify, and troubleshoot NAT and DHCP on routers.

Please be sure to look at this chapter's associated e-labs, movies, and photozooms that you will find on the CD-ROM accompanying the full text of this title. These CD elements are designed to supplement the material and reinforce the concepts introduced in this chapter.

Internet Protocol Overview

IP is the connectivity protocol of choice. IP applications are being developed at a fast rate, which means that more hosts have the possibility to be connected to the Internet. In the early stages of the Internet, PCs, workstations, servers, and routers were the only devices that were attached to the Internet. An administrator statically assigned IP addresses.

Today, PDAs, laptops, desktops, mainframes, storage devices, routers, switches, video game consoles, and security cameras connect to the Internet. There is even talk of connecting household appliances. It should become clear that without scaling options, the Internet revolution would have quickly reached its limits.

Several scaling options have been implemented over the years, including variable-length subnet mask (VLSM), *classless interdomain routing (CIDR)*, and Internet Protocol version 6 (IPv6). In this chapter, three other solutions to the scaling problem of IP are presented: private addressing (RFC 1918), address translation (NAT and PAT), and address pooling (DHCP).

Two scalability challenges face the Internet today:

- The registered IP address space is being depleted, and size of the Internet continues to increase.
- As the Internet gets bigger, so does the number of IP routes in the backbone Internet routing tables. This poses a scalability problem for routing algorithms.

IP scaling solutions are as follows:

- NAT
- DHCP
- RFC 1918 (private IP addressing)

Network address translation (NAT) is a mechanism for conserving registered IP addresses in large networks and simplifying IP addressing management tasks. NAT is standards based and is described in RFC 1631.

As a packet is routed across a Cisco IOS NAT router, the router translates the source IP address on the packet from a private internal network address to a legal IP address so that the packet can be transported over public external networks, such as the Internet. Returning traffic is translated back for delivery within the inside network. NAT is discussed in more detail later in this chapter.

The Internet has grown explosively, and it shows no signs of slowing down. Administrators must assign IP addresses, default gateways, and other necessary information to hosts that connect to the Internet. ***Dynamic Host Configuration Protocol (DHCP)*** assists administrators with issuing IP addresses to devices dynamically.

As the global Internet took off, organizations wanted to use IP for connectivity, but they did not want to expose all their hosts to the Internet. RFC 1918 deals with this by defining public and private IP address space.

The Internet Assigned Numbers Authority (IANA) sets aside three blocks of IP addresses, which are shown in Table 11-1. RFC 1918 describes best practices for employing these addresses.

Table 11-1 RFC 1918 Addresses

Class	RFC 1918 Internal Address Range	CIDR Prefix
A	10.0.0.0–10.255.255.255	10.0.0.0/8
B	172.16.0.0–172.31.255.255	172.16.0.0/12
C	192.168.0.0–192.168.255.255	192.168.0.0/16

These three ranges provide more than 17 million private addresses. *Private* means that they are not allowed to be routed through the public Internet, but organizations are free to use them as they want to. Therefore, these addresses are considered unroutable.

Both IPv4 and IPv6 addresses are assigned in a delegated manner. Users are assigned IP addresses by Internet service providers (ISPs). ISPs obtain allocations of IP addresses from a local Internet registry (LIR), from a national Internet registry (NIR), or from their appropriate regional Internet registry (RIR). These could include APNIC (Asia Pacific Network Information Centre), ARIN (American Registry for Internet Numbers), LACNIC (Regional Latin-American and Caribbean IP Address Registry), or RIPE NCC (Ráseaux IP Europeéns).

Anyone can use reserved private IP addresses. That means two networks or two million networks can each use the same private address. RFC 1918 addresses should never be seen on the public Internet; a public Internet router should never route these addresses because ISPs typically configure their routers to prevent privately addressed customer traffic from being forwarded.

If you are addressing a nonpublic intranet, a test lab, or a home network, these private addresses can be used instead of globally unique addresses. Global addresses must be obtained from a provider or a registry at some expense.

RFC 1918 addresses have found a home in production networks as well. With VLSM, you can further subnet one of the subnets left in a Class C network's address space. Although this solution is better than wasting an entire 30-host subnet on each two-host WAN link, it still costs one subnet that could have been used for future growth. A less wasteful solution is to address the WAN links by using private network numbers. In Figure 11-1, the WAN links are addressed by using subnets from the private address space 10.0.0.0/8.

Figure 11-1 Using Private Addresses in the WAN

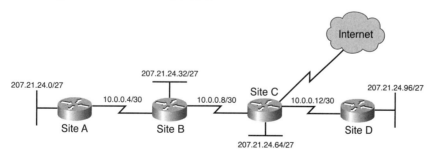

How can these routers use private addresses if local-area network (LAN) users at sites A, B, C, and D expect to access the Internet? End users at these sites should have no problem because they use globally unique addresses from the 207.21.24.0 network. The routers use their serial interfaces with private addresses merely to forward traffic and exchange routing information. Upstream providers and Internet routers see only the source and destination IP addresses in the packet; they do not care if the packet traveled through links with private addresses at some point. In fact, many providers use RFC 1918 network numbers in the core of their network to avoid depleting their supply of globally unique addresses.

One trade-off of using private numbers on WAN links is that these serial interfaces cannot be the original source of traffic bound for the Internet or the final destination of traffic from the Internet. Routers do not normally spend time surfing the web, so this limitation typically becomes an issue only when troubleshooting with ICMP, when using SNMP, or when connecting remotely with telnet over the Internet. In those cases, the router can be addressed only by its globally unique LAN interfaces.

NAT provides tremendous benefits to individual companies and the Internet. Before NAT, a host with a private address could not access the Internet. With NAT, individual companies can address some or all of their hosts with private addresses and then use NAT to access the public Internet. At the same time, these hosts connect to the Internet without necessarily depleting its address space.

NAT and PAT

NAT is the process of altering the IP header of a packet so that the destination address, the source address, or both addresses are replaced in the header by different administrator-assigned addresses. A device that is running specialized NAT software or hardware performs this swapping process. Cisco IOS NAT is designed for IP address simplification and conservation because it enables private IP internetworks that use unregistered IP addresses to connect to the Internet by translating those addresses into globally registered IP addresses. Cisco IOS NAT also increases network privacy by hiding internal IP addresses from external networks.

A NAT-enabled device typically operates at the border of a stub network. A stub network is a network that has a single connection to its neighbor network. Figure 11-2 presents a simple example of a stub network. When a host inside the stub network wants to transmit to a host on the outside, it forwards the packet to its border gateway router. In this case, the host's border gateway router is also the NAT box.

Figure 11-2 Stub Network

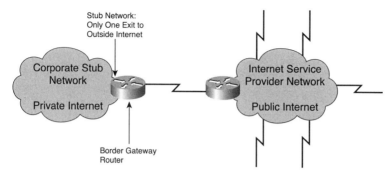

NAT operates on a Cisco router, usually connecting two networks, and it translates the private (inside local) addresses in the internal network to public addresses (inside global) before packets are forwarded to another network, as shown in Figures 11-3 through 11-5.

An internal host (10.0.0.2) wants to communicate with an external host (128.23.2.2). It sends its packet to its gateway RTA, as shown in Figure 11-3.

Figure 11-3 How NAT Works

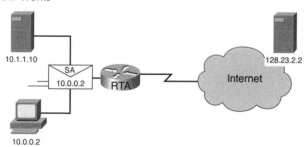

RTA sees the packet is to be routed to the outside Internet. The NAT process chooses a globally unique IP address (179.9.8.80) and replaces the local address in the source field of the pack with the global address. It stores this mapping of local to global address in the NAT table, as shown in Figure 11-4.

Figure 11-4 How NAT Works: NAT Table

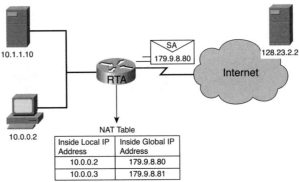

The packet is routed to its destination. In this client-server environment, the server might respond with a packet, which will come back to RTA, addressed to the global address 179.9.8.80, as shown in Figure 11-5.

Figure 11-5 How NAT Works: Reply

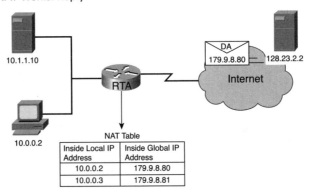

In Figure 11-6, the NAT process, seeing a packet routed from the outside to the inside will consult the NAT table for a mapping of this global address into a local address. If it finds one, it replaces the global address in the destination field of the packet with the local address, and the packet is forwarded internally.

Figure 11-6 How NAT Works: Final

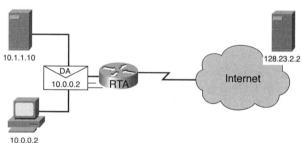

In NAT terminology, the inside network is the set of networks that are subject to translation. The outside network refers to all other addresses. Usually these are valid addresses located on the Internet.

As part of this functionality, NAT can be configured to advertise only one address for the entire network to the outside world. This effectively hides the internal network from the world and provides additional security. This feature of NAT is called static PAT, and it is shown in Figures 11-7 and 11-8. PAT is also referred to as overload in Cisco IOS configuration. Several internal addresses can be translated by using NAT compared to only one or a few external addresses by using PAT. In Figure 11-7, hosts 10.0.0.2 and 10.0.0.3 send packets to the outside world by using the single public IP address of 179.9.8.80. The router keeps track of packets for each host by appending a unique source port number to the outside IP address.

Figure 11-7 How PAT Works

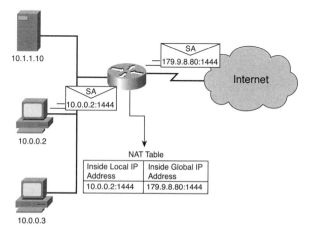

Figure 11-8 How PAT Works: Final

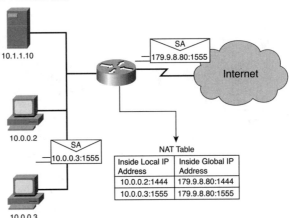

PAT uses unique source port numbers on the inside global IP address to distinguish between translations. Because the port number is encoded in 16 bits, the total number of internal addresses that can be translated into one external address by using PAT could theoretically be as high as 65,536 per IP address. PAT attempts to preserve the original source port. If this source port is already allocated, PAT tries to find the first available port number starting from the beginning of the appropriate port group 0-511, 512-1023, or 1024-65535. If no port is available from the appropriate port group and more than one external IP address is configured, PAT moves to the next IP address and tries to allocate the original source port again. This continues until PAT runs out of available ports and external IP addresses.

NAT and PAT Features

NAT can occur dynamically or statically, and you can use it for a variety of purposes. Static NAT is designed to allow one-to-one mapping between local and global addresses, as shown in Figure 11-9. This is particularly useful for inside IP hosts that must be accessible from the Internet, such as a DNS server or e-mail server.

Figure 11-9 Static NAT

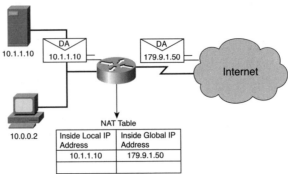

Dynamic NAT is designed to map an unregistered IP address to a registered IP address from a group of registered IP addresses, as shown in Figure 11-10.

Figure 11-10 Dynamic NAT

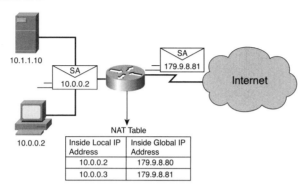

Cisco defines the following NAT terms:

- *Inside local address*—The IP address assigned to a host on the inside network that is likely to be an RFC 1918 private address.
- *Inside global address*—A legitimate IP address that the Regional Internet Registries (RIR) or service provider assigns. It represents one or more inside local IP addresses to the outside world.
- *Outside local address*—The IP address of an outside host as it is known to the hosts in the inside network.
- *Outside global address*—The IP address that the host's owner assigns to a host on the outside network.

NAT offers the following benefits:

- **Eliminates readdressing overhead, such as changing an ISP**—No longer is it necessary to readdress all hosts that require external access, which saves time and money.
- **Conserves addresses through application port-level multiplexing**—With NAT, internal hosts can share a single registered IP address for all external communications. In this type of configuration, relatively few external addresses are required to support many internal hosts, which conserves IP addresses.
- **Protects network security**—Because private networks do not advertise their addresses or internal topology, they remain reasonably secure when they are used in conjunction with NAT to gain controlled external access.

Configuring NAT and PAT

The following configuration topics are covered in this section:

- Static translation
- Dynamic translation
- Overloading NAT (PAT)

Static Translation

Static translation occurs when you specifically configure addresses in a lookup table. A specific inside local address maps to a prespecified inside global address. The inside local and inside global addresses are statically mapped one for one. This means that for every inside local address, static NAT requires an inside global address. To configure static inside source address translation, perform the tasks outlined in Table 11-2.

Table 11-2 Configuring Static NAT

Step	Action	Notes
1.	Establish static translation between an inside local address and an inside global address. Router(config)#**ip nat inside source static** *local-ip global-ip*	Enter the global **no ip nat inside source static** command to remove the static source translation.
2.	Specify the inside interface. Router(config)#**interface** *type number* Mark the interface as connected to the inside. Router(config-if)#**ip nat inside**	When you enter the **interface** command, the CLI prompt changes from (config)# to (config-if)#.
3.	Specify the outside interface. Router(config-if)#**interface** *type number* Mark the interface as connected to the outside. Router(config-if)#**ip nat outside**	

You enter static translations directly into the configuration, and they are shown in the translation table. Example 11-1 gives the command for Cisco IOS routers.

Example 11-1 *Configuring Static NAT*

```
Router(config)#ip nat inside source static 10.1.1.2 192.168.1.2
Router(config)#interface s0
Router(config-if)#ip nat outside
Router(config-if)#interface e0
Router(config-if)#ip nat inside
```

Figure 11-11 shows the use of static NAT. The router translates packets from host 10.1.1.2 to a source address of 192.168.1.2. Example 11-2 provides the gateway configuration.

Figure 11-11 Static NAT Example

Example 11-2 *Gateway Configuration*

```
hostname GW
!
ip nat inside source static 10.1.1. 2 192.168.1.2


!
interface Ethernet0
 ip address 10.1.1.1 255.255.255.0
 ip nat inside
!
interface Serial0
 ip address 192.168.1.1 255.255.255.0
 ip nat outside
!
ip nat inside source static 10.1.1.2 192.168.1.2
```

Dynamic Translation

With Dynamic NAT, translations do not exist in the NAT table until the router receives traffic that requires translation. (An administrator defines such traffic.) Dynamic translations are temporary, and they eventually time out. To configure dynamic inside source address translation, perform the tasks shown in Table 11-3.

Table 11-3 Configuring Dynamic NAT

Step	Action	Notes
1.	Define a pool of global addresses to be allocated as needed. Router(config)#**ip nat pool** *name start-ip end-ip* {**netmask** *netmask* | **prefix-length** *prefix-length*}	Enter the global **no ip nat pool** command to remove the pool of global addresses.
2.	Create an access control list (ACL) to identify hosts for translation. Router(config)#**access-list** *access-list-number* **permit** *source* [*source-wildcard*]	Enter the global **no access-list** *access-list-number* command to remove the access list.
3.	Configure Dynamic NAT based on source address. Router(config)#**ip nat inside source list** *access-list-number* **pool** *name*	Enter the global **no ip nat inside source** command to remove the dynamic source translation.
4.	Specify the inside interface. Router(config-if)#**ip nat inside**	When you enter the **interface** command, the CLI prompt changes from (config)# to (config-if)#.
5.	Specify the outside interface. Router(config-if)#**interface** *type number* Router(config-if)#**ip nat outside**	

Dynamic translation specifies the pool of global addresses that inside addresses can be translated into, as shown in Example 11-3.

Example 11-3 *Configuring Dynamic NAT*

```
Router(config)#ip nat pool nat-pool 179.9.8.80 179.9.8.95
    netmask 255.255.255.0 255.255.255.240
```

The access list must permit only those addresses that are to be translated. Remember that an implicit **deny all** exists at the end of each access list. An access list that is too permissive can lead to unpredictable results. Cisco highly recommends that you not configure access lists referenced by NAT commands with **permit any**. Using **permit any** can result in NAT consuming too many router resources, which can cause network problems.

The following commands configure the appropriate interfaces to take on the role of outside and inside:

```
Router(config)#interface s0
Router(config-if)#ip nat outside
Router(config-if)#interface e0
Router(config-if)#ip nat inside
```

NOTE

NAT will not translate the host 10.1.1.2 because it is not permitted for translation by the access list.

Figure 11-12 translates all source addresses passing access list 1 (having a source address from 10.0.0.0/16) to an address from the pool named nat-pool1. The pool contains addresses from 179.9.8.80/28 to 179.9.8.95/28.

Figure 11-12 PAT Example

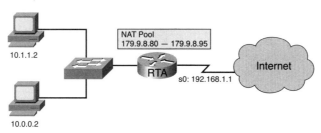

Configuration for GW is shown in Example 11-4.

Example 11-4 *Configuration for GW*

```
<output omitted>
ip nat pool nat-pool1 179.9.8.80 179.9.8.95 netmask 255.255.255.0
ip nat inside source list 1 pool nat-pool1
!
interface fastethernet0/0
 ip address 10.1.1.1 255.255.255.0
 ip nat inside
!
interface Serial0/0
 ip address 192.168.1.1 255.255.255.0
 ip nat outside
!
```

Overloading NAT

One of the most powerful features of NAT routers is their ability to use PAT. This is sometimes called a "many-to-one" NAT, or address overloading. With address *overloading*, hundreds of privately addressed nodes can access the Internet by using a single global address. The NAT router keeps track of the different conversations by mapping TCP and UDP port numbers in the translation table.

To configure overloading of inside global addresses, perform the tasks shown in Table 11-4.

Table 11-4 Configuring NAT Overload

Step	Action	Notes
1.	Define a standard access list permitting those addresses that are to be translated. Router(config)#**access-list** *access-list-number* **permit** *source* [*source-wildcard*]	Enter the global **no access-list** *access-list-number* command to remove the access list.
2.A	Establish dynamic source translation, specifying the access list that was defined in the prior step. Router(config)#**ip nat inside source list** *access-list-number* **interface** *interface* **overload**	Enter the global **no ip nat inside source** command to remove the dynamic source translation. The **overload** keyword enables PAT.
2.B	Specify the global address (as a pool) to be used for overloading. Router(config)#**ip nat pool** *name ip-address* {**netmask** *netmask* | **prefix-length** *prefix-length*} Establish overload translation. Router(config)#**ip nat inside source list** *access-list-number* **pool** *name* **overload**	
3.	Specify the inside interface. Router(config)#**interface** *type number* Router(config-if)#**ip nat inside**	When you enter the **interface** command, the CLI prompt changes from (config)# to (config-if)#.
4.	Specify the outside interface. Router(config-if)#**interface** *type number* Router(config-if)#**ip nat outside**	

Define a standard IP access list permitting those inside local addresses that are to be translated, as shown in Example 11-5.

Example 11-5 *Standard IP Access List*

```
Router(config)#access-list 1 permit 10.0.0.0 0.0.255.255
```

Establish overload translation, specifying the IP address to be overloaded as that assigned to an outside interface, as shown in Example 11-6.

Example 11-6 *Overload with an Interface*

```
Router(config)#ip nat inside source list 1 interface serial0/0 overload
```

Establish overload translation, specifying the IP address to be overloaded as that assigned to a pool name, as shown in Example 11-7.

Example 11-7 *Overload with a Pool*

```
Router(config)#ip nat pool nat-pool2 179.9.8.20 netmask 255.255.255.240
Router(config)#ip nat inside source list 1pool nat-pool2 overload
Router(config)#interface s0
Router(config-if)#ip nat outside
Router(config-if)#interface ethernet 0
Router(config-if)#ip nat inside
```

Lab Activity   Configuring NAT

In this lab, you will configure a router to use NAT to convert internal private IP addresses into outside public addresses.

Lab Activity   Configuring PAT

In this lab, you will configure a router to use PAT to convert internal private IP addresses into outside public addresses.

Verifying NAT and PAT Configuration

After NAT is configured, verify that it is operating as expected by using the **clear** and **show** commands.

By default, dynamic address translations time out from the NAT table after a period of nonuse. When port translation is not configured, translation entries time out after 24 hours, unless they are reconfigured with the **ip nat translation** command. Clear the entries before the timeout by using one of the commands in Table 11-5.

Table 11-5 Commands for Clearing NAT Table Entries

Command	Description
clear ip nat translation *	Clears all dynamic address translation entries from the NAT translation table
clear ip nat translation inside *global-ip local-ip* [**outside** *local-ip global-ip*]	Clears a simple dynamic translation entry containing an inside translation, or both inside and outside translation
clear ip nat translation protocol inside *global-ip global-port local-ip local-port* [**outside** *local-ip local-port global-ip global-port*]	Clears an extended dynamic translation entry

Translation information can be displayed by performing one of the tasks in EXEC mode, as shown in Table 11-6.

Table 11-6 Commands to Display Translation Information

Command	Description
show ip nat translations	Displays active translations
show ip nat statistics	Displays translation statistics

Alternatively, use the **show run** command and look for NAT, access list, interface, or pool commands with the required values.

Troubleshooting NAT and PAT Configuration

When IP connectivity problems exist in a NAT environment, it is often difficult to determine the cause of the problem. Many times, NAT is mistakenly blamed, when in reality, there is an underlying problem.

When you are trying to determine the cause of an IP connectivity problem, it helps to rule out NAT. Follow these steps to verify that NAT is operating as expected:

Step 1   Based on the configuration, clearly define what NAT is supposed to achieve.

Step 2   Verify that correct translations exist in the translation table.

Step 3   Verify that translation is occurring by using **show** and **debug** commands.

Step 4   Review in detail what is happening to the packet and verify that routers have the correct routing information to move the packet along.

Use the **debug ip nat** command to verify the operation of the NAT feature by displaying information about every packet that is translated by the router. The **debug ip nat** *detailed* command generates a description of each packet that is considered for translation. This command also outputs information about certain errors or exception conditions, such as the failure to allocate a global address.

Example 11-8 shows sample **debug ip nat** output for the network in Figure 11-13. In this example, the first two lines show the debugging output that a Domain Name System (DNS) request and reply produced. The remaining lines show the debugging output from a telnet connection from a host on the inside of the network to a host on the outside of the network.

Figure 11-13 Using NAT Debug Commands

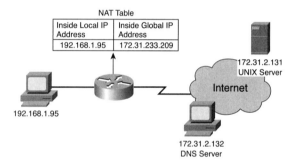

Example 11-7 debug ip nat *Output*

```
Router#debug ip nat

NAT: s=192.168.1.95->172.31.233.209, d=172.31.2.132 [6825]

NAT: s=172.31.2.132, d=172.31.233.209->192.168.1.95 [21852]

NAT: s=192.168.1.95->172.31.233.209, d=172.31.1.161 [6826]

NAT*: s=172.31.1.161, d=172.31.233.209->192.168.1.95 [23311]

NAT*: s=192.168.1.95->172.31.233.209, d=172.31.1.161 [6827]

NAT*: s=192.168.1.95->172.31.233.209, d=172.31.1.161 [6828]

NAT*: s=172.31.1.161, d=172.31.233.209->192.168.1.95 [23313]

NAT*: s=172.31.1.161, d=172.31.233.209->192.168.1.95 [23325]
```

Decode the **debug** output as follows:

- **NAT***—The asterisk (*) next to NAT indicates that the translation is occurring in the fast-switched path. The first packet in a conversation will always go through the slow path (that is, it will be process-switched). The remaining packets will go through the fast-switched path if a cache entry exists.

- **s = *a.b.c.d*—*a.b.c.d* is the source address.

- ***a.b.c.d -> w.x.y.z*—*w.x.y.z* is the address that the source was translated to.

- **d = *a.b.c.d*—*a.b.c.d* is the destination address.

- **[23325]**—The value in brackets is the IP identification number. This information can be useful for debugging because it enables correlation with other packet traces from protocol analyzers, for example.

Advantages and Disadvantages of NAT

NAT has several advantages, including the following:

- NAT conserves the legally registered addressing scheme by allowing the privatization of intranets.

- NAT increases the flexibility of connection to the public network. Multiple pools, backup pools, and load sharing/balancing pools can be implemented to help ensure reliable public network connections.

- Deprivatization of a network requires the renumbering of the existing network; the costs can be associated with the number of hosts that require conversion to the new addressing scheme. NAT allows the existing scheme to remain, and it still supports the new assigned addressing scheme outside the private network.

NAT is not without drawbacks. The tradeoff for address translation is a loss of functionality, particularly with any protocol or application that involves sending IP address information inside the IP payload. This requires additional support by the NAT box. NAT disadvantages include the following:

- NAT increases delay. Switching path delays, of course, are introduced because of the translation of each IP address within the packet headers. Performance might be a consideration because NAT is currently accomplished by using process switching. The CPU must look at every packet to decide whether it has to translate it, and then alter the IP header—and possibly the TCP header. It is unlikely that this process will be easily cacheable.

- One significant disadvantage when implementing and using NAT is the loss of end-to-end IP traceability. It becomes much more difficult to trace packets that undergo numerous packet address changes over multiple NAT hops. This scenario does, however, lead to more secure links because hackers who want to determine the source of a packet will find it difficult, if not impossible, to trace or obtain the original source or destination address.

- NAT also forces some applications that use IP addressing to stop functioning because it hides end-to-end IP addresses. Applications that use physical addresses instead of a qualified domain name will not reach destinations that are translated across the NAT router. Sometimes, this problem can be avoided by implementing static NAT mappings.

- NAT supports TCP/UDP traffic that does not carry source or destination IP addresses in the application data stream, such as HTTP, TFTP, and telnet.

Although the following traffic types carry IP addresses in the application data stream, these are some of the applications that Cisco IOS NAT supports:

- ICMP
- File Transfer Protocol (FTP) (including **PORT** and **PASV** commands)
- NetBIOS over TCP/IP (datagram, name, and session services)
- Progressive Networks' RealAudio
- White Pines' CuSeeMe
- Xing Technologies' Streamworks
- DNS "A" and "PTR" queries
- NetMeeting (2.1, 2.11, and 3.01)
- H.323v2 (H.225/245 message types except RAS - 12.1(5)T)
- VDOLive [11.3(4)/11.3(4)T and later]
- Vxtreme [11.3(4)/11.3(4)T and later]
- IP multicast [12.0(1)T] (source address translation only)

Cisco IOS NAT does *not* support these traffic types:

- Routing table updates
- DNS zone transfers
- BOOTP
- talk, ntalk
- Simple Network Management Protocol (SNMP)
- NetShow

DHCP Overview

Routers, servers, and other key nodes usually require a specific IP configuration. However, desktop clients do not require a specific address, but rather any one in a range of addresses. This range is typically within an IP subnet. A desktop client that is within a specific subnet can have any address within a range, while the other values are defaulted. These default values include the subnet mask, the default gateway, and the DNS server address for the subnet or network.

Configuring a host that is connected to a TCP/IP Internet requires several values:

- An IP address
- A subnet mask
- A default gateway
- A DNS server address

This list is the minimum; there might be other variables depending on the network environment. These variables generally have to be configured manually into every IP host. They are usually stored in a configuration file and accessed by the computer at startup.

In addition, some clients are diskless; the operating system and software are stored on ROM. The manufacturer of the ROM chip is unaware of the IP configuration values at production time; therefore, you cannot configure these values. The configuration must be supplied after booting. In these environments, you can allocate these IP values dynamically when an IP host boots. The DHCP was designed to do this particular task. Because desktop clients typically comprise the bulk of network nodes, DHCP is good news for systems administrators.

Introducing DHCP

DHCP, which works in a client/server mode, is used to enable hosts (DHCP clients) on an IP network to obtain their configurations from a server (DHCP server). This reduces the work necessary to administer an IP network. The most significant configuration option that the client receives from the server is its IP address. The DHCP protocol is described in RFC 2131.

The DHCP client is part of most modern operating systems including Windows 9x/NT/2000/XP, Solaris, Linux, and MAC OS. The client part requests the configuration values from the network. The network must have a DHCP server that manages the allocation of the IP configuration values and answers requests from clients. The DHCP server can be responsible for answering requests for many subnets. DHCP is not intended for use in configuring routers, switches, and servers because these hosts need to have static IP addresses.

DHCP works by configuring a server to give out IP information to clients. Clients lease the information from the server for an administratively defined period. When the lease is up, the host must ask for another address, although the host is typically reassigned the same one.

Administrators typically prefer to use a Microsoft NT/2000/XP server or a UNIX computer to offer DHCP services because these solutions are scalable and relatively easy to manage. Even so, a Cisco IOS feature set (Easy IP) offers an optional, fully featured DHCP server that a router can provide. It leases configurations for 24 hours by default. This feature is useful in small offices and home offices where they can take advantage of DHCP and NAT without requiring a computer-based server.

Administrators set up DHCP servers to assign addresses from predefined pools. DHCP servers can also offer other information, such as DNS server addresses, WINS server addresses, and domain names. In addition, most DHCP servers allow the administrator to define specifically what client MAC addresses can be serviced and automatically assign them the same IP address each time.

The DHCP client sends a directed IP broadcast, with a DHCP request packet. In the simplest case, a DHCP server is on the same segment, and it will pick up this request. Figures 11-14, 11-15, and 11-16 illustrate the DHCP request/reply process. The server notes that the GIADDR field is blank, so the client is on the same segment. The server notes the client's hardware address in the request packet, as shown in Figure 11-14.

Figure 11-14 DHCP Beginning Process

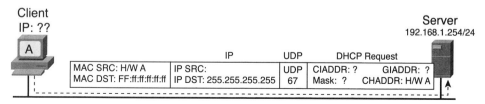

The DHCP server picks an IP address from the available pool for that segment, as well as the other segment and global parameters. The DHCP server then puts them into the appropriate fields of the DHCP packet. The server uses the hardware address of A (in CHADDR) to construct an appropriate frame to send back to the client, as shown in Figure 11-15.

Figure 11-15 DHCP Server Reply

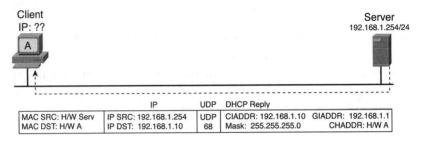

MAC SRC: H/W Serv	IP SRC: 192.168.1.254	UDP	CIADDR: 192.168.1.10	GIADDR: 192.168.1.1
MAC DST: H/W A	IP DST: 192.168.1.10	68	Mask: 255.255.255.0	CHADDR: H/W A

The DHCP client operating system uses the values in the DHCP reply to configure the IP protocol stack of that client, as shown in Figure 11-16.

Figure 11-16 DHCP Completed

DHCP uses UDP as its transport protocol. The client sends messages to the server on port 67, and the server sends messages to the client on port 68.

BOOTP and DHCP Differences

The Internet community first developed the *Bootstrap Protocol (BOOTP)* to configure diskless clients on a network. BOOTP was originally defined in RFC 951 in 1985. The predecessor of DHCP, BOOTP shares some operational characteristics. Both protocols are client/server based, using UDP ports 67 and 68, which are well known as BOOTP ports because BOOTP came before DHCP.

BOOTP provides the basic four IP parameters that have already been mentioned. However, BOOTP is not dynamic. When a client requests an IP address, the BOOTP server searches a predefined table for an entry that matches the client's MAC address. If an entry exists, then the corresponding IP address for that entry is returned to the client. This means that the binding between the MAC address and the IP address must have already been configured in the BOOTP server.

DHCP defines mechanisms through which clients can be assigned an IP address for a finite lease period, allowing for reassignment of the IP address to another client later, or for the client to get another assignment if the client moves to another subnet. Clients can renew leases and keep the same IP address.

DHCP provides the mechanism for a client to gather other IP configuration parameters (WINS, domain name) it needs to operate in the TCP/IP network.

Table 11-7 provides a summary of the differences between DHCP and BOOTP.

Table 11-7 DHCP and BOOTP

BOOTP	DHCP
Static mappings	Dynamic mappings
Permanent assignment	Lease assignment
Supports only four configuration parameters	Supports more than 30 configuration parameters
Used to send a bootable operating system to a host	Cannot be used to send a bootable operating system to a host

DHCP Features

Three mechanisms are used to assign an IP address to the client:

- **Automatic allocation**—DHCP assigns a permanent IP address to a client.
- **Manual allocation**—The administrator assigns the client's IP address, and DHCP conveys the address to the client.
- **Dynamic allocation**—DHCP assigns an IP address to the client for a limited period of time (lease).

The focus of this unit is the dynamic allocation mechanism. Some of the configuration parameters available are listed in IETF RFC 1533. A few of these parameters include the following:

- IP address
- Subnet mask
- Router (default gateway)
- Domain name
- Domain name server(s)
- Name server (such as WINS)

Refer to Figure 11-17. The DHCP server creates pools of IP addresses and associated parameters. Pools are dedicated to an individual logical IP subnet, which allows multiple DHCP servers to respond for a subnet; as such, IP clients can be mobile. If multiple servers can respond, a client can get several offers; however, a client can choose only one server. Example 11-9 shows the information the DHCP server sends this DHCP client.

Figure 11-17 DHCP Client and Server

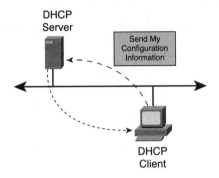

Example 11-9 *DHCP Configuration File*

```
IP Address: 192.204.18.7

Subnet Mask: 255.255.255.0

Default Routers: 192.204.18.1, 192.204.18.3

DNS Servers: 192.204.18.8, 192.204.18.9

Lease Time: 5 days
```

DHCP clients are available for a variety of operating systems and from numerous vendors, including Windows 3.1, Windows 9x, Windows NT, Windows 2000, Windows XP, Solaris, Linux, MAC OS, Novell NetWare, FTP Software, NetManage, and Cisco.

DHCP Operation

The DHCP client configuration process is shown in Figure 11-18.

Figure 11-18 DHCP Discovery Process

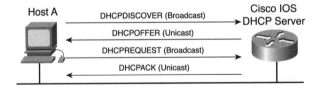

This process follows five steps:

1. **The client sends a DHCPDISCOVER broadcast to all nodes**—A client is preset for DHCP. The client sends a request for a server requesting an IP configuration (typically at boot time). Alternatively, the client can suggest the IP address it wants to use, such as when requesting an extension to a lease. The client tries to locate a DHCP server by sending a broadcast (255.255.255.255) called a DHCP-DISCOVER on its local segment.

2. **The server sends a DHCPOFFER unicast to the client**—When the server receives the broadcast, it determines whether it can service the request from its own database. If it cannot service the request, the server might forward the request to another DHCP server(s), depending on its configuration. If it can service the request, the DHCP server offers the client IP configuration information in the form of a unicast DHCPOFFER. The DHCPOFFER is a proposed configuration that might include IP address, DNS server address, and lease time.

3. **The client sends a DHCPREQUEST broadcast to all nodes**—If the client finds the offer agreeable, it will send another broadcast, a DHCPREQUEST, specifically requesting those particular IP parameters. Why does the client broadcast the request instead of unicasting it to the server? A broadcast is used because the first message, the DHCPDISCOVER, might have reached more than one DHCP server. If more than one server makes an offer, the broadcasted DHCPREQUEST lets everyone know which offer was accepted. The accepted offer is usually the first offer received.

4. **The server sends a DHCPACK unicast to the client**—The server that receives the DHCPREQUEST makes the configuration official by sending a unicast acknowledgment, the DHCPACK. Note that it is possible but highly unlikely that the server will not send the DHCPACK because it might have leased that information to another client in the interim. Receipt of the DHCPACK message enables the client to begin using the assigned address immediately.

   If the client detects that the address is already in use on the local segment, it sends a DHCPDECLINE message and the process starts again. If the client receives a DHCPNAK from the server after sending the DHCPREQUEST, it restarts the process.

5. **The client releases the IP address**—If the client no longer needs its IP address, the client sends a DHCPRELEASE message to the server. Depending on an organization's policies, it might be possible for an end user or an administrator to statically assign a host an IP address that belongs in the DHCP server's address pool. Just in case, the Cisco IOS DHCP server always checks to make sure that an address is not in use before the server offers it to a client. The server issues ICMP echo requests (ping) to a pool address before sending the DHCPOFFER to a cli-

ent. Although configurable, the default number of pings used to check for potential IP address conflict is two.

If the server is on another segment, you can use a BOOTP relay agent on the router to transport the request to that segment.

Configuring DHCP Operation

Like NAT, DHCP server requires that the administrator define a pool of addresses. The **ip dhcp** pool command defines which addresses are assigned to hosts. The command's syntax is as follows:

```
Router(config)#ip dhcp pool name1
Router(dhcp-config)#network ip-address mask
```

The first command, **ip dhcp pool** *name1*, creates a pool named *name1* and puts the router in a specialized DHCP configuration mode. In this mode, use the network statement to define the range of addresses to be leased. If specific addresses on the network are to be excluded, return to global configuration mode and use the **ip dhcp excluded-address** command. Type **exit** to get out of DHCP configuration mode.

The **ip dhcp excluded-address** command configures the router to exclude an individual address or a range of addresses when assigning addresses to clients. You can use this command to reserve addresses that are statically assigned to key hosts, such as the router's address. The command's syntax is as follows:

```
Router(config)#ip dhcp excluded-address ip-address [end-ip-address]
```

Typically, a DHCP server is configured to assign much more than an IP address. You can set other IP configuration values from the DHCP configuration mode. IP clients will not get far without a default gateway. You can set the gateway by using the **default-router** command. It is possible to configure the address of the DNS server (**dns-server**) and WINS server (**netbios-name-server**) here as well. The IOS DHCP server can configure clients with virtually any TCP/IP information.

A list of the key IOS DHCP server commands, which you enter in DHCP pool configuration mode, is shown in Table 11-8.

Table 11-8 DHCP Pool Commands

Command	Purpose
Router(config)# **ip dhcp pool** *name*	Creates a name for the DHCP server address pool and places you in DHCP pool configuration mode (identified by the config-dhcp# prompt).

Table 11-8 DHCP Pool Commands (Continued)

Command	Purpose
Router(config-dhcp)# **network** *network-number* [*mask* | */prefix-length*]	Specifies the subnet network number and mask of the DHCP address pool. The prefix length specifies the number of bits that comprise the address prefix. The prefix is an alternative way of specifying the network mask of the client. The prefix length must be preceded by a forward slash (/).
Router(config-dhcp)# **domain-name** *domain*	Specifies the domain name for the client.
Router(config-dhcp)# **dns-server** *address* [*address2 ... address8*]	Specifies the IP address of a DNS server that is available to a DHCP client. One IP address is required; however, you can specify up to eight IP addresses in one command line.
Router(config-dhcp)# **netbios-name-server** *address* [*address2 ... address8*]	Specifies the NetBIOS WINS server that is available to a Microsoft DHCP client. One address is required; however, you can specify up to eight addresses in one command line.
Router(config-dhcp)# **default-router** *address* [*address2 ... address8*]	Specifies the IP address of the default router for a DHCP client. One IP address is required, although you can specify up to eight addresses in one command line.
Router(config-dhcp)# **lease** {*days* [*hours*][*minutes*] | **infinite**}	Specifies the duration of the lease. The default is a one-day lease.

Although it is enabled by default on versions of the Cisco IOS that support it, the DHCP server process can be re-enabled by using the **service dhcp** global configuration command. The **no service dhcp** command disables the server.

Verifying DHCP Operation

Table 11-9 lists commands to display DHCP server information, while in EXEC mode, as needed.

Table 11-9 Commands to Display DHCP Server Information

Command	Purpose
Router> **show ip dhcp binding** [*address*]	Displays a list of all bindings created on a specific DHCP server.
Router> **show ip dhcp conflict** [*address*]	Displays a list of all address conflicts recorded by a specific DHCP server.
Router# **show ip dhcp database** [*url*]	Displays recent activity on the DHCP database. Use this command in privileged EXEC mode.
Router> **show ip dhcp server statistics**	Displays count information about server statistics and messages sent and received.

Troubleshooting DHCP Configuration

To enable DHCP server debugging, use the **debug ip dhcp server** privileged EXEC command. Table 11-10 lists commands to debug DHCP server information.

Table 11-10 *Commands to Debug a DHCP Server*

Command	Purpose
debug ip dhcp server events	Reports server events, such as address assignments and database updates.
debug ip dhcp server packets	Decodes DHCP receptions and transmissions.
debug ip dhcp server linkage	Displays database linkage information (such as parent-child relationships in a radix tree).

To troubleshoot the operation of the DHCP server, you can use the command **debug ip dhcp server events**, as shown in Example 11-10.

Example 11-10 *DHCP Debug Command*

```
Router#debug ip dhcp server events
Router#
00:22:53: DHCPD: checking for expired leases.
```

Example 11-10 *DHCP Debug Command (Continued)*

```
00:23:23: DHCPD: assigned IP address 172.16.13.11 to client 0100.10a4.97f4.6d.
00:27:49: DHCPD: returned 172.16.13.11 to address pool remote.
00:29:59: DHCPD: assigned IP address 172.16.13.11 to client 0100.10a4.97f4.6d.
```

This shows that periodically, the server checks to see if any leases have expired. Also, you can see when addresses are returned and when they are allocated.

DHCP Relay

DHCP clients use IP broadcasts to find the DHCP server on the segment, as seen earlier. What happens when the server and the client are not on the same segment and are separated by a router? Routers do not forward these broadcasts.

DHCP is not the only critical service that uses broadcasts. Cisco routers and other devices can use broadcasts to locate Trivial File Transfer Protocol (TFTP) servers. Some clients might need to broadcast to locate a Terminal Access Controller Access Control System (TACACS) server. Typically, in a complex hierarchical network, clients reside on the same subnet as key servers. Remote clients broadcast to locate these servers, but routers, by default, do not forward client broadcasts beyond their subnet.

Because some clients are useless without services such as DHCP, one of two choices must be implemented: to place servers on all subnets or to use the Cisco IOS helper address feature. Running services such as DHCP or DNS on several computers creates overhead and administrative headaches, so the first option is not very appealing. When possible, administrators use the **ip helper-address** command to relay broadcast requests for these key UDP services.

By using the helper address feature, a router can be configured to accept a broadcast request for a UDP service and then forward it as a unicast to a specific IP address. By default, the **ip helper-address** command forwards the eight UDP services:

- Time
- TACACS
- DNS
- BOOTP/DHCP Server
- BOOTP/DHCP Client
- TFTP
- NetBIOS Name Service
- NetBIOS Datagram Service

In the particular case of DHCP, a client broadcasts a DHCP discover packet on its local segment. Figure 11-19 shows what the DHCP message format looks like. The gateway picks up this packet, and if a helper address is configured, the DHCP packet is forwarded to the specified address.

Figure 11-19 DHCP Message Format

OP Code	Hardware Type	Hardware Length	HOPS
Transaction ID (XID)			
Seconds		Flags	
Client IP Address (CIADDR)			
Your IP Address (YIADDR)			
Server IP (SIADDR)			
Gateway IP (GIADDR)			
Client Hardware Address (CHADDR)—16 Bytes			
Server Name (SNAME)—64 Bytes			
Filename—128 Bytes			
DHCP Options			

Before forwarding the packet, the router fills in the GIADDR field of the packet with the router's IP address for the segment. This address will be the gateway address for the DHCP client when it gets the IP address, as shown in Figure 11-20.

Figure 11-20 DHCP Client Gets an IP Address

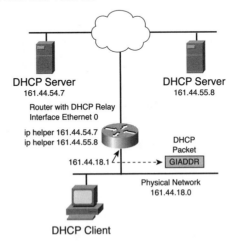

The DHCP server receives the discover packet and uses the GIADDR field to index in to the list of address pools; it is looking for a pool that has the gateway address set to the value in GIADDR. This pool is then used to supply the client with its IP address. Figure 11-21 shows a DHCP client broadcast, and Figure 11-22 shows a DHCP server unicast.

Figure 11-21 DHCP Client Broadcast

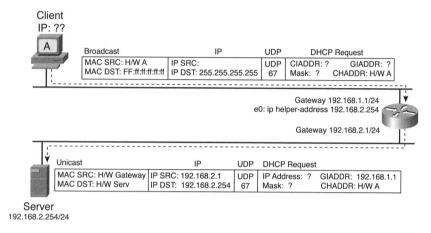

Figure 11-22 DHCP Server Unicast

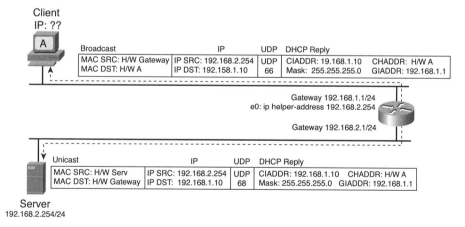

 Lab Activity   Configuring DHCP

In this lab, you will configure a router to act as a DHCP server for two different subnets: one local to the server and the other remote.

Summary

This chapter covered the following:

- As the Internet becomes larger, so does the number of IP routes in the backbone Internet routing tables. This poses a scalability problem for routing algorithms. Three solutions to the scaling problem of IP were presented.

- RFC 1918 provides background on the allocation of IP addresses for private Internets. It also provides implementation guidelines for companies that want to implement IP but do not want full connectivity to the Internet.

- NAT allows for translating private addresses into publicly usable addresses to be used within the Internet. Examples of NAT configuration and verification were shown.

- PAT allows a group of inside hosts to communicate to outside hosts and share the overloaded address in a NAT configuration. Examples of PAT configuration and verification were shown.

- DHCP provides a mechanism for allocating IP addresses dynamically so that addresses can automatically be reused when hosts no longer need them. Examples of configuration and troubleshooting were shown.

Key Terms

Bootstrap Protocol (BOOTP)   Originally defined in RFC 951 in 1985. BOOTP is the predecessor of DHCP, and it shares some operational characteristics. Both protocols use UDP ports 67 and 68, which are well known as "BOOTP ports" because BOOTP came before DHCP.

classless interdomain routing (CIDR)   Allows routers to group routes together to reduce the quantity of routing information carried by the core routers. With CIDR, several IP networks appear to networks outside the group as a single, larger entity.

Dynamic Host Configuration Protocol (DHCP)   Provides a mechanism for allocating IP addresses dynamically so that addresses can be reused automatically when hosts no longer need them.

inside global address   In a NAT configuration, the IP address that the inside local address gets translated to.

inside local address   In a NAT configuration, the IP address that is translated.

network address translation (NAT)   Only globally unique in terms of the public internet. A mechanism for translating private addresses into publicly usable addresses to be used within the public Internet. An effective means for hiding actual device addressing within a private network.

outside global address   The IP address of an outside host as it is known to the hosts in the inside network.

outside local address   The IP address that the host's owner assigns to a host on the outside network.

overloading (also known as PAT)   Uses TCP port numbers to allow a group of inside hosts to communicate to outside hosts and "share" the overloaded address in a NAT configuration.

Check Your Understanding

1. Private addresses are assigned by what?
   A. The network administrator from RFC 1918.
   B. ARIN.
   C. RIPE.
   D. Any address can be a private address.

2. Which of the following are valid RFC 1918 private addresses?

   A. 10.0.0.0/7

   B. 10.0.0.0/8

   C. 192.168.0.0/16

   D. 172.16.0.0/12

3. The BOX Company maintains its own public web server, and it is about to implement NAT. Which type of NAT will be used for the web server?

   A. Dynamic

   B. Static

   C. PAT

   D. No NAT at all

4. Which of the following applications does Cisco IOS NAT support?

   A. ICMP

   B. DNS zone transfers

   C. BOOTP

   D. FTP (including **PORT** and **PASV** commands

5. Which of the following traffic types does Cisco IOS NAT *not* support?

   A. ICMP

   B. DNS zone transfers

   C. BOOTP

   D. FTP (including PORT and PASV)

6. BOOTP supports _____ , whereas DHCP supports
   _____.

   A. Static mappings

   B. Dynamic mappings

   C. PAT

   D. NAT

7. Place the following DHCP messages in the correct order as they appear in the process.

   A. DHCPACK

   B. DHCPREQUEST

   C. DHCPOFFER

   D. DHCPDISCOVER

8. What does DHCP stand for?

   A. Dynamic Host Configuration Protocol

   B. Dynamic Hosting Configuration Protocol

   C. Dynamic Host Computer Protocol

   D. Dynamic Host Computer Port

9. NAT conserves the legally registered addressing scheme by allowing the privatization of intranets.

   A. True

   B. False

10. DHCP is not intended for use in configuring routers, switches, and servers because these hosts need to have static IP addresses.

    A. True

    B. False

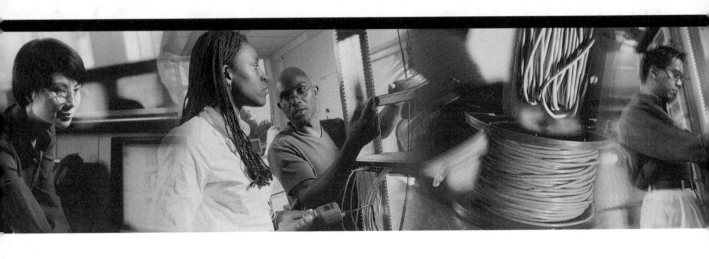

Scaling IP Addresses

The following table maps the numbering scheme used in this chapter's labs to the Target Identifiers (TIs) used in the online curriculum.

Lab Companion Numbering	Online Curriculum TI
Lab 11-1	1.1.4.1
Lab 11-2	1.1.4.2
Lab 11-3	1.1.4.3
Lab 11-4	1.1.5
Lab 11-5	1.1.6
Lab 11-6	1.2.5
Lab 11-7	1.2.8

Lab 11-1: Configuring NAT

Figure 11-1.1 Topology for Lab 11-1

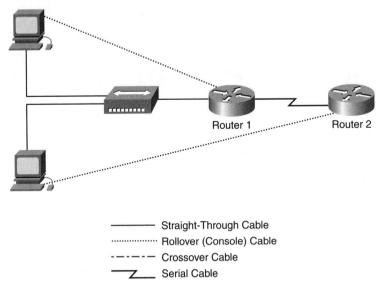

—————— Straight-Through Cable

················ Rollover (Console) Cable

— — — — — Crossover Cable

⌇ Serial Cable

Table 11-1.1 Lab Equipment Configuration

Router Desig-nation	Router Name	FastEthernet 0 Address/ Subnet Mask	Interface Type	Serial 0 Address	Loopback 0 Address/ Subnet Mask
Router 1	Gateway	10.10.10.1/24	DCE	200.2.2.18/28	NA
Router 2	ISP	NA	DTE	200.2.2.17/28	172.16.1.1/24

Enable secret password is **class** for both routers.
Enable, VTY, and Console password is **cisco** for both routers.

Objective

- Configure a router to use network address translation (NAT) to convert internal IP addresses, typically private addresses, into outside public addresses.

Background / Preparation

The ISP has allocated a company the public CIDR IP address 199.99.9.32/27. This is equivalent to 30 public IP addresses. Because the company has an internal requirement for more than 30 addresses, the IT manager has decided to implement NAT.

They have decided to reserve the addresses 199.99.9.33 to 199.99.9.39 for static allocation and 199.99.9.40 to 199.99.9.62 for dynamic allocation. Routing between the ISP and the company's gateway router is done using a static route between the ISP and gateway and a default route between the gateway and ISP. The ISP's connection to the Internet is represented by a loopback address on the ISP router.

Cable a network similar to the one in Figure 11-1.1. You can use any router that meets the interface requirements displayed in the diagram (that is, 800, 1600, 1700, 2500 and 2600 routers or a combination). Please refer to the information in Appendix D, "Router Interface Summary Chart," to correctly specify the interface identifiers to be used based on the equipment in your lab. The configuration output used in this lab is produced from 1721 series routers. Any other router used may produce slightly different output. The following steps are intended to be executed on each router unless specifically instructed otherwise.

Start a HyperTerminal session as performed in the "Establishing a HyperTerminal" session lab.

Please refer to and implement the procedure documented in Appendix C, "Erasing and Reloading the Switch," before continuing with this lab.

Step 1   Configure the routers.

Configure the hostname, console, virtual terminal, and enable passwords and the interfaces according to the chart. If you have trouble doing this, refer to the Configuration Reference Sheet at the end of this lab.

Step 2   Save the configuration.

At the privileged EXEC mode prompt, on both routers, type the command **copy running-config startup-config**.

Step 3   Configure the hosts with the proper IP address, subnet mask, and default gateway.

Each workstation should be able to ping the attached router. Troubleshoot as necessary. Hint: Remember to assign a specific IP address and default gateway to the workstation? If running Windows 98, check using **Start>Run>winipcfg**. If running Windows 2000 or later, check using **ipconfig** in a DOS window.

Step 4   Verify that the network is functioning.

A. From the attached hosts, **ping** the fastethernet interface of the default gateway router.

B. Was the ping from the first host successful? _____

C. Was the ping from the second host successful? _____

D. If the answer is no for either question, troubleshoot the router and host configurations to find the error. Then **ping** again until they are successful.

Step 5   Create a static route.

A. Create a static route from the ISP to the gateway router. Addresses 199.99.9.32/27 have been allocated for Internet access outside of the company. Use the **ip route** command to create the static route.

```
ISP(config)#ip route 199.99.9.32 255.255.224.0 200.2.2.18
```

B. Is the static route in the routing table? _____

C. What command checks the routing table contents?

_____

D. If the route was not in the routing table, give one reason why this might be so?_____

Step 6   Create a default route.

A. Add a default route, using the **ip route** command, from the gateway router to the ISP router. This will forward any unknown destination address traffic to the ISP.

```
Gateway(config)#ip route 0.0.0.0 0.0.0.0 200.2.2.17
```

B. Is the static route in the routing table?_____

C. Try to **ping** from one of the workstations to the ISP serial interface IP address.

D. Was the ping successful? _____

E. Why? _____

Step 7   Define the pool of usable public IP addresses.

To define the pool of public addresses, use the **ip nat pool** command.

```
Gateway(config)#ip nat pool public_access 199.99.9.40 199.99.9.62
netmask 255.255.255.224
```

Step 8   Define an access list that will match the inside private IP addresses.

To define the access list to match the inside private addresses, use the **access-list** command.

```
Gateway(config)#access-list 1 permit 10.10.10.0 0.0.0.255
```

Step 9   Define the NAT translation from inside list to outside pool.

To define the NAT translation, use the **ip nat inside source** command.

```
Gateway(config)#ip nat inside source list 1 pool public_access
```

Step 10   Specify the interfaces.

On the active interfaces on the router, it needs to be specified if they are inside or outside interfaces with respect to NAT. To do this, use the **ip nat inside or ip nat outside** command.

```
Gateway(config)#interface fastethernet 0
Gateway(config-if)#ip nat inside
Gateway(config-if)#interface serial 0
Gateway(config-if)#ip nat outside
```

Step 11   Test the configuration.

A. Configure a workstation on the internal LAN with the IP address 10.10.10.10/24 and a default gateway 10.10.10.1. From the PC, **ping** 172.16.1.1. If successful, look at the NAT translation on the gateway router, using the command **show ip nat translations**.

B. What is the translation of the inside local host addresses?

_____ = _____ = _____

C. The inside global address is assigned by? _____

D. The inside local address is assigned by?_____

Upon completion of the previous steps, logoff (by typing **exit**) and turn the router off. Then remove and store the cables and adapter.

Configuration Reference Sheet for This Lab

This sheet contains the basic configuration commands for the ISP and gateway routers.

```
ISP
Router#configure terminal
Router(config)#hostname ISP
ISP(config)#enable password cisco
ISP(config)#enable secret class
ISP(config)#line console 0
ISP(config-line)#password cisco
ISP(config-line)#login
ISP(config-line)#exit
ISP(config)#line vty 0 4
ISP(config-line)#password cisco
ISP(config-line)#login
ISP(config-line)#exit
ISP(config)#interface loopback 0
ISP(config-if)#ip add 172.16.1.1 255.255.255.255
ISP(config-if)#no shutdown
ISP(config-if)#exit
```

```
ISP(config)#interface serial 0
ISP(config-if)#ip add 200.2.2.17 255.255.255.252
ISP(config-if)#no shutdown
ISP(config-if)#clockrate 64000
ISP(config)#ip route 199.99.9.32 255.255.255.224 200.2.2.18
ISP(config)#end
ISP#copy running-config startup-config
Destination filename [startup-config]?[Enter]
```

Gateway
```
Router#configure terminal
Router(config)#hostname Gateway
Gateway(config)#enable password cisco
Gateway(config)#enable secret class
Gateway(config)#line console 0
Gateway(config-line)#password cisco
Gateway(config-line)#login
Gateway(config-line)#exit
Gateway(config)#line vty 0 4
Gateway(config-line)#password cisco
Gateway(config-line)#login
Gateway(config-line)#exit
Gateway(config)#interface loopback 0
Gateway(config-if)#ip add 172.16.1.1 255.255.255.0
Gateway(config-if)#no shutdown
Gateway(config-if)#exit
Gateway(config)#interface serial 0
Gateway(config-if)#ip add 200.200.200.17 255.255.255.252
Gateway(config-if)#no shutdown

Gateway(config)#ip route 0.0.0.0 0.0.0.0 200.2.2.17
```

Lab 11-2: Configuring PAT

Figure 11-2.1 Topology for Lab 11-2

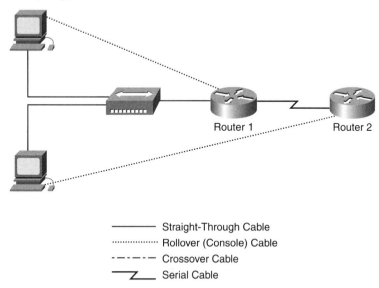

—————— Straight-Through Cable
················ Rollover (Console) Cable
– – – – – Crossover Cable
—⊻— Serial Cable

Table 11-2.1 Lab Equipment Configuration

Router Designation	Router Name	FastEthernet 0 Address/ Subnet Mask	Interface Type	Serial 0 Address	Loopback 0 Address/Subnet Mask
Router 1	Gateway	10.10.10.1/24	DCE	200.2.2.18/28	NA
Router 2	ISP	NA	DTE	200.2.2.17/28	172.16.1.1/24

Enable secret password is **class** for both routers.
Enable, VTY, and Console password is **cisco** for both routers.

Objective

- Configure a router to use Port Address Translation (PAT) to convert internal IP addresses, typically private addresses, into an outside public address.

Background / Preparation

Aidan McDonald has just received a DSL line Internet connection in his home to a local ISP. The ISP has allocated only one IP address to be used on the serial port of his remote access device. Routing between the ISP and the home router is done using a static route between the ISP and gateway routers, and a default route between the gateway and ISP routers. The ISP connection to the Internet will be represented by a loopback address on the ISP router.

Cable a network similar to the one in Figure 11-2.1. You can use any router that meets the interface requirements displayed in the diagram (that is, 800, 1600, 1700, 2500 and 2600 routers or a combination). Please refer to the information in Appendix D, "Router Interface Summary Chart," to correctly specify the interface identifiers to be used based on the equipment in your lab. The configuration output used in this lab is produced from 1721 series routers. Other routers may produce slightly different output. The following steps are intended to be executed on each router unless specifically instructed otherwise.

Start a HyperTerminal session.

Please refer to and implement the procedure documented in Appendix B, "Erasing and Reloading the Router," before continuing with this lab.

Step 1 Configure the routers.

Configure the hostname, console, virtual terminal, and enable passwords and the interfaces according to the chart. If you have trouble doing this, refer to Lab 11-1 in Chapter 11.

Step 2 Save the configurations.

At the privileged EXEC mode prompt on both routers, type the command **copy running-config startup-config**.

Step 3 Configure the hosts with the proper IP address, subnet mask, and default gateway.

Each workstation should be able to ping the attached router. Troubleshoot as necessary. Hint: Remember to assign a specific IP address and default gateway to the workstation? If running Windows 98, check using **Start>Run>winipcfg**. If running Windows 2000 or later, check using **ipconfig** in a DOS window.

Step 4 Verify that the network is functioning.

A. From the attached hosts, **ping** the fastethernet interface of the default gateway router.

    B. Was the ping from the first host successful? _____

    C. Was the ping from the second host successful? _____

    D. If the answer is no for either question, troubleshoot the router and host configurations to find the error. Then **ping** again until they are successful.

Step 5   Create a default route.

    A. Add a default route from the gateway to the ISP router. This will forward any unknown destination address traffic to the ISP. Use the **ip route** command to create the default route.

```
Gateway(config)#ip route 0.0.0.0 0.0.0.0 200.2.2.17
```

    B. Is the route in the routing table?_____

    C. Try to **ping** from one of the workstations to the ISP serial interface IP address.

    D. Was the ping successful?_____

    E. Why? _____

    F. What command checks the routing table contents?

    _____

Step 6   Define an access list that will match the inside private IP addresses.

    To define the access list to match the inside private addresses, use the **access-list** command.

```
Gateway(config)#access-list 1 permit 10.10.10.0 0.0.0.255
```

Step 7   Define the PAT translation from inside list to outside address.

    To define the PAT translation, use the **ip nat inside source** command. This command with the **overload** option will create port address translation using the serial 0 IP address as the base.

```
Gateway(config)#ip nat inside source list 1 interface serial 0 overload
```

Step 8   Specify the interfaces.

    On the active interfaces on the router, it needs to be specified if they are inside or outside interfaces with respect to PAT(NAT). To do this, use the **ip nat inside** or **ip nat outside** command.

```
Gateway(config)#interface fastethernet 0
Gateway(config-if)#ip nat inside
Gateway(config-if)#interface serial 0
Gateway(config-if)#ip nat outside
```

Step 9 Test the configuration.

A. Configure a PC on the internal LAN with the IP address 10.10.10.10/24 and a default gateway 10.10.10.1. From the PCs, **ping** the Internet address 172.16.1.1. If successful, telnet to the same IP address. Then look at the PAT translation on the gateway router, using the command **show ip nat translations**.

B. What is the translation of the inside local host addresses?

_____ = _____ = _____

C. What does the number after the colon represent?

_____

D. Why do all of the commands for PAT say NAT?

_____

Upon completion of the previous steps, logoff (by typing **exit**) and turn the router off. Then remove and store the cables and adapter.

Configuration Reference Sheet for This Lab

This sheet contains the basic configuration commands for the ISP and gateway routers.

```
ISP
Router#configure terminal
Router(config)#hostname ISP
ISP(config)#enable password cisco
ISP(config)#enable secret class
ISP(config)#line console 0
ISP(config-line)#password cisco
ISP(config-line)#login
ISP(config-line)#exit
ISP(config)#line vty 0 4
ISP(config-line)#password cisco
ISP(config-line)#login
ISP(config-line)#exit
ISP(config)#interface loopback 0
ISP(config-if)#ip address 172.16.1.1 255.255.255.255
ISP(config-if)#no shutdown
ISP(config-if)#exit
ISP(config)#interface serial 0
ISP(config-if)#ip address 200.2.2.17 255.255.255.252
ISP(config-if)#no shutdown
ISP(config-if)#clockrate 64000
ISP(config)#ip route 199.99.9.32 255.255.255.224 200.2.2.18
ISP(config)#end
ISP#copy running-config startup-config
```

```
Gateway
Router#configure terminal
Router(config)#hostname Gateway
Gateway(config)#enable password cisco
Gateway(config)#enable secret class
Gateway(config)#line console 0
Gateway(config-line)#password cisco
Gateway(config-line)#login
Gateway(config-line)#exit
Gateway(config)#line vty 0 4
Gateway(config-line)#password cisco
Gateway(config-line)#login
Gateway(config-line)#exit
Gateway(config)#interface loopback 0
Gateway(config-if)#ip address 172.16.1.1 255.255.255.0
Gateway(config-if)#no shutdown
Gateway(config-if)#exit
Gateway(config)#interface serial 0
Gateway(config-if)#ip address 200.200.200.17 255.255.255.252
Gateway(config-if)#no shutdown
Gateway(config)#ip route 0.0.0.0 0.0.0.0 200.2.2.17
```

Lab 11-3: Configuring Static NAT Addresses

Figure 11-3.1 Topology for Lab 11-3

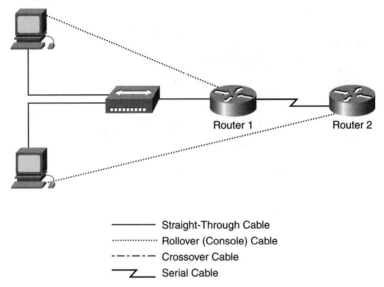

——————— Straight-Through Cable

···················· Rollover (Console) Cable

– – – – – Crossover Cable

Serial Cable

Table 11-3.1 Lab Equipment Configuration

Router Designation	Router Name	FastEthernet 0 Address/ Subnet Mask	Interface Type	Serial 0 Address	Loopback 0 Address/ Subnet Mask
Router 1	Gateway	10.10.10.1/24	DCE	200.2.2.18/28	NA
Router 2	ISP	NA	DTE	200.2.2.17/28	172.16.1.1/24

Enable secret password is **class** for both routers.
Enable, VTY, and Console password is **cisco** for both routers.

Objectives

- Configure a router to use network address translation (NAT) to convert internal IP addresses, typically private addresses, into outside public addresses.
- Configure static IP mapping to allow outside access to an internal PC.

Background / Preparation

The ISP has allocated a company the public CIDR IP address 199.99.9.32/27. This is equivalent to 30 public IP addresses. Because the company has an internal requirement for more than 30 addresses, the IT manager has decided to use NAT. They have decided to reserve the addresses 199.99.9.33 to 199.99.9.39 for static allocation and 199.99.9.40 to 199.99.9.62 for dynamic allocation. Routing between the ISP and the gateway router is done using a static route between the ISP and the gateway, and a default route between the gateway and the ISP. The ISP connection to the Internet is represented by a loopback address on the ISP router.

Cable a network similar to the one in Figure 11-3.1. You can use any router that meets the interface requirements displayed in the diagram (that is, 800, 1600, 1700, 2500, and 2600 routers or a combination). Please refer to the information in Appendix D, "Router Interface Summary Chart," to correctly specify the interface identifiers to be used based on the equipment in your lab. The configuration output used in this lab is produced from 1721 series routers. Any other router used may produce slightly different output. The following steps are intended to be executed on each router unless specifically instructed otherwise.

Start a HyperTerminal session.

Please refer to and implement the procedure documented in Appendix B, "Erasing and Reloading the Router," before continuing with this lab.

Step 1   Configure the routers.

Configure the hostname, console, virtual terminal, and enable passwords and the interfaces according to the chart. If you have trouble doing this, refer to the configuration reference sheet at the end of this lab.

Step 2   Save the configurations.

At the privileged EXEC mode prompt on both routers, type the command **copy running-config startup-config**.

Step 3   Configure the hosts with the proper IP address, subnet mask, and default gateway.

Each workstation should be able to ping the attached router. Troubleshoot as necessary. Hint: Remember to assign a specific IP address and default gateway to the workstation? If running Windows 98, check using **Start>Run>winipcfg**. If running Windows 2000 or later, check using **ipconfig** in a DOS window.

Step 4   Verify that the network is functioning.

A.   From the attached hosts, **ping** the fastethernet interface of the default gateway router.

B.   Was the ping from the first host successful? _____

C. Was the ping from the second host successful? _____

D. If the answer is no for either question, troubleshoot the router and host configurations to find the error. Then **ping** again until they are successful.

Step 5   Create a static route.

A. Create a static route from the ISP to the gateway router. Addresses 199.99.9.32/27 have been allocated for Internet access outside of the company. Use the **ip route** command to create the static route.

```
ISP(config)#ip route 199.99.9.32 255.255.255.224 200.2.2.18
```

B. Is the static route in the routing table? _____

C. What command checks the routing table contents?

_____

D. If the route was not in the routing table, give one reason why this might be so?_____

Step 6   Create a default route.

A. Add a default route, using the **ip route** command, from the gateway router to the ISP router. This will forward any unknown destination address traffic to the ISP.

```
Gateway(config)#ip route 0.0.0.0 0.0.0.0 200.2.2.17
```

B. Is the route in the routing table?

_____

C. Try to **ping** from one of the workstations to the ISP serial interface IP address.

D. Was the ping successful? _____

E. Why? _____

Step 7   Define the pool of usable public IP addresses.

To define the pool of public addresses, use the **ip nat pool** command.

```
Gateway(config)#ip nat pool public_access 199.99.9.40 199.99.9.62
   netmask 255.255.255.224
```

Step 8   Define an access list that will match the inside private IP addresses.

To define the access list to match the inside private addresses, use the **access-list** command.

```
Gateway(config)#access-list 1 permit 10.10.10.0 0.0.0.255
```

Step 9   Define the NAT translation from inside list to outside pool.

To define the NAT translation, use the **ip nat inside source** command.

```
Gateway(config)#ip nat inside source list 1 pool public_access
```

Step 10 Specify the interfaces.

The active interfaces on the router, need to be identified if they are inside or outside interfaces with respect to NAT. To do this, use the **ip nat inside** or **ip nat outside** command.

Step 11 Configuring static mapping.

A. It has been decided to use workstation #1, 10.10.10.10/24, as the public WWW server. Thus, it needs a permanent public IP address. Define this mapping using a static NAT mapping.

B. Configure one of the PCs on the LAN with the IP address 10.10.10.10/24 and a default gateway 10.10.10.1. To configure a static IP NAT mapping, use the **ip nat inside source static** command at the privileged EXEC mode prompt.

```
Gateway(config)#ip nat inside source static 10.10.10.10 199.99.9.33
```

This permanently maps 199.99.9.33 to the inside address 10.10.10.10.

C. Look at the translation table:

```
Gateway#show ip nat translations
```

D. Does the mapping show up in the output of the **show** command?

_____

Step 12 Test the configuration.

A. From the 10.10.10.10 workstation, verify it can ping 172.16.1.1

B. Is the ping successful? _____

C. Why? _____

D. From the ISP router ping the host with the static NAT translation, by typing **ping 10.10.10.10**.

E. What were the results of the ping, was it successful?

_____

F. Why? _____

G. From the ISP router, ping 199.99.9.32. If successful, look at the NAT translation on the Gateway router, using the command **show ip nat translations**.

H. What is the translation of the inside local host addresses?

_____ = _____ = _____

Upon completion of the previous steps, logoff (by typing **exit**) and turn the router off. Then remove and store the cables and adapter.

Now the router is ready for the assigned lab to be performed.

Lab 11-4: Verifying NAT and PAT Configuration

Figure 11-4.1 Topology for Lab 11-4

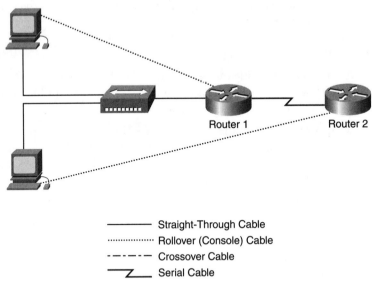

Straight-Through Cable
Rollover (Console) Cable
Crossover Cable
Serial Cable

Table 11-4.1 Lab Equipment Configuration

Router Designation	Router Name	FastEthernet 0 Address/ Subnet Mask	Interface Type	Serial 0 Address	Loopback 0 Address/ Subnet Mask
Router 1	Gateway	10.10.10.1/24	DCE	200.2.2.18/28	NA
Router 2	ISP	NA	DTE	200.2.2.17/28	172.16.1.1/24

Enable secret password is **class** for both routers.
Enable, VTY, and Console password is **cisco** for both routers.

Objectives

- Configure a router for Network Address Translation and Port Address Translation
- Test the configuration and verify NAT/PAT statistics

Background / Preparation

The ISP has allocated a company the public CIDR IP address 199.99.9.32/30. This is equivalent to four public IP addresses. Because the company has an internal requirement for more than 30 addresses, the IT manager has decided to use NAT with PAT. Routing between the ISP and the gateway router is done using a static route between the ISP and the gateway and a default route between the gateway and the ISP. The ISP connection to the internet will be represented by a loopback address on the ISP router.

Cable a network similar to the one in Figure 11-4.1. You can use any router that meets the interface requirements displayed in the diagram (that is, 800, 1600, 1700, 2500, and 2600 routers or a combination). Please refer to the information in Appendix D, "Router Interface Summary Chart," to correctly specify the interface identifiers to be used based on the equipment in your lab. The configuration output used in this lab is produced from 1721 series routers. Any other router used may produce slightly different output. The following steps are intended to be executed on each router unless specifically instructed otherwise.

Start a HyperTerminal session.

Please refer to and implement the procedure documented in Appendix B, "Erasing and Reloading the Router," before continuing with this lab.

Step 1 Configure the routers.

Configure the hostname, console, virtual terminal and enable passwords and the interfaces according to the chart. If there is trouble doing this, refer to the NAT configuration lab.

Step 2 Save the configurations.

At the privileged EXEC mode prompt on both routers, type the command **copy running-config startup-config**.

Step 3 Configure the hosts with the proper IP address, subnet mask, and default gateway.

Each workstation should be able to ping the attached router. Troubleshoot as necessary. Hint: Remember to assign a specific IP address and default gateway to the workstation. If running Windows 98, check using **Start>Run>winipcfg**. If running Windows 2000 or later, check using **ipconfig** in a DOS window.

Step 4 Verify that the network is functioning.

A. From the attached hosts, **ping** the last ethernet interface of the default gateway router.

B. Was the ping from the first host successful? _____

C. Was the ping from the second host successful? _____

D. If the answer is no for either question, troubleshoot the router and host configurations to find the error. Then **ping** again until they are successful.

Step 5 Create a static route.

  A. Create a static route from the ISP to the gateway router. Addresses 199.99.9.32/27 have been allocated for Internet access outside of the company. Use the **ip route** command to create the static route.

  ```
  ISP(config)#ip route 199.99.9.32 255.255.255.252 200.2.2.18
  ```

  B. Is the static route in the routing table? _____

  C. What command checks the routing table contents?

  _____

  D. If the route was not in the routing table, give one reason why this might be so?_____

Step 6 Create a default route.

  A. Add a default route, using the **ip route** command, from the gateway router to the ISP router. This will forward any unknown destination address traffic to the ISP.

  ```
  Gateway(config)#ip route 0.0.0.0 0.0.0.0 200.2.2.17
  ```

  B. Is the route in the routing table? _____

  C. Try to **ping** from one of the workstations to the ISP serial interface IP address.

  D. Was the ping successful? _____

  E. Why?_____

Step 7 Define the pool of usable public IP addresses.

  To define the pool of public addresses, use the **ip nat pool** command.

  ```
  Gateway(config)#ip nat pool public_access 199.99.9.32 199.99.9.35
  netmask 255.255.255.252
  ```

Step 8 Define an access list that will match the inside private IP addresses.

  To define the access list to match the inside private addresses, use the **access-list** command.

  ```
  Gateway(config)#access-list 1 permit 10.10.10.0 0.0.0.255
  ```

Step 9 Define the NAT translation from inside list to outside pool.

  To define the NAT translation, use the **ip nat inside source** command.

  ```
  Gateway(config)#ip nat inside source list 1 pool public_access overload
  ```

Step 10 Specify the interfaces.

The active interfaces on the router, need to be identified if they are inside or outside interfaces with respect to NAT. To do this, use the **ip nat inside** or **ip nat outside** command.

```
Gateway(config)#interface fastethernet 0
Gateway(config-if)#ip nat inside
Gateway(config-if)#interface serial 0
Gateway(config-if)#ip nat outside
```

Step 11 Test the configuration.

A. From the workstations, **ping 172.16.1.1**. Open multiple DOS windows on each workstation and telnet to the 172.16.1.1 address. Next, view the NAT translations on the gateway router, with the command **show ip nat translations**.

B. What is the translation of the inside local host addresses?

_____ = _____ = _____

Step 12 Verify NAT/PAT statistics.

A. To view the NAT and PAT statistics type the **show ip nat statistics** command at the privileged EXEC mode prompt.

B. How many active translations have taken place?

_____

C. How many addresses are in the pool?

_____

D. How many addresses have been allocated so far?

_____

Upon completion of the previous steps, logoff (by typing **exit**) and turn the router off. Then remove and store the cables and adapter.

Configuration Reference Sheet for This Lab

This sheet contains the basic configuration commands for the ISP and gateway routers.

```
ISP
Router#configure terminal
Router(config)#hostname ISP
ISP(config)#enable password cisco
ISP(config)#enable secret class
ISP(config)#line console 0
ISP(config-line)#password cisco
ISP(config-line)#login
ISP(config-line)#exit
ISP(config)#line vty 0 4
ISP(config-line)#password cisco
ISP(config-line)#login
```

```
ISP(config-line)#exit
ISP(config)#interface loopback 0
ISP(config-if)#ip address 172.16.1.1 255.255.255.255
ISP(config-if)#no shutdown
ISP(config-if)#exit
ISP(config)#interface serial 0
ISP(config-if)#ip address 200.2.2.17 255.255.255.252
ISP(config-if)#no shutdown
ISP(config-if)#clockrate 64000
ISP(config)#ip route 199.99.9.32 255.255.255.224 200.2.2.18
ISP(config)#end
ISP#copy running-config startup-config


Gateway
Router#configure terminal
Router(config)#hostname Gateway
Gateway(config)#enable password cisco
Gateway(config)#enable secret class
Gateway(config)#line console 0
Gateway(config-line)#password cisco
Gateway(config-line)#login
Gateway(config-line)#exit
Gateway(config)#line vty 0 4
Gateway(config-line)#password cisco
Gateway(config-line)#login
Gateway(config-line)#exit
Gateway(config)#interface loopback 0
Gateway(config-if)#ip address 172.16.1.1 255.255.255.0
Gateway(config-if)#no shutdown
Gateway(config-if)#exit
Gateway(config)#interface serial 0
Gateway(config-if)#ip address 200.200.200.17 255.255.255.252
Gateway(config-if)#no shutdown
Gateway(config)#ip route 0.0.0.0 0.0.0.0 200.2.2.17
```

Lab 11-5: Troubleshooting NAT and PAT

Figure 11-5.1   Topology for Lab 11-5

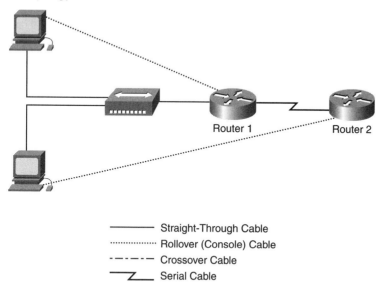

```
──────── Straight-Through Cable
············· Rollover (Console) Cable
─ ─ ─ ─ Crossover Cable
───z─── Serial Cable
```

Table 11-5/1   Lab Equipment Configuration

Router Designation	Router Name	FastEthernet 0 Address/ Subnet Mask	Interface Type	Serial 0 Address	Loopback 0 Address/ Subnet Mask
Router 1	Gateway	10.10.10.1/24	DCE	200.2.2.18/28	NA
Router 2	ISP	NA	DTE	200.2.2.17/28	172.16.1.1/24

Enable secret password is **class** for both routers.
Enable, VTY, and Console password is **cisco** for both routers.

Objectives

- Configure a router for Network Address Translation and Port Address Translation.
- Troubleshoot NAT and PAT using **debug**

Background / Preparation

The ISP has allocated a company the public CIDR IP address 199.99.9.32/30. This is equivalent to four public IP addresses. Because the company has an internal requirement for more than 30 addresses, the IT manager has decided to use NAT and PAT. Routing between the ISP and the gateway router is done using a static route between the ISP and the gateway, and a default route between the gateway and the ISP. The ISP's connection to the Internet will be represented by a loopback address on the ISP router.

Cable a network similar to the one in Figure 11-5.1. You can use any router that meets the interface requirements displayed in the diagram (that is, 800, 1600, 1700, 2500 and 2600 routers or a combination). Please refer to the information in Appendix D, "Router Interface Summary Chart," to correctly specify the interface identifiers to be used based on the equipment in your lab. The configuration output used in this lab is produced from 1721 series routers. Any other router used may produce slightly different output. The following steps are intended to be executed on each router unless specifically instructed otherwise.

Start a HyperTerminal session.

Refer to the erase and reload instructions at the end of this lab . Perform those steps on all routers in this lab assignment before continuing.

Step 1   Configure the routers.

Configure the hostname, console, virtual terminal, and enable passwords and the interfaces according to the chart. If there is trouble doing this, refer to the NAT configuration lab.

Step 2   Save the configurations.

At the privileged EXEC mode prompt on both routers, type the command **copy running-config startup-config**.

Step 3   Configure the hosts with the proper IP address, subnet mask and default gateway.

Each workstation should be able to ping the attached router. Troubleshoot as necessary. Hint: Remember to assign a specific IP address and default gateway to the workstation. If running Windows 98, check using **Start>Run>winipcfg**. If running Windows 2000 or later, check using **ipconfig** in a DOS window.

Step 4   Verify that the network is functioning.

A. From the attached hosts, **ping** the fast ethernet interface of the default gateway router.

B. Was the ping from the first host successful? _____

C. Was the ping from the second host successful? _____

D. If the answer is no for either question, troubleshoot the router and host configurations to find the error. Then **ping** again until they are successful.

Step 5 Create a static route.

A. Create a static route from the ISP to the gateway router. Addresses 199.99.9.32/27 have been allocated for internet access outside of the company. Use the **ip route** command to create the static route.

```
ISP(config)#ip route 199.99.9.32 255.255.255.252 200.2.2.18
```

B. Is the static route in the routing table?

_____

C. What command checks the routing table contents?

_____

D. If the route was not in the routing table, give one reason why this might be so?_____

Step 6 Create a default route.

A. Add a default route, using the **ip route** command, from the gateway router to the ISP router. This will forward any unknown destination address traffic to the ISP.

```
Gateway(config)#ip route 0.0.0.0 0.0.0.0 200.2.2.17
```

B. Is the route in the routing table? _____

C. Try to **ping** from one of the workstations to the ISP serial interface IP address.

D. Was the ping successful? _____

E. Why? _____

Step 7 Define the pool of usable public IP addresses.

To define the pool of public addresses, use the **ip nat pool** command.

```
Gateway(config)#ip nat pool public_access 199.99.9.32 199.99.9.35
   netmask 255.255.255.252
```

Step 8 Define an access list that will match the inside private IP addresses.

To define the access list to match the inside private addresses, use the **access-list** command.

```
Gateway(config)#access-list 1 permit 10.10.10.0 0.0.0.255
```

Step 9 Define the NAT translation from inside list to outside pool.

To define the NAT translation, use the **ip nat inside source** command.

```
Gateway(config)#ip nat inside source list 1 pool public_access
overload
```

Step 10 Specify the interfaces.

On the active interfaces on the router, it needs to be specified if they are inside or outside interfaces with respect to NAT. To do this, use the **ip nat inside** command.

```
Gateway(config)#interface fastethernet 0
Gateway(config-if)#ip nat inside
```

Step 11 Test the configuration.

A. Turn on debugging for the NAT process By typing **debug ip nat translations** at the privileged EXEC mode prompt.

B. Does the **debug** command show any output?

_____

C. Were the pings successful?

_____

D. If translation was taking place there would be output from the debug command. In reviewing the running configuration of the Gateway router, it is seen that the **ip nat outside** statement has not been entered on the serial 0 interface. To configure this enter the following:

```
Gateway(config)#interface serial 0
Gateway(config-if)#ip nat outside
```

E. From the workstations, **ping 172.16.1.1**.

If the **ip nat outside** statement was entered correctly there should be output from the **debug ip nat** command.

F. What does the NAT*: S=10.10.10.? -> 199.99.9
mean?_____

G. To stop the debug output, type **undebug all** at the privileged EXEC mode prompt.

Upon completion of the previous steps, logoff (by typing **exit**) and turn the router off. Then remove and store the cables and adapter.

Configuration Reference Sheet for This Lab

This sheet contains the basic configuration commands for the ISP and gateway routers.

```
ISP
Router#configure terminal
Router(config)#hostname ISP
ISP(config)#enable password cisco
ISP(config)#enable secret class
ISP(config)#line console 0
ISP(config-line)#password cisco
ISP(config-line)#login
ISP(config-line)#exit
ISP(config)#line vty 0 4
ISP(config-line)#password cisco
ISP(config-line)#login
ISP(config-line)#exit
ISP(config)#interface loopback 0
ISP(config-if)#ip add 172.16.1.1 255.255.255.255
ISP(config-if)#no shutdown
ISP(config-if)#exit
ISP(config)#interface serial 0
ISP(config-if)#ip add 200.2.2.17 255.255.255.252
ISP(config-if)#no shutdown
ISP(config-if)#clockrate 64000
ISP(config)#ip route 199.99.9.32 255.255.255.224 200.2.2.18
ISP(config)#end
ISP#copy running-config startup-config
Destination filename [startup-config]?[Enter]


Gateway
Router#configure terminal
Router(config)#hostname Gateway
Gateway(config)#enable password cisco
Gateway(config)#enable secret class
Gateway(config)#line console 0
Gateway(config-line)#password cisco
Gateway(config-line)#login
Gateway(config-line)#exit
Gateway(config)#line vty 0 4
Gateway(config-line)#password cisco
Gateway(config-line)#login
Gateway(config-line)#exit
Gateway(config)#interface loopback 0
Gateway(config-if)#ip add 172.16.1.1 255.255.255.0
Gateway(config-if)#no shutdown
Gateway(config-if)#exit
Gateway(config)#interface serial 0
Gateway(config-if)#ip add 200.200.200.17 255.255.255.252
Gateway(config-if)#no shutdown

Gateway(config)#ip route 0.0.0.0 0.0.0.0 200.2.2.17
```

Lab 11-6: Configuring DHCP

Figure 11-6.1 Topology for Lab 11-6

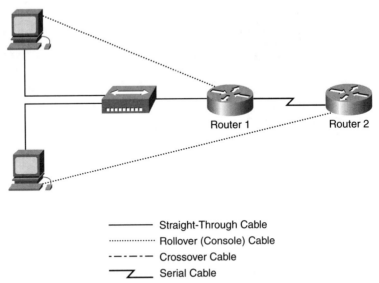

—————— Straight-Through Cable

·············· Rollover (Console) Cable

- — - — - Crossover Cable

⌇ Serial Cable

Table 11-6.1 Lab Equipment Configuration

Router Designation	Router Name	FastEthernet 0 Address/ Subnet Mask	Interface Type	Serial 0 Address	Loopback 0 Address/ Subnet Mask
Router 1	campus	172.16.12.1/24	DCE	172.16.1.6/30	NA
Router 2	ISP	NA	DTE	172.16.1.5/30	172.16.13.1/24

Enable secret password is **class** for both routers.
Enable, VTY, and Console password is **cisco** for both routers.

Objective

■ Configure a router for DHCP to dynamically assign addresses to attached hosts.

Background / Preparation

Routing between the ISP and the campus router is by way of a static route between the ISP and the gateway, and a default route between the gateway and the ISP. The ISP connection to the internet is identified by a loopback address on the ISP router.

Cable a network similar to the one in Figure 11-6.1. You can use any router that meets the interface requirements displayed in the diagram (that is, 800, 1600, 1700, 2500, and 2600 routers or a combination). Please refer to the information in Appendix D, "Router Interface Summary Chart," to correctly specify the interface identifiers to be used based on the equipment in your lab. The configuration output used in this lab is produced from 1721 series routers. Other routers may produce slightly different output. The following steps are intended to be executed on each router unless specifically instructed otherwise.

Start a HyperTerminal session as.

Please refer to and implement the procedure documented in Appendix B, "Erasing and Reloading the Router," before continuing with this lab.

Step 1   Configure the routers.

Configure the hostname, console, virtual terminal, and enable passwords and the interfaces according to the chart. If there is trouble doing this, refer to the NAT configuration lab.

Step 2   Save the configurations.

At the privileged EXEC mode prompt on both routers, type the command **copy running-config startup-config**.

Step 3   Create a static route.

A. Addresses 199.99.9.32/27 have been allocated for Internet access outside of the company. Use the **ip route** command to create the static route.

```
ISP(config)#ip route 172.16.12.0 255.255.255.0 172.16.1.6
```

B. Is the static route in the routing table?

_____

Step 4   Create a default route.

A. Use the **ip route** command to add a default route from the campus router to the ISP router. This will provide the mechanism to forward any unknown destination address traffic to the ISP.

```
campus(config)#ip route 0.0.0.0 0.0.0.0 172.16.1.5
```

B. Is the route in the routing table?

_____

Step 5 Create the DHCP address pool.

To configure the campus LAN pool, use the following commands:

```
campus(config)#ip dhcp pool campus
campus(dhcp-config)#network 172.16.12.0 255.255.255.0
campus(dhcp-config)#default-router 172.16.12.1
campus(dhcp-config)#dns-server 172.16.1.2
campus(dhcp-config)#domain-name foo.com
campus(dhcp-config)#netbios-name-server 172.16.1.10
```

Step 6 Excluding addresses from pool.

To exclude addresses from the pool, use the following command:

```
campus(dhcp-config)#ip dhcp excluded-address 172.16.12.1
  172.16.12.10
```

Step 7 Verifying DHCP Operation.

A. At each workstation on the directly connected subnet configure the TCP/IP properties so the workstation will obtain an IP address and DNS server address from the DHCP server (see Figure 11-6.2). After changing and saving the configuration, reboot the workstation.

Figure 11-6.2 TCP/IP Properties Dialog Box

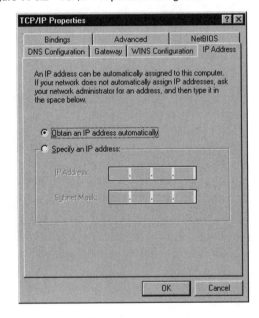

    B. To confirm the TCP/IP configuration information on each host use **Start>Run>winipcfg**. If running Windows 2000, check using **ipconfig** in a DOS window.

    C. What IP address was assigned to the workstation?

    _____

    D. What other information was automatically assigned?

    _____

    E. When was the lease obtained? _____

    F. When will the lease expire? _____

Step 8   View DHCP bindings.

    A. From the campus router, the bindings for the hosts can be seen. To see the bindings, use the command **show ip dhcp binding** at the privileged EXEC mode prompt.

    B. What were the IP addresses assigned?

    _____

    C. What are the three other fields listed in the output?

    _____

Upon completion of the previous steps, logoff (by typing **exit**) and turn the router off. Then remove and store the cables and adapter.

Lab 11-7: Configuring DHCP Relay

Figure 11-7.1   Topology for Lab 11-7

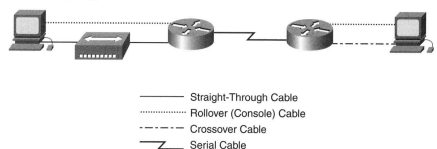

——————— Straight-Through Cable

················· Rollover (Console) Cable

– – – – – Crossover Cable

⎯⎯Z⎯⎯ Serial Cable

Table 11-7.1 Lab Equipment Configuration

Router Designation	Router Name	FastEthernet 0 Address/ Subnet Mask	Interface Type	Serial 0 Address
Router 1	campus	172.16.12.1/24	DCE	172.16.1.6/30
Router 2	remote	172.16.13.1/24	DTE	172.16.1.5/30

Enable secret password is **class** for both routers.
Enable, VTY, and Console password is **cisco** for both routers.

Objectives

- Configure a router for DHCP
- Add the capability for workstations to remotely obtain DHCP addresses and dynamically assign addresses to the attached hosts.

Background / Preparation

A DHCP client uses IP broadcasts to find the DHCP server. However, these broadcasts are not forwarded by routers, so in the case of the remote LAN, the workstations will not be able to locate the DHCP server. The router must be configured with the **ip helper-address** command to enable forwarding of these broadcasts, as unicast packets, to the specific server.

Routing between the remote and the campus router is done using a static route between the remote and gateway routers and a default route between the gateway and remote routers.

Cable a network similar to the one in Figure 11-7.1. You can use any router that meets the interface requirements displayed in the diagram (that is, 800, 1600, 1700, 2500, and 2600 routers or a combination). Please refer to the information in Appendix D, "Router Interface Summary Chart," to correctly specify the interface identifiers to be used based on the equipment in your lab. The configuration output used in this lab is produced from 1721 series routers. Other routers may produce slightly different output. The following steps are intended to be executed on each router unless specifically instructed otherwise.

Start a HyperTerminal session.

Please refer to and implement the procedure documented in Appendix B, "Erasing and Reloading the Router," before continuing with this lab.

Step 1   Configure the routers.

Configure the hostname, console, virtual terminal, and enable passwords and the interfaces according to the chart. If there is a problem completing this, refer to the NAT configuration lab.

Step 2   Configure routing on the remote router.

Use OSPF as the routing protocol, set up the network as area 0 and the process ID as 1.

```
remote(config)#router ospf 1
remote(config-router)#network 172.16.1.0 0.0.0.255 area 0
remote(config-router)#network 172.16.13.0 0.0.0.255 area 0
```

Step 3   Configure routing on the campus router.

A. Use OSPF as the routing protocol, set up the network as area 0 and the process ID as 1.

```
campus(config)#router ospf 1
campus(config-router)#network 172.16.1.0 0.0.0.255 area 0
campus(config-router)#network 172.16.12.0 0.0.0.255 area 0
```

B. Are there OSPF routes in the routing table?

_____

Step 4   Save the configurations.

At the privileged EXEC mode prompt on both routers, type the command **copy running-config startup-config**.

Step 5   Create the campus DHCP address pool.

To configure the campus LAN pool, use the following commands:

```
campus(config)#ip dhcp pool campus
campus(dhcp-config)#network 172.16.12.0 255.255.255.0
campus(dhcp-config)#default-router 172.16.12.1
campus(dhcp-config)#dns-server 172.16.12.2
campus(dhcp-config)#domain-name foo.com
campus(dhcp-config)#netbios-name-server 172.16.12.10
```

Step 6   Create the remote DHCP address pool.

To configure the remote LAN pool, use the following commands:

```
campus(dhcp-config)#ip dhcp pool remote
campus(dhcp-config)#network 172.16.13.0 255.255.255.0
campus(dhcp-config)#default-router 172.16.13.1
campus(dhcp-config)#dns-server 172.16.12.2
campus(dhcp-config)#domain-name foo.com
campus(dhcp-config)#netbios-name-server 172.16.12.10
```

Step 7 Exclude addresses from pool.

A. To exclude addresses from the pool, use the following commands:

```
campus(dhcp-config)#ip dhcp excluded-address 172.16.12.1
  172.16.12.10
remote(dhcp-config)#ip dhcp excluded-address 172.16.13.1
  172.16.13.10
```

This defines the address range to be excluded from dynamic issue by the DHCP server.

B. Why would addresses be excluded?

Step 8 Verify DHCP operation on the campus router.

A. From the workstation directly connected to the campus router configure the TCP/IP properties for the workstation to obtain its IP properties automatically from DHCP. These properties include the IP and DNS server addresses (see Figure 11-7.2).

Figure 11-7.2 TCP/IP Properties Dialog Box

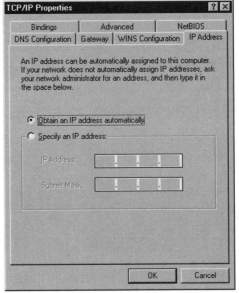

B. After changing the configuration, reboot the workstation. View the TCP/IP configuration information on each host. If running Windows 98, go to **Start>Run>winipcfg**. With Windows 2000 or higher, use **ipconfig** in a DOS command prompt window.

C. What IP address was assigned to the workstation?

Step 9   Verify DHCP operation on the remote router.

    A. Repeat the last step using the workstation attached to the remote router.

    B. Is there a valid address assigned from the DHCP pool?

    _____

    C. What IP address was assigned to the workstation?

    _____

    D. What does this address (if any) represent?

Step 10   Configuring DHCP relay.

Configure the remote router with the **ip helper-address** command to enable forwarding of broadcasts, as unicast packets, to the specific server. This command must to be configured on the LAN interface of the remote router for DHCP to function.

```
remote(config)#interface fastethernet 0
remote(config-if)#ip helper-address 172.16.12.1
```

Step 11   Repeat verification of DHCP operation on the remote router.

    A. Reboot the workstation attached to the remote router.

    B. Is there a valid address assigned from the DHCP pool?

    _____

    C. What IP address was assigned to the workstation?

    _____

    D. If there is no IP address, troubleshoot the workstation and router configurations and repeat Step 11.

Step 12   View DHCP bindings.

    A. From the campus router, the bindings for the hosts can be seen. To see the bindings, use the command **show ip dhcp binding** at the privileged EXEC mode prompt.

    B. What are the IP addresses assigned to the hosts?

    _____

Upon completion of the previous steps, logoff (by typing **exit**) and turn the router off. Then remove and store the cables and adapter.

NOTES

NOTES

NOTES